William J. Stockton, MD

NOW IT ALL
MAKES SENSE

Recovery through self-knowledge, told in the actual dialogue
of ten patients and their self-knowledge therapist.

NOW IT ALL MAKES SENSE

Recovery through self-knowledge, told in the actual dialogue of ten patients and their self-knowledge therapist.

William J. Stockton, MD

Free Will Publishing, L.L.C.
Charlottesville, VA

ISBN# 0-9769141-0-7

Cover Art Copyright © 2005 Bill Garner
Typesetting and page design E. Estela Monteleone, Borderlands Press—www.borderlandspress.com

Printed in the United States of America

1st Printing May 2005

Free Will Publishing, L.L.C.
Charlottesville, VA

www.nowitallmakessense.com

Dedication

To my Momma Choc, and Daddy Will, who gave me life and made all the stars and planets line up just right for me.

To my wife and soulmate, Irma, and my three daughters, Becky, Kathy and Debbie, who have made my life rich beyond measure.

To my many teachers, mentors, colleagues, and friends who inspired me to use my talents and fulfill my destiny.

To my many patients who enriched my life by sharing their lives with me and gave me the privilege of helping them enrich their lives.

To my enemies, failures, and critics whose challenges demanded I develop the strengths to overcome adversity.

And to my editor, Deborah Stockton, for whose ruthless blue pencil, patience, and encouragement in writing this book, my gratitude has no bounds.

Contents

Foreword

Dr. William Stockton has written an important clinical book, *Now It all Makes Sense*. He addresses "mind" in its multilayered complexity, including "mind's" rich connections with heart and soul. In clear, unadorned prose he avoids both biological and psychodynamic reductionism while speaking out cogently against the trend, driven substantially by for-profit entities, to turn psychiatrists into prescribers and psychiatry into a primarily medication prescribing profession. Through gripping clinical vignettes he documents, among other things, that medications, " . . . no matter how precisely designed . . ." cannot ". . . resolve emotional conflicts that impair the decisions and actions required of a productive person."

An experienced, mature clinician, he describes psychotherapy work as a creative, courageous, healing patient/doctor endeavor he terms "*self*-knowledge" or "*self*-understanding" therapy. In so doing he sets aside some of the negative aspects of psychoanalysis while retaining its enduringly positive elements.

His case presentations describe the *self*-understanding process in motion, stressing the importance of both intellectual and emotional learning. This sort of rich presentation of complex situations in motion is all too rare in modern psychiatric writing and will prove to be of enor-

9

mous interest and value to those legions of psychiatric residents and colleagues wishing to hone their psychotherapy skills. It is the equivalent of a master's series for dancers or writers.

In these powerful and moving vignettes that, in more than one instance, moved me to tears, he places himself squarely within a small group of literate clinical psychiatric writers including Paul DeGenova, Peter Kramer in his book, *Moments of Engagement*, and Robert Coles in *The Call of Stories*.

Now It All Makes Sense speaks eloquently to both the lay and professional reader as it demystifies and destigmatizes mental illness. It is a most worthy and valuable contribution that deserves the widest possible readership.

Harold Eist, M.D.
Past-President, American Psychiatric Association
April, 2005
Bethesda, Maryland

1

Now It All Makes Sense

On my first visit to Greece, I recalled with fascination my high school study of Ancient Greece's beliefs in innumerable gods and goddesses. Some were half mortal, and a separate one was assigned for every detail of earth, life, death, the heavens, and the underworld. Zeus, spiritual father of all gods, Hera, his wife, queen of heaven and guardian of the sanctity of marriage, Athena, virgin goddess of wisdom, and, Ares, god of war, were chief among unique deities for entities such as fire, light, poetry, music, sun, moon, invention, debauchery, and death. None of this seemed to make any sense.

But one night during my trip, as I returned to Athens by ship from Rhodes, a great storm arose on the Mediterranean making me deathly seasick. Puzzled at being subjected to such misery, I suddenly realized the perfectly logical explanation: that very afternoon at a topless beach I had lusted for a beautiful, full-breasted young woman, so Hera, goddess of women and first lady in the kingdom of gods, became jealous of my attraction to one of her rivals and ordered Poseidon, god of the sea, to punish me. Having discovered the organized logic in the Greeks' theology, "Ah," I thought, "now it all makes sense."

At a more rational level, learning about how the Ancient Greeks accommodated their inner disharmony by

11

believing in innumerable discordant gods helped me appreciate Saint Paul's first century A.D. virtually overnight success converting the Greeks from pantheism to Christianity. Worshipping one unified God, incarnated on Earth as His loving, nonrebellious Son, was far more settling to the human mind than keeping track of a bunch of fragmented, self-centered, jealous, constantly fighting deities.

Understanding the plight of Ancient Greeks and their mind-strengthening solution also helped me, two thousand years later, to grasp more fully how my daily practice of self-knowledge therapy, based on a comprehensible theory of psychology derived from the scientific study of how the human mind and brain work, helps people make sense of their conflicted thoughts and feelings.

Ancient people, like each of us, had to grapple with a brain whose 100 billion nerve cells fire off an astronomical number of signals that include disturbing unorganized thoughts, painful feelings, and prohibited urges, plus the emotional defenses, subconscious and conscious, against these raw outputs of the mind.

The Ancient Greeks relieved their confusion by attributing the causes of their inner chaos to forces outside themselves in the form of their deities, just as I relieved my distress by blaming my seasickness on Hera's jealousy and Poseidon's tempest. Yet the Greeks' solution left them with vain, independent, demanding gods and goddesses who were no more ordered than the Greeks' own human experiences.

From its earliest history humanity has sought explanations, magical and reasoned, for inexplicable ideas and acts of nature. Before the Ancient Greeks, the Egyptians, Chinese, and Hindus found answers for mysterious human events in the relative positions and movements of the sun, moon, planets, and other celestial bodies observed through the discipline of astrology, humankind's first known science.

Philosophers of Ancient Greece, despite the polytheism of their contemporaries, were also the progenitors of applied reason who sought rational explanations for man's experiences. Warren Carroll, in *The Founding of Christendom* (Christendom Press, 1985), wrote:

Aristotle was a student of Plato [who was himself a student of Socrates] at Athens, and Aristotle refined reason itself into a system, providing for the first time in history explicit standards for intellectual judgment universally valid at any time and in any culture. Through Aristotle's teaching the mind could know itself, know that it knew external, objective reality, and know how it knew that reality—an achievement of enormous magnitude for one man so early in the history of thought.

Though the Greeks stopped worshipping their multiple diverse gods, humanity's need to rely on magical explanations and external solutions continued.

Magical solutions are deeply compelling, since, beginning with our undeveloped mind of early childhood, they are our first, most powerful avenue for feeling, while not actually achieving, that we have overcome whatever ails us. Some Middle Ages societies, for example, blamed mysterious supernatural "demons," believing those demons inhabited the bodies of their victims, then infected innocent unsuspecting others in the way we now know of certain diseases. Explanations for the causes of "demons" were no more civilized or scientific than their everyday magical remedies of brutality, starvation, isolation, bleeding, and purging. Some cultures felt that demons could be completely destroyed and contagion prevented only if the body of the person housing the evil spirits were obliterated; burning the afflicted person alive was the surest way.

While our emotions wish to rely on magic, our inquisitive sound intellect wants reasonable, logical answers. We seek to know what makes us think the way we do so we can understand and master our inner chaos and conflicts that, left unattended, lead to self-created emotional pain and self-defeating behaviors.

As the scientific revolution evolved in the late nineteenth century, a group of pioneers began developing theories about how the mind worked. Most notable among them were Sigmund Freud (1856-1839), a research neurologist curious about the brain's psychological function, the mind, then later, Carl Jung (1875-1961) and Alfred Adler (1870-1937). Their attempts to explain human emotions and the behaviors proceeding from them were the first scientific approach to the mind as an entity whose traits could be defined and understood. When these researchers pursued their theories with emotionally troubled patients, they soon found that the self-knowledge their patients gained during the research studies gave those individuals mastery over, and relief from, their troubled emotions. This fortuitous discovery was the breakthrough that launched what would become the science of self-mastery acquired through self-knowledge. Self-knowledge is achieved through the process of understanding, intellectually and emotionally, how one's mind works to cause its chaos and conflicts.

The skepticism often prompted by Freud's name and many of his rightfully discredited sexual theories has tainted and obscured the momentous breakthrough he and his fellow pioneers made. Their discovery of how the mind works and the great advances in psychology it spawned have provided avenues for obtaining rational solutions to our irrational thoughts and feelings.

When these researchers learned the value of self-knowledge, they naturally wanted to give their great finding a name. Excited and thinking like cold laboratory scientists rather than concerned healers who sensitively responded to the needs of people, they coined the sterile, detached term "psychoanalysis" to apply to their discovery, never considering its affect on the people who would need the self-knowledge their discovery made possible. Not only did the field of self-knowledge therapy get stuck with the term "psychoanalysis" but inevitably the term's impersonal nature, however intellectually acceptable, would, at least subliminally and subtly, affect how later therapists and patient or client users of this discovery would respond to the term's implied meaning. Prospective patients would not take kindly to feeling they would become a clinical subject of "analysis," as if they were experimental animals undergoing microscopic dissection, and therapists would look upon their work as "analyzing" a patient or client rather than working with him to master his troubled emotions. For that reason, in this and the following chapters I use the terms "self-knowledge" and "self-understanding" therapy to reflect and stress the spirit of these terms' intent that is not fully evident in the word "psychoanalysis."

Although our mind constantly confronts us with its felt helplessness to its demons, most people usually find their distress minor enough not to seek the mastery self-understanding provides. When anxiety, inexplicable fears, and self-defeating behaviors become unacceptable, however, self-knowledge makes possible our ability to sort out and decode their root emotions by understanding their disguised meanings and sources.

A simple, everyday analogy to this process occurs when we see a hodgepodge of papers on our desk, then feel, however mildly, unsettled about the mental confusion the clutter causes until we give ourselves control and a sense of ease by organizing the documents into their appropriate categories. Similarly, when we are lost on a trip we feel restless until we locate ourselves on a map, or when we are in the dark we feel uneasy until we turn on a light.

A more in-depth analogy to the process of mastering our bewildering thoughts and feelings would be if we tried to interpret a foreign language or decipher an obscure code. An interpreter or cryptographer must know, beyond mere vocabulary, the structure and nuance of the codes or languages' words and terms.

Our sense of helpless confusion often results in fears and other feelings we cannot account for through reason or logic. Childhood fears of places like attics, basements, or haunted houses, or of animals like mice, crickets, and roaches are normal and typically fade with maturity. Many other fears, such as of open spaces, high places, or bogeymen, however, hide in the recesses of our mind and do not disappear on their own. These fears, usually caused by emotions and ideas masked by the arcane language of the subconscious mind, require self-knowledge to be resolved or overcome.

My personal history, that I relate in detail in Chapter Five, "It's All My Fault She's Sick," provides an illustration of this. At seventeen, I began having frequent episodes of terror from my images of eternity after death that were brought on by my subconscious reaction, unknown to me at the time, to knowing I would be left behind alone when my family moved to Oklahoma. In spite of this small town Texas boy's attempts to relieve these disturbing feelings through religion and philosophy, I suffered my symptoms for over ten years. Finally, in my late twenties, when I was a medical intern, I discovered the science of self-knowledge and overcame my crippling obsessional dreads by learning how my mind had worked to cause them.

Widespread apprehensions about the sensitive, taboo content involved in personal struggles have often made the revelations of how the mind works a convenient butt of humor and ridicule. The concept of early life patterns being revealed as the root causes of adult problems is difficult for some people to swallow, and their discomfort leaves them having to cope with their skepticism by poking fun at or dismissing what they do not understand. This atmosphere, and the wish for privacy, has led most of those who gain, and those who help others gain, self-knowledge not to publicly reveal their experiences, thus depriving most people of knowing the often life-saving value of self-knowledge. The experience of self-understanding abounds with successes like mine and those described in Chapters Two through Eleven, yet public awareness of such triumphs is almost nonexistent.

Psychiatric and self-knowledge therapy organizations, as well as their members who provide treatment through self-understanding, have all contributed to this failure of communication. While medical specialties devoted to treating the body have publicized their advances, proponents of the science and practice of self-understanding have largely maintained an aloof silence about its accomplishments. Most therapists who offer help in obtaining self-knowledge have been too immersed in honing their skills to devote efforts to making the value of their work well-known. Yet even those competent in public communication have been reluctant to advance their patients or clients' cause with the forceful advocacy necessary for any endeavor involving large numbers of people.

In 1967 when Christiaan Barnard in South Africa performed the first successful heart transplant operation, the entire world knew about it within hours. Yet when a person receives a "new heart" through self-knowledge, the "operation" remains a secret.

We all rejoice with those who benefit from the life-saving procedure of heart transplant surgery, though that procedure affects far fewer people than does the operation of breathing new life into one's mind and emotions through self-knowledge. People can identify with a successful heart transplant as if it applied directly and immediately to them, while the life successes that come through understanding the meaning and functions of one's deep emotions, whose benefits are available to everyone, are often viewed as irrelevant.

While we are all eager to learn about a heart transplant's miraculous implicit promise, the fear of encountering painful, conflicted emotions created by our mind drives us away from the promise that self-knowledge offers the way to a successful career, healthy relationships, and fulfilled dreams. Ironically, in our "bare all" society of today where the presence of deep emotions is accepted by almost everyone, most people still choose not to face these emotions' significance to how we feel and think, or to overcome the troubles they create. Even among those who acknowledge that their emotions are critical in causing pain and failure, many feel too intimidated by their fear of knowing these culprits to confront their feelings.

The wish to avoid knowing intimately the deep layers of our mind is natural, since they house the scary, disturbing feelings of primitive fears, raw anger, taboo body pleasures, and helplessness. Resistance to knowing fearsome feelings also becomes an internal saboteur that makes us vulnerable to complying with others, such as drug treatment oriented managed care companies, who would try to discourage us from exploring our minds.

I have written *Now It all Makes Sense* to demystify and destigmatize the general public's perception of this sometimes controversial treatment by revealing how the process of self-knowledge therapy works to help people overcome their resistances and fears. When one is not afraid to "know thyself," as inscribed on the temple of Apollo at the Delphic Oracle, c.650-550 B.C., one is not held hostage to his fears. Self-knowledge gives one freedom to use all his personal resources to fulfill his goals, just as self-knowledge saved my and countless others' lives, careers, and relationships, and allowed us to live our dreams and goals.

When a person is desperate for relief from the inner torment of anxiety, depression or panic, her desperation can override her fear of feeling these feelings as they surface. In my own instance, my terror of eternity was so fierce that facing ideas or feelings lurking in my subconscious mind was a relief. I knew that nothing I could discover in my mind's deepest recesses could possibly feel as unbearable as my terror of eternity. This was equally true of Mr. Masters in Chapter Ten, "Only One Escape," who felt overwhelmed by panic about high places and feeling trapped.

Self-defeating behaviors, as when one acts as if one is above the laws of nature, common sense, and society, are a different matter. Individuals with such behaviors often deny their peril by being contented with, pleased with, proud of, or rewarded by, those behaviors. Yet those wishing to change their pattern of self-defeat must uncover its root emotions in the same way as one who wishes to free himself of severe anxiety. When a person so endangers himself by his self-contentment, the therapist often must bolster the person's drive to acquire the mastery of self-knowledge by helping the client or patient remember his treatment goals. For example, a patient who bragged about the cleverness of his kleptomania "successes" breezed into my office one morning cheerfully asking, "What should we talk about today?" I responded, "How about jail?"

The stories of Mr. Tucker in Chapter Three, "Hey, No

Problem," whose procrastination almost ended his outstanding legal career, and Mr. Morris in Chapter Eight, "I
Can't Do It All By Myself," whose inability to act alone
ruined two marriages and threatened his livelihood, illustrate the problems faced by those who may be comfortable
with their self-defeating behaviors, but whose outside world
is not and demands that they overcome their unacceptable
conduct or face its consequences. Such people usually
have no conscious anxiety about their behaviors.

When a client has no conscious anxiety, or when signs
of his problem are not apparent to him, the therapist must
have a full comprehension of the mind's subconscious
structure so she can help the client recognize the root emotions of his behaviors. Therapists lacking this understanding are helpless even to begin searching for the problem's
underlying cause.

One gains self-knowledge by confronting feared, disordered emotions one would ordinarily ignore or pretend
do not exist. Then, by observing the emotions while si-
multaneously experiencing them and understanding their
functions, one demystifies and defangs the feelings so one
can master them.

Professionals superficially trained in analytic therapy
can sometimes offer what appears to be in-depth knowledge of a person's problem by intellectually describing the
problem and its emotional components, while not actually
helping the patient or client gain access to or understand
his crucial emotions. Though intellectual understanding
of emotions is necessary, it alone is insufficient for helping resolve conflicted emotions. Unless the therapist herself has an intimate awareness of her own emotions,
achieved only by experiencing those emotions herself, the
self-knowledge therapeutic process is little more than an
intellectual exercise.

Freedom to experience feared feelings should not be
heard as saying that one should act out the feelings, since
deciding whether a given act is appropriate should be determined by one's judgment. Experiencing feared feelings means making the feelings available to oneself so she

can become aware of the specific conflicts of her internal struggle. This confusion arises most frequently when the one acquiring self-knowledge is grappling with aggressive or sexual urges then fears that if she allows herself to fully experience the feelings she will harm someone, be unfaithful to a loved one or moral code, or disgrace herself. Knowing one's feelings means gaining mastery over them, not becoming their slave who yields to their felt demands. This struggle is vividly described by Ms. Lewis in Chapter Eleven, "At One," as she mastered her feeling of losing body boundaries.

When the science of self-knowledge treatment developed into a distinct medical field during the mid-twentieth century, it came to influence many facets of society, including literature, entertainment, and the law. Most importantly, by the mid-twentieth century it became the foundation of psychiatric education, revolutionizing psychiatric practice from a discipline that had been attempting to cure mental illnesses by using the few, ineffective medications available at the time, and other physical treatments, like electroshock, into a specialty that sought to treat all mental conditions through self-understanding.

As psychoanalysts and conventional psychiatrists gained experience however, they discovered that while self-knowledge treatment was extremely effective with emotional conditions involving inner conflict and self-defeating behaviors, it was distinctly ineffective as the sole or primary treatment for schizophrenia, profound depression, and other severe mental illnesses. At the same time, beginning in the late 1950's, new drugs that were achieving unprecedented effectiveness in controlling symptoms of insanity, particularly delusions of persecution, hearing voices, and the inability to distinguish internal fantasies from external reality, became available. Newly developed antidepressant drugs also demonstrated their capacity to treat severely and suicidally depressed people, saving many lives.

The great successes of these medications, though real, engendered in the psychiatric profession and drug industry a false confidence in the seeming unlimited power of drugs to cure all mental-emotional conditions. This unwarranted confidence also spared many psychiatrists the hard work, and sometimes sense of helplessness, required in responding to some patients' incomprehensible and demanding feelings, for which psychiatrists frequently were not prepared. As a result, during the 1980's and 1990's the pendulum of psychiatric treatment philosophy swung back a hundred and eighty degrees, so that drug treatment came to be, and has remained, the basis of psychiatric training and essentially the sole form of treatment used by most psychiatrists for all mental-emotional conditions.

As mentioned, for schizophrenia and suicidal depression drug treatment is not only medically indicated, it may be life saving, and far preferable to self-knowledge therapy as the sole form of treatment, although the latter is invaluable as supplemental treatment to help the patient sort out and manage issues of daily life. But the financial benefits of drug treatment have motivated insurance companies and business providers of insurance to create an ill conceived, one-size-fits-all general trend that excludes the needs of patients whose primary symptoms are anxiety, non-suicidal depression, and self-defeating behaviors, for which only the mastery gained through self-knowledge provides enduring relief.

The false promise and consequent misuse of drug treatment for two such conditions are illustrated by Ms. Poland's experience told in Chapter Four, "Vodka Leaves No Odor," and by Ms. Green's story in Chapter Seven, "The More He Mistreats Me, The More I Love Him." Ms. Poland's general practitioner prescribed an antidepressant for her alcohol-induced depression and Ms. Green's divorce attorney referred her to me because she could not "cooperate in her own defense." A trial of antidepressant medication prescribed by a drug-oriented psychiatrist had failed to dent her self-destructive attitude since it was due to emotional conflicts, not a depressive illness.

Lack of public awareness about this practice has created a monstrous problem for people who suffer from troubled emotions and desperately seek the answers provided only through self-understanding. When this source of relief is unavailable, these people become vulnerable to the claims of massive advertising campaigns that imply magical properties of a drug, as if its sometimes capacity to relieve the immediate pain of certain acute symptoms also means that the drug eliminates the symptoms' underlying causes. Everyday clinical observations show us that when a problem's cause is left unresolved it is likely to exact its price in other, more costly ways, such as career failure, divorce, self-destruction, and death.

While for some people drugs are lifesaving, no drug, no matter how precisely designed, can resolve the emotional conflicts that impair the decisions and actions required of a productive person. However one conceptualizes the basis of self-defeating behaviors, such behaviors are driven by emotions gone awry, and the only detailed access to fixing these emotions is through the conscious awareness of their subconscious causes made possible by self-knowledge.

The public, uninformed of this radical change in psychiatric philosophy, is not aware that, in general, one no longer can categorically expect psychiatrists to offer mental health treatment that provides knowledge of how the mind works. During the 1980's and 90's, in response to this travesty of psychiatric education, psychologists, social workers, and other mental health therapists with advanced degrees began acquiring further education in helping people understand how their mind works and became the predominate professionals offering self-knowledge therapy.

Lack of public awareness is especially critical today, since many people seek psychiatric help with the expectation of resolving inner conflicts only to find that the psychiatrist they have consulted is limited to seeing a person's emotional problem as due simply to some unexplained disturbance in brain chemistry.

We often forget that our mind is the body organ that runs our life, and that we must keep our mind in the best running order possible if we expect our life to go as we plan and desire. When our mind works against rather than for us, self-knowledge gives us the mastery to make our mind run well.

The foremost challenge for anyone seeking self-understanding is to remain honest with oneself while enduring emotions felt to be unbearable long enough to detoxify the fear of those emotions. People come to me with the willingness to pay their hard earned money for me to help them understand how their mind works in causing their pain and self-defeat, but when I ask them to explore with me their underlying thoughts and feelings, they, figuratively, plug up their ears and shout, "Don't say that, I can't bear it," or "I don't want to talk about it." Of course, most people work through this defense then proceed to work out the problems involved, but the reaction illustrates the forces of resistance that must be overcome.

People ask, "Why can't I learn self-knowledge by myself?"

The answer is one can, as long as the troublesome emotion is not so disturbing that one would rather ignore it than encounter and understand it. In those instances, as a colleague said when asked why self-analysis doesn't work, "Simply put, it doesn't work because there's no one to keep you honest."

Overcoming resistance requires a safe environment where one feels free to expose his feared feelings. This safety is provided by the therapeutic alliance between therapist and client. The therapeutic alliance is a union of the client's trust in the self-knowledge therapist that allows the client to contribute his emotional experiences, and the therapist's ability to merit that trust by sharing her scientific knowledge of the human mind to help the client understand the meaning of what he is feeling.

While the therapeutic alliance is the single most basic and important element in acquiring self-knowledge, and is possible only if the client so chooses, it also may create resistance of its own, since it is often felt as a threat to one's independence and self-identify. Even when a client begins self-knowledge therapy with a genuine attitude of "I need your help," the threat to his autonomy can quickly arouse the feeling "I want to do this by myself." Many people so take this wish for granted they neither express the idea nor even recognize its presence. Far too often the desperate subconscious drive not to feel dependent deprives one of acquiring self-knowledge through work with another person. The therapeutic alliance, however, provides the framework for working through this as well as other forms of resistance.

Self-knowledge therapy has long been accused of being an "elitist" treatment available only to the well-to-do. When I entered the field of self-knowledge therapy and heard it described in this way, I was puzzled since I was not rich, famous, or particularly successful. I came to learn that this "elitism" actually applied to those who were willing to do the hard work of acquiring self-knowledge regardless of their social position or financial status. Self-knowledge helps best those who take personal responsibility for their problems and are motivated to use their mind to master those problems through an in-depth understanding of their causes. This applies to anyone, famous or unknown, already successful or not yet achieved.

Self-knowledge treatment began as an inherently complex science in an unknown field seen by the public, then as now, through a lens ground by millennia of fear, superstition, and the wish for magic. Progress in the field was further encumbered for many years by certain psychological hypotheses, especially Freud's theories about "penis envy" in women, and "castration fears" in men. Overcoming these challenges has provided the self-knowledge therapy discipline with opportunities for growth and refinement not afforded more recent, less in-depth, less tested therapies.

For example, when Freud's "penis envy" and "castration fears" theories were not verified in actual practice, they were rejected by most mental health professionals. Too, we now know that sexual conflicts and fears in a woman are more likely due to the shame, humiliation, terror of body harm, and unfounded subconscious guilt she felt in childhood as a victim of seductive, sadistic actions forced on her by older, physically and emotionally more powerful males when she was too young to understand what was happening to her and too physically helpless to protect herself from the abuse. Sexual fears also arise from a child's having formed distorted impressions of sexual encounters caused by exposure to visual images of sexual events before she was old enough to comprehend that such events would apply to her only when she became a fully developed, grown woman, not to her little body at the time. The story of Portia Tillman in Chapter Two, "Only the Powerful Survive," illustrates childhood trauma due to the sexually sadistic actions of an older brother, while the account of Angela Armagh in Chapter Nine, "So Big and Long," exemplifies a child's reaction to mental pictures aroused by her sexual curiosity.

Hindering the public perception of self-knowledge therapy in a different way has been the commitment of many analytic therapists, particularly highly placed academic psychoanalysts, who until recently dominated the profession, to the purity of "psychoanalysis," an influence that spilled over to the field of self-knowledge therapy. Psychoanalysis is a highly specialized form of analytic therapy (with which it is often considered synonymous) frequently involving five or more sessions per week. It is extremely valuable as part of the educational requirements for self-knowledge therapists and to patients or clients whose emotional condition specifically requires it, allowing that they have the time and money to invest in it. The grand notion that intensive psychoanalysis was God's gift to the world as the panacea for all people's needs, however, resulted in its well-deserved unfavorable ivory tower reputation that has rubbed off on self-knowledge therapy and misled the public from recognizing the latter's value to countless people when appropriately applied.

While this book is informative for anyone interested in how the mind works, it will be especially valuable for people who wish to make the most of their lives in a world offering great opportunities. In particular this applies to those who have the abilities to fulfill their goals but have been unable to match their aspirations with achievements because they have blunted or defeated their strengths with emotions gone awry.

A major factor in the persistence of self-defeating behaviors is a person's lack of awareness or unreadiness to accept that his failure is due, even partly, to his self-defeating behavior. For example, a person may dismiss his failure as simply caused by "bad luck," or blame it on another person, an unfair society, ethnic or religious prejudice, an institution, "the Establishment," or a whole range of outside forces—rationalizations that solve nothing and leave in place the personal emotional sources of his failure to achieve his goals. Some may have tried such self-corrective measures as "assertiveness training," "rage control," medications, or, "If I just try harder," to overcome their problem, only to find the benefit non-existent or short-lived.

Just as true mastery arises from Francis Bacon's (1561-1626) scientific precept "Knowledge is Power," so our promise of mastery is that of any scientific endeavor. Using modern telescopes, astronomers are able to provide us with a sense of mastery of time and space never known before. By applying geometric principles to track the movement of stars, the laws of physics to measure the speed of light, and knowledge of mathematics to calculate the distance travelled by light emitted from suns thirteen and a half billion years ago, these scientists tell us our universe is approximately fifteen billion years old. More down to earth, archaeologists and paleontologists, through the science of carbon-dating, can determine the age of artifacts hundreds and thousands of years old.

Similarly, though less precisely due to the mind's unique complexity, those who know how the mind works can "carbon-date" the childhood period in which mental-emotional structures originated, since certain strengths, weaknesses, and conflicts are likely formed during a specific developmental phase. Severe depressions that are especially resistant to treatment, for example, are more apt to have begun from the early loss, between the ages of a few months to three or four years old, of a parent or primary caregiver, while less severe depressions that are more responsive to treatment are apt to have originated in deeply ingrained feelings of inferiority and helplessness from four on. The story of Mr. Stetson in Chapter Six, "Ooooh, My God," illustrates a depression stemming from this later period.

Despite the ultimate promise of living your dreams by knowing your mind, therapists who provide self-understanding usually do not make specific promises to patients. This reluctance is due to the mind's willingness to use any idea for defensive purposes as it seeks to avoid the pain of hard therapeutic work. Given a promise, the subconscious mind, with the knee-jerk reflexivity of a teenager taking on her parent, will sabotage the treatment by setting out to prove the therapist and her promise wrong. For example, if I promised a patient that her treatment would be achieved in six months, her self-protective emotions, would, however subtly, tempt her to use the promise to avoid her painful feelings and conflicts by subconsciously assuming that by just attending the sessions for six months her problem would be solved without her having to truly engage the painful feelings responsible for her self defeating behavior.

Giving advice to a patient or client, except under rare and extreme circumstances, is even more perilous, not only because advice inevitably includes the values, attitudes, and conflicts of the advice-giver rather than the advice-receiver, but also because giving in to someone else's directive usually makes a person, like the aforementioned teenager, want to prove the other person wrong.

I can speak here of the promise of self-knowledge because I know from experience that and how self-understanding gives us the tools to overcome our problems, and in writing this book I do not suffer the constraints of an individual clinical situation. As illustrations in the following chapters will show, the curative effects of self-honest self-knowledge work are as sure as is gravity in making an apple fall.

The process of gaining self-knowledge includes what I describe in detail in Chapter Two as "Emotional Debridement," a psychological corollary of the standard surgical method, "debridement," for treating wounds of the flesh. Its three steps involve: identifying the emotional problem, cleaning the emotional wound by learning its underlying causes, then encouraging healthy emotional growth using one's own already proven strengths.

Emotional debridement is specifically valuable in helping a person "root out" and overcome deeply felt feared feelings that required defenses, usually self-defeating, to protect him from the fear of their pain. Emotional debridement differs from surgical debridement in that surgical debridement is entirely in the hands of a surgeon, while each step of emotional debridement is decided solely by the patient or client.

In word for word dialogue, Chapters Two through Eleven tell the stories of ten patients, or clients, nine with myself as the therapist and one about myself as the patient. Each story is used as a vehicle to illustrate specific emotional problems, conscious and subconscious, these men and women of various backgrounds, occupations, and relationships faced, and to show how each person mastered these problems by uncovering, piece by piece, then overcoming, through emotional and intellectual understanding, the mind's seeming mysteries that determine how we feel and think in creating our painful anxieties and self-defeating behaviors.

Some of the individuals had conditions that emitted painful signals to alert them that something inside was wrong, while others needed their outside world to warn them that their behaviors were incompatible with their career goals, personal life, and even survival. But all had one objective: they yearned to realize their goals and dreams of successful, productive careers and healthy, fulfilling relationships, rather than having to accept failure because their mind worked against instead of for them.

2

Only The Powerful Survive

Ten minutes past our appointed time, Ms. Portia Tillman stalked into the waiting room, nodded politely at me, glowered when I greeted her, then strode, all business, into my office. Her handsome dark blue suit and red and white striped scarf enhanced her natural attractiveness, and her worried eyes stared at me as she sat in the chair I indicated. She raised her eyebrows as if to say, "Well, what do you want?"

"When you called you said you needed to talk about a crisis at work. Is that a good place to start?" I asked.

With narrowed eyes and clenched jaw she stared at me, not answering for a full minute.

"I'm not the one having a crisis; I'm the one being blamed for it," she said, at last, as if grinding nails.

"What happened?" I asked.

"One of my subordinates, Carmen's her name," Ms. Tillman made a disgusted face, "was ten minutes late to work yesterday, so I reprimanded her. Then she ran to my boss and had a tantrum, so I'm being told I need help."

"How so?" I responded.

She shrugged. "Apparently, some of my employees saw what happened and told the CEO they would quit unless I stopped what they called my 'mean, humiliating behavior.' And then all hell broke loose."

29

"How did that turn into all hell breaking loose?" I asked.

"Alex panicked!" she exclaimed. "You can't molly-coddle your employees and still get the job done. Any CEO who doesn't know that is a fool. If you don't come down hard on them, they'll try to get away with anything they think they can, and the damn unions and government will back them up."

"Alex is your CEO?" I asked.

"Yes, and any executive who knuckles under and lets workers bully management ought to be the one in here, NOT ME. When you're dealing with people, only the powerful survive," she declared, red-faced.

"What do you do at your company?" I asked.

"I'm the Chief Operations Officer of a software production firm, and I oversee more than five hundred employees. I do a damn good job, too." She abruptly stopped herself, then added, "And if an employee can't keep up, she shouldn't work there."

"The only reason I'm here is because they gave me an ultimatum," she said, and clenched her jaw again.

"What kind of ultimatum?" I asked.

She glared at me. "Alex said, 'Get help or else.' This was the third time in six months those same people had complained about me. They grumble all the time, but I've never been threatened before. Alex just knuckled under this time." She crossed her arms and continued glaring.

"Say more about Alex knuckling under?" I asked.

"She said they had to find some solution that would work for both the employees and me. Well, screw them. For one thing, they put me in the same category as my employees."

"It feels humiliating?" I asked.

"What do you mean, 'It feels?'" she cried out, furious. "That's psychobabble, it's just one of the ways you people have of blaming the victim. It's humiliating to be treated as if this is my problem rather than Carmen's, or Alex's, for that matter, for being such a coward."

I realized I had been slightly surprised when, referring

to Alex, Ms. Tillman had said "she," so I asked, "When you spoke of Alex, you said 'she'?"

"Yes. Why do you ask?" she snapped.

"I must have thought that Alex was a man," I said.

"There you go. You're just like all other men. You assumed that if someone was a CEO, he'd have to be a man. Alex is a woman, and our Board Chair is also a woman, just like my workers. Almost everyone there is a woman. A group of women put together an all-women firm, and, so far, they've kept it that way. We have some token men on the Board and cleanup and utility crews, but most of the others are women. Maybe I didn't actually say so, but I thought you knew it."

When Ms. Tillman had first described her "crisis," I had jumped to the conclusion she was being abused by a bunch of sexist males who resented a woman's very presence and Ms. Tillman's aggressive authority even more. I was primed for this view because I regularly see professional and business women who are treated unfairly at work, to the point where women lawyers, for example, intimidated by this abuse and concerned about vulnerability at their firms, are much more apt than men to cancel our appointments when work activities conflict. Women often do not feel as free as men to tell demanding superiors, possessive clients, or colleagues to "buzz off" for an hour while they attend to personal, even medical, business.

This was one of my many moments of personal growth resulting from experiences in my career. I had no reason to know Ms. Tillman worked for an all women firm, but my assumption that her CEO was a man told me a part of my mind was still behind the times, since women increasingly are in high business positions, just as in the professions. Because acquiring self-knowledge involves working intensely with other people, a therapist is constantly faced with his or her blind spots and shortcomings and must accept every opportunity to grow with the challenges that arise in work with patients or clients.

"Before I asked you to clarify that Alex was a woman, you were annoyed that I hadn't understood that Alex and the Board had actually humiliated you when they treated this as your problem, rather than Carmen and Alex's, and that it was not just some feeling you had," I said.

She looked at me and nodded slightly. "Alex and the Board Chair also said, and I know it even better than they do, that if I left, the company wouldn't have anyone with my experience to come in overnight and replace me, and they'd face a production crisis. We've got a contract to deliver 100,000 pieces of software in ten days and that means I have to stay on top of every detail twenty-fours a day until the job's done. I also know that the company doesn't want the headaches that unions, and government agencies, and lawyers cause when they scream about the poor workers suffering injustices. So what do the idiots do? Instead of standing up for me, they humiliate me, they 'help me' arrange the time and expense of meeting with you," she sneered. "Well, BIG DEAL! Fuck 'em. I don't want their goddamn help."

"They're way off base when they think they're doing a good thing?" I asked.

"What do you mean, 'a good thing'?" she demanded.

"I think I may not have used the right term, because it appears, from what you said, that they want to keep people happy so the production wheels will turn, and you're having to pay the price for it."

"They're feeling so damn self-righteous when they ought to be hanging their heads in shame. I know the real reason Alex kowtowed to them and didn't fire their asses was because she and the Chair didn't have the guts to face down the workers and tell them we will not tolerate Carmen or anybody else not getting to work on time. They're all cowards, and they're treating me like I'm a nut," she yelled.

"You feel especially bitter about having to see me?" I asked.

"There you go again with your psychobabble when you say I *feel* bitter, like the problem was how I 'feel.' I don't *feel* bitter, I am bitter because I have stupid bosses, and frankly I don't think you're much different. I had no say in the matter; it was this or get fired. I've put my heart and soul into this company for years, and I don't want to jeopardize my career, and they know it, so after all I've given them, they stab me in the back. It's blackmail. Even if they think I need help, this wasn't the way to do it. I hate people," she clenched her fist, "who misuse their authority and throw their weight around."

"It was in the midst of all that that you got my name?" I asked.

"When it became clear I didn't have a choice, I got your name from Mary Forester, who said she'd seen you a few years ago."

"Had anything like this ever happened before?" I asked.

Her frown eased slightly. "No, I've had a good career. I know I have exceptional organizational skills—I became COO by the time I was thirty-three—and I expect to make CEO when Alex leaves. A member of the Board told me the company has been more productive in my three years than under any other COO since the company began twelve years ago. That's what's crazy about this whole thing. How the hell," she threw her hands in the air, "do they think I've been so productive?" then slammed her hands down on the arms of her chair. "They act like they don't know the reason I've been successful is that I know how to handle employees and get the job done."

"The way you said that suggests Alex's attitude came as a surprise," I said.

Nodding, she scowled again. "Alex told me, 'Your production and management abilities are superior, but,'" Ms. Tillman sneered, "'your insensitive and abusive behavior of employees is unacceptable and will get you fired.' Then she went on and on about 'legally enforceable respect for human rights these days.' I can't tell you how much I hate anybody who talks down to me and tries to control me that way."

"Alex seems not to have held anything back in getting her point across," I said.

Looking at me as if I were an idiot, she replied, "You make it sound as if what happened was a good thing, so obviously you don't understand. Alex is presumptuous, heavy-handed, mean-spirited, and the worst CEO I know about misusing authority. After her ultimatum and lecture about human rights, Alex told me that I reminded her of Maria Callas, the opera singer, about how she was the world's greatest soprano, but was fired by every major opera house because, 'her behavior caused more trouble than her singing was worth.'"

"What about her behavior?" I asked.

"Alex said it was 'abusive and insensitive.' Well, screw you Alex! A singer's and my situations are completely different. Maria Callas was just a self-important prima donna, not someone who has to be clear-minded and strong in managing a bunch of trouble-making employees. My position is much closer to the opera house manager's who has to handle people like Maria Callas in order to produce the opera."

I said, "You said your position was like the opera manager's rather than Maria Callas', and of course you're absolutely right about the strengths necessary to be an effective manager. One must be firm, as well as clear-minded, about the organization's goals in order to gain the respect necessary to get the best from your personnel in achieving the task. So I'm not yet clear how the problem arose."

She gave me a disgusted look. "The problem arose," she said with disdain, "because little Miss Priss Carmen thought she could get away with ignoring my warnings and come to work late again, and Alex was totally irresponsible in not supporting the way I handled Carmen."

I replied, "Certainly both of them are responsible for their part in all this, but I'm sure you recognize that you are the only person who has any control over your response to whatever they do, and, in the end, that is all you and I can work with here. It sounds like a tough bunch that's ganged up on you, but can you say more about what Carmen reacted to and what Alex and the Board Chairman were upset about when they made you call me?"

She shot back immediately, "Well, first of all, stop patronizing me. I don't need you to tell me they're a 'tough bunch that's ganged up' on me, I'm strong enough to deal with this myself without you treating me like I'm a child.

The answer to your question is that I don't know what Carmen reacted to, and that doesn't make any difference anyway because she's just bitching about my coming down on her for being late. But Alex was upset because she said I 'overreacted.'" Ms. Tillman's voice was heated.

"Can you say more about 'overreacted'?" I asked.

"You're doing it again," she yelled. "You've already taken their side! You told me to say more about 'overreacted' as if that's what I actually did. That's not what I said. What I said was, 'Alex *said* that I overreacted.'" With fire in her eyes and breathing heavily, she continued. "I don't know why I came here anyway. I knew you were a man and wouldn't understand, you're all alike. When Mary recommended you I started not to come because I knew a man couldn't understand how a woman feels, but when I told Mary my misgivings, she said, 'Yes, he's a man, and I know how you feel, but this one's okay.' I'm not sure now, though."

I responded, "I agree that a woman feels and experiences many things that a man can't understand—being the victim of male sexism and delivering a baby, to name only two—but what you've described is having not been understood by the women in your firm."

Ms. Tillman's face became expressionless as she stared at me for a few moments, then she turned and looked through the big picture window into my wooded back yard and the park beyond. While October's red, deep orange, and yellow leaves, and squirrels frisking on the oaks offer many people diversions from their emotional focus, the appeal of these scenes did not distract Ms. Tillman, too caught up in her reaction to notice.

She continued, "I need to think about that, but I guess our time is up today, because I heard someone come into the waiting room."

"Can you meet at this same time on Thursday?" I asked.

She paused a moment. "This is Tuesday, that'll be at ten two days from now." After entering a note in an appointment book she had taken from her purse, she said, "Fine, I'll see you then."

On Thursday, she again arrived ten minutes late, marched aggressively into the office, and, after taking her seat, said, "I want to begin where we left off last time."

With her finger pointed accusingly at me, she began, "You people aren't telling me anything new. I already know I have a short fuse."

"Can you say more about 'short fuse?'" I asked.

Her hand dropped to her lap, and she glared at me.

"Jennifer, my best friend since elementary school, told me she thinks I overreact to 'everyday slights,' and that I carry the anger around for hours."

"Say more about what she's referring to?" I asked.

Ms. Tillman opened her mouth to speak, then closed it and looked away. After a moment she opened her mouth again, then immediately closed it, pressing her lips together tightly.

"You started to say something and then stopped yourself. Do you know what was on the tip of your tongue?" I asked.

Tears formed in the corners of her eyes, then she looked away and swallowed hard. Turning back to me, she said, "I'm just not comfortable discussing this."

"I know this is difficult, but of course that's nature's way of saying how important it is for us to talk about it. What about 'not comfortable'?" I asked.

She stared out the window, then at me, before answering. "I get upset when I don't control myself better, so for Jennifer to tell me about it, then to have to tell you, is humiliating. I don't know which is worse, not controlling myself, or for Jennifer to be right, or telling you about it. Whatever it is, it's too upsetting."

"Are you saying it starts with being upset with yourself?" I asked.

She took a deep breath.

"Jennifer says I'm one of those people you read about with 'road rage.'" She looked mortified, and shook her head.

"You stopped yourself. Was something hard to say?" I asked.

She did not answer for a few moments. "Almost every day I get furious and flip 'the bird' at drivers who cut me off. Once I told a waiter, 'PISS OFF,' when he gave me a sarcastic 'Thank you' because I'd given him a small tip for his poor service." She gave a slight triumphant smile. "Another time, I had to talk a policeman out of arresting me when I cursed him for giving me a parking ticket, and when things like that happen I stay so angry and upset I can hardly sleep at night." Her voice was calm and her expression straightforward.

"That's what you meant about your friend saying you overreact?" I asked.

"Yes," she stated firmly.

"What do you think kept you from following up on her comments?" I asked.

Her frown had a puzzled, frustrated look.

"What do you mean, 'Following up?'" she asked. "I already told you I know what the problem is. Being independent is the most important thing in my life. I've always been able to handle my problem by myself, and I sure as hell don't need somebody like Alex telling me what to do. Even when I went along with the idea of seeing you, I thought, 'What the hell did I agree to?'"

"Say more about the importance of being independent?" I asked.

She gaped at me, as though momentarily lost for words, then sat back in her chair and set her jaw.

"Are you saying you don't understand why being independent is important?" she demanded.

I responded, "I think I understand, because being able to be independent is important to all of us. In fact, autonomy is usually a major goal of self-understanding. I think, though, I misstated the question. I asked if you could say more about the importance of being independent, when what you had said was not that it was just important, but that it was 'the most important thing in my life,' and you said it with a tone of almost desperate imperative. And that's really what I was asking you to say more about."

She crossed her arms and considered my question.

"Well, coming here is a perfect example. The company used their power over me to make me do this, and now look where I am. Everybody thinks I'm crazy, I'm humiliated in front of my workers, and my medical record shows I saw a psychiatrist. These things don't happen to you if you're independent." She sounded resigned, though her voice was hard.

"I can give you a thousand more examples just like that, and I don't need to go far to do it. It's happening right now. Here. Hear that noise?!"

Moments before, someone next door had begun creating an almost deafening roar by cleaning up fallen leaves with a gasoline powered blower.

"Those people are making so much noise we can't hear each other talk, and they don't give a damn about how much it bothers us. I know people like that. They enjoy having power over us while you and I sit here helpless. There are supposed to be laws against noise pollution, but the government doesn't do a damn thing to stop it, and you and I can't do anything about it."

Her tone reflected the frustration most people feel in such circumstances, though not the rage she had expressed earlier when talking about the factory workers' mutiny and Alex's sending her for treatment, rather than supporting her over the workers.

"That's why I'm independent. If it were up to me, I'd go out there right now and tell the bastards they'll have to do that some other time. I guess you're concerned about the people who live there, but I can tell you that if I had neighbors as inconsiderate as yours, I'd tell them I wouldn't put up with it. If you're not independent, people will walk all over you," she asserted, and recrossed her arms.

"Coming here is especially difficult because it makes you feel dependent?" I asked.

With a snort of disgust, she shook her head. "No, it doesn't make me feel dependent, it makes me *look* dependent. But seeing you was the least of the evils of the options I had and the main reason I was willing to accept treatment at all."

"Can you say more about options?" I asked.

She grimaced in annoyance.

"When Alex told me I had to get help or get fired, my first thought, once I got past my shock that they were serious about making me do this, was to get this 'help' business over as soon as possible, like a weekend group therapy marathon. But in the back of my mind, something told me that it would take more than a few days to figure this out and deal with it. I also knew drug treatment was out of the question because my job requires me to make specific, split-second decisions under pressure, which I'm told I excel at, and I can't afford to walk around like a zombie.

"And anyway, and probably most important, if anything's going to change, I have to understand why and how it's happening, just like I fix other problems at work, or in myself. I know that half-assed solutions don't work," she said, with a slight smile.

She took a deep breath, looked out the window, then turned to me raising one eyebrow. "So, here I am. What do we do?"

I responded, "Well, the one-line answer is, 'Actually, just what we've been doing already,' but I have the impression from the way you spoke of having to 'understand why and how' things happen that you already have some sense of how this process of gaining self-knowledge works."

Her face slightly relaxed, and she leaned back in her chair.

After a long pause, she looked directly at me. "If we're going to do this, and it looks like I have to, do you know how you can help me most?"

"How—?" I started to ask, but she cut me off.

"You can shoot straight with me," she went on, "and keep me honest with myself. I need to understand what my problems are and what I can do about them. Even when my friends and family try to tell me what I do wrong and what I should do instead, they don't know what else to say. And I don't either. Sometimes they get frustrated and yell at me, and then I make it worse by lashing back at them."

She scowled. "One of the hardest parts of doing this is having to accept that Evelyn was right—Evelyn is my cousin. When I told her about what happened at work, and that I couldn't ask for anybody's help because I have to do things my way, Evelyn said, 'But your way isn't working.'" She heaved a big sigh. "I have to admit she was right, at least in this instance. But it's only because Alex and the company didn't back me up.

"I can talk to Evelyn about most things, she's an intelligent and kind person, but she won't challenge me, because when I start complaining about how people upset me, she feels so sorry for me she won't say anything she thinks might hurt me."

Ms. Tillman gazed out the window. "The trees are really pretty this time of year," she said, then sighed and turned back. "Sometimes I get a glimmer of what I do that causes me trouble, but it doesn't last very long, because when I try to think about it, other things start coming into my mind."

"Can you sense what happens inside to make you think about 'other things'?" I asked.

"I don't know, I just can't stay focused. That's what I mean about keeping me honest with myself, and why I need you to help me think about what's wrong long enough for me to do something about it. I solve my company's operational problems all the time, and I can solve my own, too, if I just know what they are and what I can do to fix them."

She paused momentarily and opened her mouth to speak but then stopped herself.

"You started to say something. Can you say what was on your mind?" I asked.

"I just realized we were near the end of the session, and I didn't want to start something new unless we'd have time to talk about it," she said.

"Perhaps you could give us some idea about it and then we can go into it more fully next time," I responded.

She heaved a deep sigh. "My meeting with Alex reminded me of something that's been in the back of my mind. I've been in my current job three years, and during the first two I had very good relations with my employees, and my operational methods were highly productive. My problems with the workers didn't begin until this past year." She paused and looked thoughtful. "Uh, uh, I've always known I want to get back at people when they irritate me, but, uh, I never had trouble controlling it until, uh, these last several months."

The hesitancy in her voice led me to ask, "You seem puzzled about what you just said?"

"Yes," she replied. "I've never thought much about why I get angry with people who upset me, because I've always had what I thought were good reasons, and I knew I could control my reactions, but I can't control my lashing out now, and I don't know why."

"What occurs to you?" I asked.

She narrowed her eyes.

"Well, I don't know how anyone could be expected to deal with an infant like Carmen and not call her down for being ten minutes late, because that's what a competent and responsible manager should do. She'd been late more times than I could count, and I'd already warned her, privately and quietly, a dozen times. And I'm absolutely sure she put the others up to complaining about me so she could get me off her back."

Ms. Tillman looked through me for several moments. After refocusing her eyes, she said, "I'm not a total dummy, though. I can justify being angry at her, but I've never handled people by losing my temper and laying into them so hard before. I'm running a division of five hundred employees, for God's sakes, not fighting in some drunken street brawl, but that's what I did with Carmen."

She covered her face with her hands, then averted her eyes in embarrassment.

"What did you mean, 'That's what I did with Carmen'?" I asked.

She said, "I knew I'd have to tell you sometime. I didn't just bawl out Carmen, I said things I shouldn't have. I was almost screaming, and I, . . ." She looked away, red-faced.

After several moments, I asked, "Something's hard to say?"

She screwed up her face, as if in pain. "I said something like, 'You're lazy just like everybody else that comes across the border.' And of all the things I could have said, that was the worst. Apart from being politically incorrect with her personally, what made it terrible was that fifty percent of our employees are immigrants, and what I said was absolutely untrue anyway. Our best workers are immigrants, I just said it in a fit of rage and didn't mean it at all.

"I've known for a long time something was wrong, although I don't know why." She looked worried. "But until this thing with Carmen happened, I still believed I could control myself. I've always been able to rely on will power, and I kept thinking I still could. Even when I knew I looked bad to other people, I didn't stop it or even consider doing something about it."

Sensing we were running late, we both looked at the clock and discovered we were well beyond our scheduled time.

"Can you meet at this same time next Tuesday?" I asked.

"I'll be here," she nodded, with a slight smile, and left.

She began the next session as she walked through the door. "I've felt better about doing this since last time, so I want to go back and tell you what I realized before I got here today."

She relaxed into her chair.

"I know we didn't come up with any deep answers last time, but I could tell we were on the right track of understanding why I am the way I am so I can do something about it.

"Like I said last time, I've always used will power to control myself; I give myself lectures and bite my tongue. But at some point that stopped working. It's gotten easier just to say my workers are irresponsible, or that my CEO doesn't support me, but I know that doesn't solve anything either, because blaming and railing at a person can't make her be someone she's not.

"Then over the last several months, and I can't say exactly when, I could sense that when I got angry, something inside me was driving me to lash out, but even then I thought I could control myself. I don't know why I had to wait for this crisis, which could have ruined me, before I was ready to do something about it."

"When do you think the realization finally crystallized in your mind?" I asked.

She snickered. "Only when Alex laid down her ultimatum."

Resuming her serious expression, she continued.

"When you thought, in the first session, that Alex was a man, that was helpful, although I wasn't about to say it at the time, because it helped me think more about why I'm here. I often react to men and their sexist attitudes the way I did with Carmen, and then I think that men are my problem. But obviously my reaction to Carmen was not because she's a sexist male, so this problem has to be about more than men. The people who complain about me at work are not men, they're all women. And it's not just my employees either. Alex told me the senior executives, including Alex herself, said they'd had enough of 'your resentful attitude and dragging your feet every time they give you a directive.'"

She frowned in silence.

"If the frown could talk, what would it say?" I asked.

Raising her eyebrows, she smiled in surprise. "I didn't realize I was frowning. I guess it was because I hate to accept that this thing doesn't just involve men. I was frowning in concentration, because now that I'm starting to see what my problem is not, I'm becoming more clear what it is, that it's with anyone who tries to dominate or abuse me, not just men."

By now, Ms. Tillman's excessive rage that had spilled over into her every word and act had subsided enough for me to see her outstanding qualities that could make her an outstanding leader in any endeavor, whether industry or some other field. She was intelligent, well organized, and, when not defensively angry, likeable, sensitive to the needs of her employees, and clear and firm in implementing business goals. As she, herself, once said in passing, "I've always known I was a 'diamond in the rough' and had it in me to make it to the top, but, at the same time, I also knew that unless I found a way to smooth out my rough edges, I never would."

Likewise, her personal goals were sound, realistic, and unconflicted. In addition to her skills, she had an outstanding reputation and was determined to climb the corporate ladder to become her company's CEO.

But she also knew that her self-defeating behaviors were colliding with her career ambitions and her industry's high-performance demands, and that she must overcome these behaviors or likely have to sacrifice her goals. The crisis she had inflicted on herself had been inevitable, since her behaviors had arisen from deep-seated subconscious demons she only vaguely knew existed, much less identify and surmount.

The process that allows you to know your mind is no supernatural mystery and does not rely on magic. The procedure, "Emotional Debridement," for identifying and overcoming emotional demons, is based on the same principles used in the surgical technique "debridement."

Surgical debridement, the standard method for treating wounds of the flesh, involves three basic steps: first, identify and remove the harmful debris and no-longer-viable tissue from the injured area; second, analyze the removed debris and dead tissue to provide information for further treatment; and third, with the wound freed of inhibiting foreign substances, normal, healthy tissue can grow and heal the injured flesh. In surgical debridement, these three stages—identification and removal, analysis and study, and healthy growth—occur largely as separate, distinct steps.

Overcoming flawed emotions through emotional debridement is incalculably more complex than surgical debridement, yet the steps are analogous: first, identify the flawed emotional structures, such as anxious dreads and self-defeating behaviors; second, eliminate the flawed structures by understanding their underlying causes; and third, supplant the removed troublemakers with one's own already proven, healthy strengths.

Emotional debridement is made possible by the capacity of one's mind to observe and master feelings and ideas at the same time one is experiencing those same feelings. While one part of the mind is experiencing an emotional pattern, another part of the mind can observe the pattern's meanings by studying its quality, function, origin, history, and associated feelings and ideas. A person can then decide whether the pattern has outlived its usefulness, and, if so, relinquish it.

Two critical distinctions differentiate surgical and emotional debridement. First, in surgical debridement, the steps are sharply defined and demarcated from each other, whereas in emotional debridement the steps overlap and become intertwined, with each step's advancement facilitating the progress of the others.

The second distinction is fundamental and crucial: in surgical debridement, the treating physician decides which, if any, noxious tissue to remove, while in emotional debridement, any decision to change one's emotional makeup is made entirely by the person seeking relief. The person desiring internal change is the one who decides whether or not to take each critical step of relinquishing painful anxieties and self-defeating behaviors, rooting out demons, and expanding her use of healthy, well-functioning emotional structures.

Ms. Tillman's mastery of her self-defeating behaviors, active-aggressive ones toward her employees and passive-aggressive ones toward her superiors, lay in her discovering and overcoming the demons underlying these behaviors, and then integrating this knowledge into her emotions. Her common sense told her that her real strengths gained from her new self-knowledge, would make unnecessary her illusory *felt* strengths of self-defeating "fierce independence" and non-verbal defiance.

The emotional changes resulting from emotional de-bridement do not happen simply by one person telling another what is wrong with him; they result from a working alliance between two people who make individual, indispensable contributions. A patient, or client, contributes his unique awareness of his troublesome thoughts and feelings, a self-honest willingness to study and understand them, and the motivation to endure the arduous steps necessary to make internal changes. A self-knowledge therapist brings her ability to detect even subtle versions of self-defeating mental-emotional patterns, a balanced objectivity and emotional interest in the therapeutic work, and the verbal skills to communicate that understanding and commitment to the client.

Still, no matter how much one wishes to overcome self-defeating patterns, the emotions underlying these patterns have tender spots that tenaciously, and often vehemently, resist being exposed; once the mind realizes it is in danger of pain, it protects itself by pushing the painful emotion out of conscious awareness. Since the mind fiercely resists meddlers, including therapists or even oneself, when they try to help one gain self-knowledge by making disturbing feelings accessible to one's observing mind, the therapist's empathic sensitivity and communication skills become critical. To achieve the rapport and trust necessary for focusing on tender emotions and painful conflicts, the self-knowledge therapist must be especially sensitive to, and respectful of, a patient or client's attitudes and feelings.

Resistance to exposing dreaded feelings is a normal, recurrent part of the process of achieving self-knowledge. Overcoming this resistance involves defining the resistance itself and is often achieved only a small measure at a time. When a person seeking change needs help in facing and overcoming her resistances, the self-knowledge therapist must be emotionally and intellectually prepared to do whatever is necessary to help the procedure. This includes not only gentle nudges, but also firm confrontations when indicated and appropriate for the individual. In certain instances it means sensitively holding the person to the task by bringing her attention back, again and again, to the dreaded emotion, as Ms. Tillman's emotional debridement often required.

The therapist can ease this process, but the patient or client herself must be willing to expose her painful emotions to the work of gaining self-understanding, often using sheer will power to confront opportunities to experience and temporarily endure the disturbing feelings. The process can be helped by the person remembering her goals, as frequently as necessary, and contrasting them with the consequences of self-defeating alternatives, then to continue to do so until emotional debridement is accomplished and new, healthy patterns become ingrained.

After several weeks of working through her resistance to accepting emotionally what she had come to know intellectually—her subconscious emotions' role in creating her self-destructive behavior that resulted in her explosion at Carmen—Ms. Tillman began a session, "You've asked me several times to talk about the importance of being independent, but I've never answered you because your question implies that something is wrong with what I've always thought was a normal and desirable attribute. I think I can answer now because I finally realize you haven't meant normal independence; you've been asking about my 'fierce independence,' and I'm more aware now of how much trouble it's caused me."

Because independence not involved in conflict ordinarily is a healthy and beneficial emotion and character trait, her use of "fiercely" had caught my attention early on. It said this was a particularly strong emotion whose meaning and function would be important to understand in overcoming her most self-defeating character trait.

Immature behaviors are normal and constructive in a two year old child who is experimenting with her world and testing the limits of acceptable behavior. A young child's crude pseudoindependence, stubbornness, and demanding tantrums are vital building stones for the refined adult strengths of autonomy, self-assertion, determination, and mastery. But infantile behaviors preserved in their original forms are completely out of place in the adult world, and almost always result in self-defeat. A production manager cannot reasonably expect to maintain high morale in five hundred employees if she inflicts tantrum-like castigations on subordinates in the presence of their peers.

Since Ms. Tillman had indicated her readiness to talk about her fierce independence, and because the timing and sequence of mental-emotional events is as central to understanding the mind as physical events are to diagnosing and treating the body, I asked, "Has something happened recently that has made you especially aware of the trouble your drive for 'fierce independence' causes you?"

She winced. "That question has occurred to me for some time, but this morning it hit me like a sledgehammer. I had to rearrange my office to make room for a new filing cabinet, and when Nancy, my secretary, saw me start to move my heavy oak desk, she came to help me, and, without thinking, I reflexively told her, 'No, I'll do it,' and then I couldn't move the desk, and I strained my back trying. You may have noticed me leaning to the left when I came in here today. It's really hurting, but I didn't mention it because, and this is for the same reason we're talking about, an independent person doesn't let herself sound like a needy whiner."

"Say more about wanting not to sound like a 'needy whiner'?" I asked.

She curled her lips as though she had a foul taste in her mouth.

"People who whine make me so sick I feel like I want to vomit," she said.

"Are you saying, then, that letting Nancy help you not strain your back would make you a needy whiner?"

"It's the same thing, it's admitting you're weak and helpless, and I dread that; I'd rather die first. I'll do *anything* to be independent."

Emotions are as basic to our mind as heartbeats are to our body and are present in our earliest days, even though we usually have little conscious memory of them. Our earliest experiences, even in infancy, of powerful feelings that create conflict and problems become particularly important when we later try to understand our perception of those feelings. Knowing the history of Ms. Tillman's weak and helpless feelings was critical to understanding her imperative to be strong and independent.

"What comes to mind from the past about feeling weak and helpless?" I asked.

She looked at me for a moment then glanced out the window, distracted by the rapid movements of one squirrel chasing another up the large oak tree near the window. After a moment, she turned back with a slight smile. "I'd rather think about those squirrels, but I guess that wouldn't get me anywhere.

"I usually don't let myself think about feeling weak and helpless. I've tried to be strong and independent as long as I can remember. I never let anyone help me or tell me what to do unless I've already decided I want them to. It's had advantages, too, because a lot of people, like other kids when I was growing up, admire me and compliment me, and look to me as their leader. I remember those times most, but, when I let myself think about it, I have the feeling that the way I insist on being so independent puts a lot of people off, and they don't take to me as friendly as I wish they would. Then I think that whatever I get from being independent may not be worth it. I usually don't remember those times, and I would have forgotten about turning down Nancy's help and how I got this back pain, except that I can't ignore it so easily since this work has made me more aware of what I'm doing."

As she changed her position she winced again. I sensed that her expression reflected her awareness of how people are put off by her "fierce independence" as much as it did her back pain.

"You put people not taking friendly to you together with not telling me about the back pain," I said.

"They're the same. When people hurt me or avoid me, it's like I'm on the outside looking in, like a weak, whining child pressing her face against the window, pleading to let me inside where everything important is happening, and that's how I would look if I whined to you about my back hurting. You'd think I was weak."

"Can you say more about 'pleading for someone to let you in?'" I asked.

Her eyes filled with tears.

"You asked me the same kind of question a few minutes ago, and I didn't know what to say, but maybe I can now," she said, struggling to speak as she cried. "The memory that flashed through my mind for just a second, and then I couldn't get back for a moment, was of when I was five, and my mother was in the hospital after she'd been in a car accident." Ms. Tillman closed her eyes for a moment. "I desperately wanted to see her because I was afraid she was gone forever, but the hospital people wouldn't let me, because they said I was too little, and that I would have to be six before I could go in. I felt so scared and helpless I was frantic, and I cried and cried, but they wouldn't let me in. My father let me talk with her on the phone, but that only helped a little because I wasn't really sure it was her or where she was."

She covered her eyes with her hands, and cried several moments without speaking.

While she was crying, I heard my next patient—a man who felt especially wronged and devalued if he were kept waiting—open and close the waiting room door, and when I checked the clock I saw that Ms. Tillman's and my time was already up. I did not mention my observation, though, until her crying had subsided, by when she too had become aware we would have to stop. She wiped her tears, stood, and said, "I'll see you next time." I nodded and she left.

The next session she arrived thirty minutes late, upset and agitated, and immediately, while still standing, said, "I'm so sorry to have kept you waiting. I had a crisis with a customer, and I had no choice but to take care of it right away. And then I was flustered and worried about being late, so I got away without my cell phone and couldn't call you, and I figured it would delay us even more to stop at a pay phone. I really apologize; this kind of thing doesn't happen very often."

"But when it does, we have to take care of first things first," I responded, "and it looks like this was one of those times."

She sat and took a few moments to compose herself. "In spite of this flap today, though, things seem to have stabilized and are going better at work, but I want to pick up where we left off last time. I told you about what happened when Mother was in the hospital, but I didn't get a chance to tell you about the other thing I thought of when you asked me about being weak and helpless."

She stopped talking, looked out the window, and crossed her arms across her chest as though to help hold back tears.

"It was my brother, Kyle. In one way I love him, but I hate him for what he did to me."

"What he did to you?" I asked.

As she looked at the floor, her jaw muscles tightened.

"Starting when I was six and he was eleven, he sexually molested me, and I was too little to fight him off," she replied with a voice that almost shook with anger. "At first he tickled my ribs until I couldn't breathe, and then he put his hand between my legs. Once he tried to put his penis in my mouth, but I got so sick and vomited he didn't try to do that again. I was so scared I didn't know what do. He was so much bigger than I was, and he would force me to lie still while he put his hands all over my body."

She became still, then clasped her hands over her mouth, as though trying not to vomit, and her face went absolutely white.

"What did you think of just then?" I asked gently.

Tears poured from her eyes, and her whole body began to shake. She cried for several minutes, the silence broken only by her gasping for breath. When her breathing became more regular, she reached for some tissues to dry her face, and I waited for her to continue.

"I remembered," she whispered, "other times when he tried to do that."

I asked, "It's too upsetting to talk about what you remembered?"

She closed her eyes tightly, and nodded. After a few moments, she opened her eyes and said, "He tried to put his penis in my mouth other times, and I fought him off, but I get so sick when I think of it, the memory goes away."

Tears ran down her cheeks, but she continued her story as she wiped them with a tissue.

"I begged Mother to make him stop, but she must not have understood me or didn't believe me because he kept doing it. I never did know whether she told him to stop. I was too helpless to make him quit until I was almost twelve and got to be strong enough to fight him off myself. Being weak felt so terrible I swore I'd never let anyone treat me that way again. But it wasn't just being vulnerable, I felt humiliated and degraded; my friend's brothers didn't do things like that to them. I think I learned the meaning of independence before I could even say the word, because I knew I'd never let anyone make me feel that way again."

Still crying, she paused and stared in the direction of the tree just beyond the window.

"What are you thinking?" I asked.

Sniffling, she answered, "I didn't tell you this a few minutes ago because it all happened so fast, but when I saw those two squirrels, I thought for just a moment how I hated the big male for chasing the scared little girl, and I felt so sorry for her because she was too helpless to protect herself."

Ms. Tillman's perception of the squirrels' behavior so closely followed the memories she had been describing, I asked, "What about what you just said?"

"I know what I just said, I heard myself as I said it. There actually was no big or little one, those squirrels were about the same size, and I couldn't tell you whether either was a male or female. But it seemed so natural to think that way, that the one chasing the other was a big male bully, and the one running for its life was a frightened little girl who couldn't protect herself. That's how I felt around Kyle until he went away to college."

She looked at her watch, and, somewhat alarmed, said, "Oh my God, we've run out of time again. I'm awful sorry about being late, although this time I'm not just apologizing to you, I'm sorry for myself for having missed the time. There's always so much more to say."

Ms. Tillman had expressed vividly the helplessness a small child feels in an adult world, especially when faced with emotional trauma perpetrated by bigger people, and how these feelings become profoundly etched into and preserved in one's timeless subconscious mind. Her whole life she had been fearing vulnerability as if the conditions of her actual weakness as a small child still existed and would continue forever with the same intensity she felt when she first experienced the trauma.

To cope with these feelings, she had developed the defense of "fierce independence," a mechanism that made her feel strong and beyond the hurt and harm of others.

While little Portia's emotional survival as a small child relied on developing extreme independence and dominion over others, Ms. Tillman as an adult no longer actually needed these outmoded mechanisms; rather, they defeated her goals. Because she now was neither physically small nor emotionally immature, the bases of her original dreads of extreme helplessness and vulnerability no longer existed; as a strong, grown woman she could protect herself physically and tolerate her painful emotions.

A crucial step in Ms. Tillman's mastery of her feelings occurred when she allowed herself to become consciously aware of how she had used her fierce drive for independence to dominate others in order to protect herself from her dread of vulnerability and helplessness.

She began the next session while walking through the office door. "I've been anxious to get here and follow up what we talked about last time. When I saw my own feelings in a couple of playful squirrels, I recognized how these feelings have been in me my whole life, and then I got to wondering why I've been so much more harsh this past year."

"Can you wonder out loud?" I asked.

She continued as she sat down. "I think it has something to do with Alex."

"What about Alex," I asked.

"She came here from another company a year ago. Even though I respect and like her in some ways, I've bitterly resented her ever since she got here. I felt hurt and betrayed by the Board when they chose her to be CEO instead of me, although I think the Board members were influenced mostly by the previous CEO who'd recommended Alex. I know this wasn't Alex's fault, but I've been angry with her ever since she came, especially when she gives me orders and quotas. I deserved that position, not her," she said, slamming her fist on the arm of her chair.

"You felt helpless and betrayed by the Board the same way you did when the hospital authorities wouldn't let you in to see your mother and when Kyle abused you," I said with a question in my voice.

"Finding this out about myself doesn't come as a surprise. I've always sensed I had these feelings, I've just never really talked about them or tried to work them out. Other people apparently have seen this in me for a long time. Friends at work, who knew me before Alex came, have asked me, 'What's happened to you since Alex got here?' Even Alex asked me, 'I've heard you were such a pleasant person before I came, have I done something I don't know about, or do I rub you the wrong way?' I couldn't answer her, of course, in part because I didn't really know myself, and I certainly didn't realize how much it showed."

Aware of her anger toward Alex and the Board, but no longer consumed by it, Ms. Tillman's tone and manner were forthright, free of rage and tears.

Then she became silent and looked into space.

"Can you think out loud?" I asked.

She remained quiet for several moments. "The more we talk about how independent and aggressive I've been since Alex came, the more I'm aware of something else I do—you'd probably call it a 'defense mechanism'—that keeps me from feeling vulnerable and degraded. I said before how much I've resented Alex for getting the job I wanted, but I didn't say why it was so critical. I'm sure everyone has their own reason for being ambitious, but mine seems more specific than most people's." She crossed her arms, then crossed her legs, with one ankle resting on the other knee. "Now that I know why being independent is so important to me, I recall that by the time I was five or six I thought that big people, like my parents and the hospital director, and then Kyle, had so much power no one could hurt them or make them do things, and I decided right then that I wanted to be big and powerful as quick as I could. I had thought for a couple of years before Rhoda, the previous CEO, left that I would get her job, so It really hit me hard when they gave the job to Alex."

"It felt like the sooner you could be big and powerful, the sooner you could be protected from feeling helpless and vulnerable?" I asked.

"Yes, and I guess it blinded me to the facts of reaching high places: you have to have training and experience, and you have to be a known quantity. Alex was forty-eight at the time she got the CEO job, and I was only thirty-five. She'd had thirteen more years in corporate work than I'd had, and people knew her and what she could do. I'd thought she got there because Rhoda influenced the Board, but later I learned that wasn't true. The Board had known about Alex and her work a long time. I had been with the company only a couple of years, and that was nothing compared to Alex, she'd been in the software business with another company for ten years. I've already succeeded well, and I'm sure I'll do even better in the future, but I think now that no success, no matter how and when it came, would have been enough to soften the blows of hurts and disappointments."

She uncrossed her arms and legs, leaned forward, and pointed at me. "One thing is for sure though, I can see now I really don't need to be 'ferociously independent' any more." She smiled.

The several months of work that culminated in this insight were the most trying during her pursuit of self-knowledge, but its painstaking, step-by-step emotional debridement of her fear of helpless vulnerability had allowed her to relinquish her self-destructive mechanism of ferocious independence. By exposing herself to this dreaded feeling within the session, where she felt safe and had no actual need for her illusory power, she discovered she could bear the dread, and, in doing so, eliminated not only the dread's mystery and power but her need for excessive independence as well.

She found that, in the end, the threatening feeling was, though powerful, simply a fearsome childhood emotion that had persisted into her adulthood where it no longer applied, an emotion that made her feel as if she were still a helpless five year old forcibly restricted from seeing her mother, or a vulnerable six year old forced into sexual submission by a sadistic older brother, conditions that had not existed for almost twenty-five years. With these discoveries she came to know, emotionally, as well as intellectually, that she no longer had to fear the helpless and humiliating subjugation that had caused her "fierce independence."

Intellectual awareness of subconscious emotions is necessary for emotional debridement and repair. But intellectual awareness alone is not sufficient: it must be accompanied by knowing intimately, and wishing to change, one's troublesome emotions. Emotional growth usually comes naturally as one gains self-knowledge, particularly for strongly motivated people like Ms. Tillman. Without this incentive to change one's troublesome emotions, intellectual awareness of subconscious thoughts and feelings, including the insights of writers and poets, renders such awareness no more useful for making emotional change than are abstract platitudes.

The third step of Ms. Tillman's emotional debridement —extending the growth and use of already well-functioning, properly employed strengths—came easily for her, as it does most people. Strongly motivated by her company's ultimatum and her own good judgment, she willingly relinquished her excessively aggressive behaviors and replaced them with her real capacities for even-tempered tact and personal persuasion, abilities that had already played a major role in her business and personal success.

Ms. Tillman had ready access to subordinates and superiors who were, unknowingly, willing and eager in the normal work day to test her tender spots, and she used those opportunities to take several steps in achieving mastery over her internal saboteurs. She dealt with her aggravation toward others by deliberately behaving maturely, then bringing her reflexive anger to our work where she could learn how her mind had caused it, while regularly reminding herself that her highest priority was not to bash offenders with her destructive urges, but to achieve her prized life goals.

By then her dreaded feelings had either dissipated completely or were lessened to such a degree she rarely thought of them.

Three years to the month after Ms. Tillman's almost ruinous tirade against her employees, her CEO took a position with a larger company, and, before leaving, recommended Ms. Tillman to succeed her. Ms. Tillman's employees respected and no longer feared her, and the Board members admired her work and did not question her stability. The Board of Directors immediately asked Ms. Tillman to be the new CEO, and she accepted.

3

Hey! No Problem

On a Friday afternoon in the late 1990's, a state court clerk closed her office and left for the day, puzzled that a court ordered document had not been filed in time to meet the judge's deadline. The legal brief, crucial to the defendant's case in a personal injury lawsuit, had not arrived because the defendant's attorney had failed to do his job.

Postponements and continuances are well recognized in legal proceedings, and procrastination and lateness are well known lawyer habits, but Robert Tucker had already missed many important deadlines. In his long history of dilatory behavior on critical, time sensitive matters, he had often counted on his stellar reputation and silver tongue to bail him out short of absolute disaster. This time, though, he could not easily smooth over the consequences of his failure.

In defying the court order, Mr. Tucker incurred the wrath of Judge Landis, a small town southwestern state court judge well known for his stern reactions to big-city types and his intolerance of lawyer incompetence. Judge Landis immediately held Mr. Tucker in contempt of court, fined him substantially, and referred his case to the Bar Association's Ethics Committee.

By jeopardizing the reputation of his respected personal injury law firm, Mr. Tucker provoked the firm's managing partner, Allen Bailey, irate with a beet red face, to look Robert Tucker squarely in the eye, slam his fist on his desk, and yell, "This is the last straw!"

Mr. Tucker sat stone faced.

"You will show me concrete evidence that you are serious about overcoming this problem by doing something about it immediately or you are out of here!" Mr. Bailey demanded, in angry tones.

When Jack Sanders, Mr. Tucker's most trusted colleague, heard a few minutes later about the confrontation, he tried to convince his good friend that he must take steps to overcome his problem, to demonstrate his "good faith" toward keeping his job if nothing else. Faced with having to choose between procrastination and his career, Mr. Tucker reluctantly decided to get help. Mr. Sanders gave him my name, and Mr. Tucker called and made an appointment for the next afternoon.

Several hours before Mr. Tucker was due, Mr. Sanders, recognizing Mr. Tucker's resistance to the entire process, called to give me background on the seriousness of Mr. Tucker's situation, including describing the events above. "I told Bob I'd call you, so he knows we're talking. Bob's an ambitious man, and everyone at the firm knows he wants to be the best in his field. Many of us think he already is. He's our smartest partner, our best writer and speaker, he's a natural to argue in the courtroom and to deal with difficult clients, and, unless stringent deadlines are involved, we can always count on him to handle and win the complicated cases. His personal charm also makes him our best rain maker, and he always wins our beauty contests [law firms' jargon for competition with other firms for obtaining new clients].

"But we've always known that, sooner or later, he'd put the firm in serious jeopardy if he didn't stop missing deadlines. Any partner's behavior, particularly one of Bob's prominence, can affect everyone else, and his colleagues' resentment can hurt the whole firm's morale." Mr. Sanders hesitated a moment. "But the main reason I called is to be sure Bob's lack of concern doesn't mislead you into thinking he's not in real trouble. Let there be no question that the firm has run out of patience and will fire him if he doesn't turn around, immediately."

That afternoon, a tall, handsome, well groomed, fortyish Mr. Tucker smiled politely when he arrived fifteen minutes late, nodded his head, and responded with only a slight smirk when I said, "Hello, I'm Dr. Stockton."

He offered no explanation for being late, noticeable only because most people usually apologize, at least perfunctorily, and said nothing as he entered the consultation room and sat in the chair I had motioned to.

I began immediately. "Well, as I'm sure you know, Mr. Sanders called to fill me in," then, extending my open hands, added, "but it's important for us to know how you think about what brought you here."

He looked into space for two or three minutes before turning back to me. "They call me a procrastinator."

"What about 'procrastinator'?" I asked.

"What is there to talk about?" he sneered, with an air of dismissal. "That I'm late sometimes? Hey, no problem. What's the big deal? I've been late my whole life."

"Say more about 'my whole life'?" I asked.

He rolled his eyes, and heaved an impatient sigh.

"I don't get to the office before ten, but neither do other lawyers. I'm usually later than most everyone else, and I miss some professional deadlines, but I always win my cases so my clients and colleagues accept that it's nobody's business but my own." He crossed his arms and stared at me.

"You said you've been late 'my whole life.' That suggested this pattern has been around for some time," I said.

His eyes widened in surprise, then his face slowly went blank.

"Sometimes I got to school late, and I used to cram the night before tests," he droned, "but I always made good grades so there was no problem." He crossed his leg and idly bounced his foot. "In high school and college I wasn't always on time for debate team practice, and when we had contests at other schools I sometimes missed the team bus, but someone was usually around to drive me, and I always won my debate." He stared at me, then gave a short laugh. "My mother once joked, 'I had a long labor with Robert because he refused to be delivered when the doctor expected him,' so she was even amused by it."

"Are you saying you're surprised when people are upset with you?" I asked.

He threw up his hands. "I don't know why people get so wired about this, I always get the job done, like when I stayed up to study the night before tests and still made A's." A hint of defiant pride had come into his voice.

After several moments, I said, "Does that seem to be all there is to it? What else occurs to you?"

He gave me a look of annoyance, then cleared his throat.

"My clients respect my work enough to tolerate my lateness. Building contractors never meet the deadlines they promise, but they stay in business because they do good work. My wife, Dorothy, gets on my case because I sometimes get home after I say I will, but she should be grateful to me for working so hard and being a good provider. And anyway, I'm usually home in time to say goodnight to the kids." He glanced around the room, looking bored.

I noticed he had not acknowledged, in any form, the aggravation and problems he caused others.

"Your habits upset your wife like they did the judge?" I asked.

He shrugged.

"I guess so, Dorothy's always angry." He sat up, switched his crossed legs, and resumed bouncing his foot. "She says, 'You never live up to your promises.' A year ago, she threatened to divorce me if I didn't stop leaving her and the kids in the lurch, but I talked her out of it, and she didn't bring it up again until this thing with the judge."

He looked out the window.

"If your looking out the window could talk, what would it say?" I asked.

Turning back to me, he said, "What kind of question is that? Looking can't talk. I'll tell you what I was thinking, though. If it weren't for my daughters, I wouldn't mind so much my wife divorcing me. My daughters are my only real joy in life." His eyes moistened. "I don't know what I'd do without them." Then he looked out the window again. "What are you thinking?" I asked.

This time his face was grim. "I was thinking about Dorothy and why I said I wouldn't mind losing her. Last night when I told her about the judge and the firm coming down on me, she said, 'I'm sorry for your predicament, but thank God somebody's doing something about the way you treat people, and I'm not going to tolerate it much longer either.'" He pulled a tissue from a box on the lamp table next to him to wipe a tear. "She may mean it this time, although she may not be so eager to leave when she realizes that the trouble I'm having could end up hurting her and the girls as well as me." His stiff, unemotional tone had returned. "But, I'll just have to wait and see what she does." Then he added, "But that's between my wife and me, and it's not any of Bailey's business."

"What about Bailey's business?" I asked.

"What do you mean?" he asked, raising an eyebrow.

"Mr. Sanders said you're in hot water," I said.

He waved a dismissive hand. "Oh that'll settle down, it always has. Al Bailey overreacts so much you can't take him seriously, and he's making 'much ado about nothing' about this anyway."

"You said, 'it always has.' What did you mean?" I asked.

His foot froze a moment, then continued its rhythm.

"Well, this kind of thing comes up now and then, but it dies down pretty soon and people forget about it," he said and began drumming his fingers on the lamp table.

"This has happened before?" I asked.

"Oh, yeah," he said, with another dismissive wave. Then he glanced out the window, before adding, "Well, maybe the importance of this case makes the stakes to the firm higher than usual."

Abruptly, he became still and his face paled, then he shook his head rapidly, as if to shake off what he was hearing himself say.

"But that doesn't make any difference, these things always turn out to be a tempest in a teapot, and I'm sure this one will too." He nodded, as if reassured.

"So you don't really think you have to treat Mr. Bailey's threats seriously?" I asked.

"Bah, I'll talk to him and he'll forget all about it," he said with a forced smile, as he tapped his fingers on the arm of his chair.

"And Judge Landis?" I asked.

His eyes locked on me as he again became still, then resumed tapping his fingers and bouncing his foot. "Well, I hadn't thought much about him because I've never had a judge react like that before. But I don't think there's anything to worry about there either." He began to rub the back of his neck. "I was so busy working on the case I forgot the deadline. These things happen all the time, people get upset and complain, but you can't let them bother you," he said.

Looking at his watch, he realized our time was up, then asked, "When are we supposed to meet next?"

"What about the same time on Friday?" I suggested.

"You mean Friday of this week?" he asked with alarm. "That's only three days from now!"

I nodded.

He regarded me a moment. "See you then."

The next session he walked in late frowning and began talking the instant he sat down.

"A lot has happened since I saw you, and none of it's good." His crossed leg moved in vigorous circles.

"How so?" I asked.

"I talked to Al Bailey again and he was madder than he was the first time. He said he wants to talk to you, as he put it, 'to make damn sure your shrink understands the trouble you're in.' I don't know what's wrong with the son of a bitch," Mr. Tucker said, throwing up his hands. "He acts like I didn't hear him the first time. Anyway, I told him it's okay with me for him to talk with you, but that it wasn't necessary because Jack already had." He rubbed the back of his neck. "So he's going to see Jack before he does anything else." He began tapping his fingers. "The bastard said something else, too, that I really resented. He said the reason he wanted to talk to you is that he thinks I've got some kind of problem that makes me 'stubborn' about obeying legal procedures or simple rules of courtesy, or even listening to someone trying to reason with me about it. I don't know where the hell he's coming from." As Mr. Tucker spoke, he stretched his head around as though trying to relieve a stiff neck.

"You suggested something else happened, too?" I asked.

He pursed his lips. "Let's see, we met on Tuesday," he thought a moment, "then on Wednesday I met in court with Judge Landis, and he laid out the details of my contempt citation, and uh, . . ."

Pale faced, he looked at me and clicked his teeth several times.

I said, "You stopped yourself in mid-sentence, as if you couldn't go on. What did you think about?"

He swallowed, clenched his jaw, and took a couple of deep breaths. "Judge Landis fined me $10,000 and gave me a copy of the letter he sent to the Bar Association Ethics Committee."

"What happened?" I asked.

"I never thought things would get this far. And there's more," he said, wide-eyed, nodding his head. "On Thursday I got another registered letter, this one from the Ethics Committee, saying they want to meet with me next Tuesday at three o'clock. In certain ways this letter is worse than the one from Judge Landis because I know that the Committee doesn't usually act this quickly, either to send the original notice after receiving the complaint, or to demand a meeting with the defendant so quickly after sending the notice. And I also know that when they say three o'clock, they mean three o'clock, not a second later."

"Well, let's see where we can best take this," I said with a question in my voice.

He rolled his head while he massaged his neck. "I've never had anything get to me like this before."

"Get to you, how?" I asked.

"I can't concentrate on my work. I've hardly slept a wink for the last two nights. I was all right Tuesday night after I saw you and then talked with Bailey when I got back to the office, but after I saw Judge Landis on Wednesday and then got the letter from the Ethics Committee yesterday I haven't slept at all." Rubbing the back of his neck again, he grimaced. "Can you give me something to help me sleep?"

I said, "There are several sleeping medicines one can use, but I think you'll find that in the long run you'll benefit most if we take advantage of your pain to understand how you got yourself into this trouble, so you won't be as apt to be in the same place again in the future."

He knit his brow, slowly nodded, and said, "Okay," with great reluctance. "But I hope it won't take long, being awake for hours at night is awfully hard." Raising his eyebrows, he asked, "What's next?"

"Earlier you talked about having these behaviors your whole life. I see our time is up now, but perhaps we can start next time with what more you remember about them?" I said.

Again, he nodded slowly.

At our next appointment, again arriving late, he began as if we had had no interruption.

"I've been thinking that maybe I ought to talk about my procrastination. I'm not sure where to begin, so I'll start by telling you about my family. I was an only child. My father was an accountant, and my mother was a junior high school English teacher. I know they loved me by the way they were so involved in my life, but they ran a tight ship. My father treated me like I was numbers at his office, and Mother expected me to behave the way she wanted her eighth graders at school to behave. She set my alarm for one full hour before the school bus came and insisted I get up immediately, and," he half smiled and shook his head, "it was even worse after school.

"You're not going to believe this, but my father scheduled my first study session from four to six, dinner from six to seven, second study period from seven to ten, and lights out at ten-thirty. I had to come to dinner on time with my hands washed and ready to discuss, with proper grammar, whatever ideas and events they wanted to talk about. And even when I was a teenager, they demanded I keep my room neat and orderly."

"That sounds worse than the military," I said with a sympathetic grin. "How did it feel to be controlled so much?"

"I hated it!" he exploded, slamming his fist on the arm of his chair. Taking a deep breath, he shook his head. "But I didn't realize how much I hated it until after I'd left home."

"What happened after leaving home that let you know?" I asked.

He scowled. "When I was in college near Boston, I went to visit my cousins and Aunt Helen, Mother's younger sister, and I saw my mother in Aunt Helen from the moment I got there until I left three hours later."

He wadded up the tissue he had used to blow his nose and fired it into the wastebasket.

"She told her children what to do, and how and when to do it. Unlike me, though, they knew they hated it, and they said so. One of my cousins, Jerry, screamed at her, 'GET OFF MY BACK.'"

He breathed heavily for several moments.

Looking at me with hard eyes, he said, "If it isn't obvious already, the answer to your question about what happened to let me know how angry I felt about being controlled at home was I realized how mad I got at Aunt Helen for trying to control my cousins, just like my mother and father did with me.

"One time," Mr. Tucker said, with disbelief, "she literally told Jerry, who's thirteen, 'Go to the bathroom,' when he kept shifting from one foot to the other while he was talking to his brother and me." He shook his head. "Jerry was obviously embarrassed that she would treat him like a little child in front of his friends, but it didn't stop him from screaming at her, 'I'm old enough to know when I need to go to the bathroom, so leave me alone.'" Mr.

Tucker's voice was thick with resentment. "I never could have done what he did, but it made me remember how bitter I felt when my parents did that kind of thing to me."

He stared out the window, then looked at me. "When I said I never could have done what Jerry did when he yelled, 'Get off my back and leave me alone,' I knew Jerry thought it was all right to get mad at his mother in a way I never could."

"What about it not being all right?" I asked.

"I wasn't just intimidated by my parents, I would have felt too guilty and afraid to talk to them that way."

"Say more about guilty and afraid," I urged.

His shoulders bowed, and he sighed deeply.

"I never could have gotten angry like Jerry did. My parents were very proper high Episcopalians, and no reason would ever have been good enough for them."

Over the following months, as Mr. Tucker deepened his knowledge of the causes of his procrastination, he became aware that his reactions of anger, guilt, and fear of feeling controlled had been a recurring problem throughout his life.

"I don't remember when I was little, like before I started to school," he began one session, "but they tell me that I was a real hellion and never obeyed anyone, that I was stubborn, and that I fought them and had temper tantrums any time I didn't get my way, even before what people call the 'terrible twos.'" He looked smug, then after a moment added, "Hm, I just realized that, 'stubborn,' is what Al Bailey called me."

He threw up his hands and shrugged.

"Like I said, I don't remember any of that, but I do remember that when I was in first grade, my parents kept telling me that the Bible said, 'Honor thy father and thy mother.' Then they made me read it as if it were part of my studying, and I read it so many times I recall the exact passage: Exodus, Chapter 20, verse 12, and that it goes on to say, ' . . . that thy days may be long upon the land which the Lord thy God giveth thee.' And that's when I started worrying about being good and that something bad would happen to me, like my days on this land wouldn't be very long, if I didn't honor and obey my parents." He grimaced and shook his head.

"There was more to that chapter, too. It's where the Ten Commandments and all the 'Thou shalt nots' come from, and also, and I remember exactly what it says, 'He that smiteth a man, so that he die, shall be surely put to death,' and then it says an eye for an eye, a tooth for a tooth, hand for hand, foot for foot. And then I got afraid that if I hit or kicked someone, like my mother or father, God would cut off my hand or foot. And then later, I don't remember exactly when, I studied the history and religion of those mideast countries, and I learned that people who commit crimes with their hands, like pickpockets, get them cut off, so I knew my fears were real." He closed his eyes and shuddered.

"And that same chapter in Exodus," he resumed, "also says something about 'a stiff necked people,' and I thought it was saying that if I got a stiff neck it meant I had been bad, so I learned to rub my neck so it wouldn't get stiff, then God wouldn't think I'd been bad. And a little later, when I learned that stiff-necked means stubborn, and people said I'd been stubborn, I worried that I wouldn't be long on this land." With a wry smile, he added, "How could one argue with that kind of authority?" He tilted his head and stared at nothing for a moment. "There's 'stubborn' again. Maybe the reason I got so mad at Al Bailey was that what he said was the same thing people have said about me my whole life, and it rankles me every time I hear it."

Before I could ask him to follow up his thoughts about 'stubborn,' he rushed on.

"That all happened when I was six, and I never told anyone about my worries, but Mother mentioned many times how good going to school had been for me because that was when I started behaving so well.

"I don't remember being unhappy before I started to school, but I do know that that was when I started being afraid to disagree with my parents, and I certainly could never have talked back to them the way Jerry did to Aunt

Helen. I don't really know what I was afraid of." He sounded puzzled. "After I got to be a teenager, they weren't any bigger than I was, but I always took for granted that you mind your parents and don't question it. They were so strong willed and intolerant of any disobedience and, worst of all, so goddamn self-righteous!" he exclaimed. "I think I must have gotten my fear of disobeying them mixed up with being afraid God would kill me or cut off my hand for not honoring them."

Mr. Tucker's recognition that his fear of disobeying his parents had become mixed up with his fear God would punish him marked the beginning of his insight into understanding his motive for creating his self-defeating defenses.

As we explored this issue over several months, his resistance to facing his active role in forming his defenses constantly emerged, until, one day, he entered the room on time, and, with no comment, began by focusing his eyes on mine.

After several moments, he said, "You have to understand something about the way my parents tried to convince me of the value of what they made me do. The reasons they gave for making me study and having those dinner discussions were so rational I couldn't argue with them. When I got to be a teenager, they said that all they wanted was to help me develop my mind so I'd be prepared for whatever career I would choose. The problem was not the dinner discussions themselves, I enjoyed them to some degree, it was that they were part of the way my parents, even at that age, controlled everything I did!"

"You're talking about these memories as we explore the problem that got you into trouble with the judge and your firm. Can you sense how they belong together?" I asked.

He frowned. "I don't know. I hadn't thought about it that way. Actually I was thinking about something else."

"Can you think out loud?" I asked.

"Oh, it's not important, just a PTA meeting my wife and I went to several years ago when our kids were in elementary school."

"What do you remember about the PTA meeting?" I asked.

He chuckled, "I guess I remember it because there was a psychiatrist like you there."

"What about the psychiatrist?" I asked, smiling.

Looking embarrassed, he said, "I feel silly talking about some psychiatrist at a PTA meeting ten years ago, but she was a child specialist who talked about how children handle their anger. You may know her, her name was Marjorie somebody, and she said that when children are afraid to show their anger, they have to learn ways of expressing it so they won't be punished." He thought a moment. "She said something like, 'If a child learns that saying, "I won't," will get him in trouble, but that whining, "I can't," especially if he has a good excuse, will get him sympathy, there is little question which method most children will choose.' I remember that when she said it, it struck a familiar chord. I didn't think any more about it at the time, but it's always stuck in the back of my mind."

I asked, "Are you saying you couldn't have said 'I won't' to your parents like Jerry did because you were afraid God would punish you, but you could whine 'I can't' when you had a good enough excuse?"

He shifted his weight from one side of the chair to the other, as he considered my question.

"Yes, but I couldn't think of any excuses for not studying, or talking at dinner, since the reasons my parents gave me for doing them were so reasonable. I couldn't think of who the psychiatrist might've been talking about, because I never wanted to say 'I can't," and I certainly wouldn't have said, 'I won't.' What excuse could I give when I, myself, enjoyed learning and preparing for a career as much as they wanted me too?" he asked, raising his eyebrows.

"Are you saying then that your 'I can'ts' and excuses happen when other people expect or demand something of you that you don't want to do?" I asked.

He sat up straight, and looked at me sharply. "What do you mean that I say 'I can't' when other people expect or demand something of me? I don't do that."

"I was thinking of what your actions said to the Judge, 'I couldn't deliver the brief on time because I was working so hard preparing it that I didn't remember the deadline,'" I responded.

He stared at me. "Well, they're hardly the same," he asserted. "The psychiatrist was talking about little children. The brief was a professional matter, and anyway, I wouldn't have run into problems if the judge hadn't been such a hard-nosed son of a bitch." He rubbed the back of his neck.

The degree of Mr. Tucker's denial of his contribution to causing the threat to his professional life, his attribution of blame to others, and his rationalizations for his behavior, told me I would have to confront him about his own role much more than usual if my efforts to help him overcome his problems were to succeed.

"You said earlier that when the psychiatrist talked about children who say, 'I can't,' and then give a good excuse for refusing to do what they're told, that it struck a familiar chord. Could that have been because you were remembering something about yourself?" I asked.

"No, I never did anything like that. I don't understand why you keep asking me." He crossed his arms and glowered at me.

I said, "I recall your mentioning in our first session something like, 'Sometimes I got to school late, but I always made good grades so there was no problem.' Are you saying that wasn't the same as, 'I can't because I've got a good excuse'?" I asked.

"No, because it didn't cause any problems except for the teacher getting upset, but she didn't count because that was her job," he snapped.

I said, "You also included in that first session that you weren't always on time for debate practice, and that when you missed the team bus for contests, someone else had to drive you. Are you implying that people tolerated your being late, and you assumed that your behavior was acceptable, because you always won your debate?"

His face red with fury, he looked at his watch. "I see

the time is up," he said abruptly, and left.

In fact, our time had not been up; he had left five minutes early. Ordinarily we both acknowledged our partings by confirming when we would meet next. In this instance, though, I had not responded because I felt I had already stretched his tolerance of my confrontations too thin, and his angry tone had told me he was in no mood to hear anything resembling a peaceful overture.

Such moments are always disquieting for a therapist. My moments with Mr. Tucker this day raised questions in my mind about whether what I did was or was not helpful. Had I misjudged his capacity for growth, the severity of his continued denial, and the degree to which he would go to avoid looking at this part of himself? Had I been insensitive in the terminology and phraseology of my confrontations? Had I not left enough time to help him settle his reactive emotions? Did he feel so threatened he would call and terminate his work with me, or just not show up the next session?

I would have to live with these uncertainties until our next session, which, fortunately, had already been scheduled for the following day.

The next day I heard the outside door open and close ten minutes before his appointed time, and when I entered the waiting room, he greeted me with an embarrassed smile and a muted, "Hi."

After walking silently into the office, he took his seat as usual, then I waited for him to begin.

"You probably thought I was mad at you yesterday, and in a way I was, but mostly I was mad at what you were saying," he said, more subdued than usual.

"What part of what I said?" I responded.

"I've always known I could never have said what Jerry did because I was convinced as a child that God would 'put me to death,' so that didn't come as a surprise. But when you kept going on and on about how many ways I've whined 'I can't,' and then avoided blame by giving all those excuses, and refused to listen to anybody about what I was doing, I realized you were talking about my being stubborn." His voice was almost shrill. "And then I heard my parents and teachers and Al Bailey and so many others, and now the judge, saying a thousand times, 'stubborn, stubborn, stubborn,' and 'excuses, excuses, excuses,' and I had to leave, because I couldn't stand it any more." He shifted from side to side in the chair, all the while rubbing the back of his neck.

"Couldn't stand what about 'stubborn' and 'excuses'?" I asked.

"Because people don't say it the way you and I," he gestured toward me and then himself, "talk about things here. When you describe something I do, it's objective, like we were talking about any medical problem, but when other people say, 'You're being stubborn,' what they really mean is, 'You're bad.' And I don't intend to be bad, it's just that being stubborn is the only way you can deal with some people. Like the judge. He's a damn dictator who abuses his privilege, and I'm totally powerless to do anything to get back at him."

"Like you felt as a child under the dictates of your parents and teachers?" I asked.

"Yes! And I really do hate people like that, even my parents when they treated me that way, and especially sons-a-bitches like Judge Landis! That child psychiatrist was right, being stubborn is one of the few ways you can get back at someone like that, and I knew it was the only way I could fight my parents." He grinned broadly. "People really get upset when you frustrate them or defeat their plans."

I replied, "To notice that someone is frustrated or upset is one thing, to observe it with glee is something else. If your smile could talk, what would it say?"

His smile vanished.

"What do you mean?" he demanded. "I just smiled because it's a nice thing to do when you're talking to someone. I smile a lot when I'm talking," he said, glaring at me.

"I know you enjoy talking with people," I said, "so naturally that would be your first explanation for your smile, but a minute ago your smile was especially wide, so let's see what occurs to you next about frustrating or defeating someone."

"I don't know what you're talking about. It sounds like you're accusing me of enjoying upsetting people, but I don't believe that at all, I've never been that kind of person," he said, rubbing the back of his neck.

"As you know by now, we all have lots of feelings about what we think and do, so maybe you could say some of the other thoughts that come to mind?" I asked.

He looked daggers at me, then stared into space.

"If there is anything to what you said, it's not for the reason you said. I don't like to upset anyone. When I used to tell teachers I was late for school because I studied late the night before, or when I told my parents I was late getting home because I had helped the teacher after school, I felt like I had more control than they did."

In my question about the meaning of his smile, I had not intended, as he suggested, to imply that he enjoyed seeing other people suffer from his action, rather to ask him to examine his facial expression that seemed not to match the content of his words. But I chose not to take up, at that time, his attribution to me of his own idea, so as not to interrupt his work on the primary meaning of his smile.

"How did it feel to have more control than they did?" I asked.

"I liked it," he declared.

"Maybe that's what I picked up in your smile. Can you say more about liking it?" I asked.

He looked outside.

"This is one of those times when my intelligence tells me I have to admit to a feeling I don't want to accept, because it sounds so childish and mean, but it does feel good to frustrate people who have more authority than I do. Those people usually tell me to do things, but this gives me power over them," he said, raising his fist in a Tiger Woods victory gesture, then his face fell. "That's why I got so upset when you kept talking about my being stubborn and having good excuses for it, because it seemed like you were trying to take away from me what little control I have in life."

"Do you know why your parents and teachers let you get away with all this?" I asked.

He looked startled, then gave me a self-satisfied smile. "No one ever asked me that. I guess the reasons I gave were so convincing no one ever doubted me."

"It sounds like you were as good a lawyer then as you are now. But what else occurs to you about people accepting your excuses for being late?" I asked.

"I know, uh, I know, uh . . . ," he smiled and shook his head. "This is harder than my bar exam. Let me try again." He frowned in concentration and took a deep breath. "I've always been a little surprised at how people have gone along with my explanations, at least until Judge Landis. No one ever questioned me, and the more people went along with me the more control I felt I had over them."

"What do you think about allowing yourself to get away with your rationalizations?" I asked.

He took another deep breath. "Deep inside, I never really felt honest about it. But my parents always went along with me, so it seemed like I was somehow special, like I could ignore the rules because both my parents took my side when my teachers, or anyone else, complained about me. I can remember, more than once, when my parents got really angry and took on the principal when he tried to punish me for disrupting some event with my lateness, and he must have felt so bullied that he just gave in."

He loosened his collar and, with an anxious frown, asked, "Is it hot in here?"

"Are you saying the feelings are heating up inside?" I asked.

He shot me a hostile look.

"I suppose so," he said warily and chewed on a hangnail for a moment. "Mother always believed my reasons. She really went to amazing lengths to keep me from getting into trouble. Once she drove me 250 miles to a debate contest because I'd been, 'too busy preparing for an exam to catch the team van,' and you can be sure I didn't tell her the exam was two weeks away and that I never prepared for a test that early anyway," he said, looking sheepish.

"But I can tell you that right now, even though I'm talking about this objectively, I still feel like I'm entitled to being treated special because it seems like if my parents thought I was, then I must be." He stared out the window, then turned back, looking pained.

"I didn't bargain for this."

"Didn't bargain for what?" I asked.

He shook his head. "I know where this is going, and I don't like it."

"Say more about where it's going that you don't like?" I asked.

With a twisted smile, he responded, "You want to take away my special feeling, and I don't like it because it's the only feeling of control I've ever had."

"You said that frustrating others has given you power and control as if that were still true, as if you still needed it, and as if those emotions didn't know that now, as an adult, you have many strengths and sources of power and control that you never dreamed of as a boy," I said.

His face went blank, as it frequently had in the beginning of our work.

"That's a logical thought," he said, in a monotone, "but it never occurred to me. I'll have to think about it."

By then, we were beyond our time, and Mr. Tucker had heard my next patient in the waiting room. As he rose to leave, he said, "I'm sure we'll continue this next time."

He began the next session by saying, "It took a while to sink in, but when I finally realized where this work is headed, I knew I wouldn't be here another minute if I weren't under the gun." Breathing heavily, he sat in stony silence glaring at me.

"How did you know where it is headed?" I asked.

"Doing this means I'll have to give up the only feeling of power and control I've ever known."

"What are you saying about how that feels?" I continued.

"I'll talk about that in a minute," he responded, "but first I want to ask you if we can meet for double sessions rather than these single ones. It always takes me so long to get started that our time is almost up before I really get into the work. That's what happened last time, and I knew when I left that there was still so much we hadn't yet talked about."

"I feel the same way you do," I replied, "so I'll try to work out the time by our next appointment."

"Okay. Now I'll answer your question about how it feels to think of giving up my only sense of power and control."

I nodded in assent.

He looked at me with a sad, angry expression for a full minute.

"I don't know how to say this, because I'm not used to talking about feelings, but it felt like I was," he searched for words, "lost, and, I guess," he thought again, "empty, is the word."

"What about 'lost' and 'empty'?" I asked.

He sighed, as if defeated. "I felt lost because upsetting others has been the only strength I've ever known, and I don't know how I could live without it. But I'm not just losing a feeling of control, I feel empty, too." He became silent.

"Empty?" I asked.

"Yes, it feels like I'll lose my mother and father, too. They made me feel special because they always sided with me when people complained about me. Now I won't need them any more, and that sounds like it would be good, and in some ways it is, but it also means I'll lose them." Appearing embarrassed, he shook his head. "It sounds silly for a grown man to talk this way, my father's been dead for ten years and my mother's almost eighty, and after I left home I never talked with either of them about my career problems, but I've always had the feeling they were there and would take up for me anyway. I know I've got to get over this feeling if I'm going to save my professional life, and my marriage, but it's hard." His voice was brittle. Then he looked directly at me with intense, piercing eyes.

"If your expression could talk, what would it say?" I asked.

His eyes blazed.

"I didn't realize it until after I left last time, but I hate what we're doing, and I wouldn't be doing it if Bailey weren't making me," he said, breathing heavily. "You're part of this whole damn thing, too, and I've never been as mad about anything as I am toward you for making me do this." His voice grew louder. "I feel the same about you as I do Bailey, and Judge Landis, and every other fucking son of a bitch who tries to control my life or tell me what to do, whether it was my teachers, or my clients and law partners, and now my wife!"

He rubbed his mouth while allowing his anger to settle down.

"Civility won't let me feel it and say it like I did with you, but this rage is always there just below the surface, so I guess I've had to do what the little boy did when he whined, 'I can't,' by telling people to go to hell in a way they can't object to because I give good reasons." He momentarily smiled his victory smile. "I can usually gauge a person's tolerance of how far I can push them, like with clients or my wife, and then back off, but that's not always true, like when I went too far with the judge, and then I have to deal with their reaction. I've tried cases in front of Judge Landis before, and I've always had a quiet contempt for the bastard, so maybe he picked it up, and this time he felt he'd had enough. Fuck him," he said as he raised his middle finger to flip the bird at Judge Landis.

I said, "Your anger went to Al Bailey and Judge Landis, and the others, at the moment you said you'd never felt as mad toward anyone as you do toward me. Could it have felt safer to focus your anger on them than continue with the anger about me?"

He stared at me.

"I've felt this way about you from the very beginning when Bailey sent me to you so you could turn me into someone he wants me to be, and I detest people like you because you're just his stooge, and the judge's, too, for that matter. Maybe I'm just more aware of how I feel about you, because we talk together, and I never speak to them, but I come here and you sit over there so goddamn smug and arrogant and play me like a violin." His voice was harsh and shrill.

"You make me talk about my problems, but never yours, and I know you have problems, too, because psychiatrists have more than anyone. You're just like my teachers, you think you know everything, especially what's best for me, and I have to toe the line, or otherwise I flunk, because if I don't come out of this the way you and Bailey and the judge want me to, then the firm will kick me out, and God only knows what the judge will do." His expression suddenly shifted to a worried frown. "Which reminds me, my lawyer got another continuance of the Ethics Committee hearing, so it'll probably be a while before I know what they'll do. Actually, he'd gotten two postponements before this, but I think I was so pissed at the time that I didn't mention them to you."

He looked at the floor, and said, "I don't know where all this anger gets me," in a subdued voice, then looked up at me.

I replied, "You seem to be saying that where the anger gets you is away from the helplessness you feel in the hands of those, like your parents and teachers, or the judge and me, you see as making you toe their line, but that the way you handle the anger can backfire and then you wind up, like with Judge Landis and the Ethics Committee, being more helpless in your real world than you were before."

He answered, "When I said how I felt about you in the beginning, I realized it's those feelings that've made me come late, like the stubborn ones we talked about before. I especially remember feeling that way when I thought I had to be here on time. It made me feel like a supplicant begging for help, like Oliver Twist pathetically pleading for 'more' soup and like when I had to follow the judge's orders or suffer the consequences. And I hate that feeling more than anything. Well, screw you too!"

Until children grow up enough to rely on self-discipline, parental controls helps them cope while they learn to control themselves. This civilizing process teaches children appropriate responses to their primitive urges and provides them security against fears that their impulses will become unmanageable. Ordinarily, parents strike a balance between imposing controls and being sensitive to the child's need to learn by making his own mistakes, but if a parent inflicts excessive controls, the child can be overwhelmed by helplessness and rage that he is not yet equipped to manage.

Children who must submit to this excessive parental control often feel the same oppression as do subjects of political tyranny. Adults are relatively free to revolt or elect new leaders when authorities abuse their privileges, but since children are captives, who can neither mutiny nor overtly rebel, they must handle their reactions internally, and their reactions are as varied as there are individuals.

Rather than accept and face the emotions we fear, we protect ourselves, both as children and adults, from these painful feelings of rage and fear by turning to defenses in the forms of other emotions, ideas, or behaviors. This process generally is subconscious and happens automatically without any thought process. When a feared emotion occurs, we suppress or deny it and then find expression for the feeling in ways that allow us not to feel threatened. In a child this may take the form of behavioral problems, preoccupation with fantasies that result in easy distractibility, and lack of goals. In adults, it may occur as workaholism; professional rigidity or clashing with others in our career; avoidance of responsibility; compulsive housecleaning; and abusive behaviors in our family life.

Robert turned to passive-aggressive procrastination early in his life as a compromise that allowed him to partially satisfy two wrenching and conflicting emotions: his rage at his parents' severe control and his fear of the consequences of his rage. Robert's denial of his rage and replacement of it with passive-aggressive procrastination allowed him to express his hostility without appearing to be hostile; he could comply with authorities by doing his job, but doing it contemptuously and with the intent of punishing the person in power.

Resolution of Mr. Tucker's problems began by identifying his compulsion to procrastinate and his denial that his procrastination threatened his career and personal life, the two problems that had caused him to see me.

Though our work focused on both demons, overcoming his denial mechanism took precedence, since we could not work in depth on his compulsion to procrastinate until he could acknowledge that it was a problem.

Denial is one the earliest defense mechanisms we develop, and, while it serves to protect us from terrifying helplessness when we are infants, persistence of denial into adulthood can be extremely harmful. Denial does not merely cause simple avoidance of unpleasantries; it can treat a painful reality, no matter how dangerous, as if that reality did not exist, usually replacing it with a pleasurable, or more acceptable, fantasy or delusion.

In its most severe form, people afflicted with paranoid schizophrenia frequently deny horrifying paranoid delusions, such as being victimized by the FBI or CIA, by replacing them with grandiose, omnipotent notions of being Jesus Christ. Alcoholics and drug addicts on a one-way road to hellish death often rhapsodize, "Look at all the great writers who were alcoholics, it certainly didn't hurt them," never mind that the writers they refer to died by drinking themselves to death or some other form of suicide. Mr. Tucker replaced the pain of recognizing the consequences of his behavior with the lofty notions that he always, "made good grades," "won my debate," or "win my cases."

Mr. Tucker began overcoming his denial mechanism as he, reluctantly, saw in himself the child psychiatrist's observation that a child who expresses some version of, "I can't," as a way of refusing to comply with expectations of him, is much less likely to be punished than one who baldly declares, "I won't." While Mr. Tucker eventually did acknowledge his defiant procrastination, his steadfast denial of its consequences required my repeated reminders of Judge Landis and Al Bailey's ultimatums and that this continued behavior would inevitably result in sabotaging his goals.

Our animal ancestors developed a "fight or flight" reaction as nature's way of protecting them from danger, and
we humans have refined this internal alarm by developing
a conscience that allows us to recognize the difference
between acceptable and unacceptable behavior. A healthy
conscience emits a danger signal that warns, and therefore
motivates, us not to commit unacceptable acts, or at least
to think twice before doing so. But Mr. Tucker's denial
was so strong he could not allow himself to hear when the
outside world warned him, "You're doing something
wrong, and, sooner or later, you will pay the price."

When one's anxiety feels too great to bear, however,
protective defenses like denial can become so strong that
a danger signal cannot break through, and one is deprived
of this healthy, and often life saving, internal alarm to alert
him to his peril. When this happens, the person must use
other mechanisms, including his sound judgment, to provide the motivation necessary for resolving his conflicts
and ensuring his safety and well-being. The result of this
psychological flaw is similar to that of a person with lep-
rosy whose extremities, and other body parts, are in constant danger of harm, such as being burned or cut, because
his disease deadens his sensory nerves, so he has no warning signal to protect him.

Denying the consequences of one's behavior may also
result from the message one receives from his outer world,
particularly during his early development, that his behaviors are acceptable, and he does not need to discipline himself. Even if this misconception holds true under specific
circumstances in his childhood, as it did with Robert while
living with his parents, an adult soon finds that the outer
world is not so tolerant, and he must change his ways.

By getting Robert out of tight spots, Mr. Tucker's parents, instead of holding him accountable for his actions,
failed to help him develop a healthy alarm structure, and
by indulging his passive-aggressive procrastination that did
not consider others' needs, they reinforced his certainty of
personal entitlement rather than strengthening his sense of
responsibility.

Robert continued his dilatory behaviors into adulthood where he was no longer safeguarded by his parents, and pushed his procrastination to the limit, assured by his false confidence that his intelligence and talents would always rescue him. His behavior was like that of people who lead physically reckless lives, certain their skills will save them, only to be surprised when they wake up dead from having believed their illusion of invincibility.

If one is writhing from crushing anxiety and panic, one is usually willing to search for internal saboteurs as the cause of his pain. Mr. Tucker, having silenced his emotional warning signals through a lifetime of denial, was pain free and even felt good about his behavior so he, like many people, needed the motivation of an external threat to overcome this resistance and motivate the healing process, a threat generously supplied by Al Bailey's warning and Judge Landis' court order.

Mr. Tucker had not been able to rely on his own judgment to save himself because his denial did not permit him to recognize how he, himself, had created his problems.

Mr. Tucker's emotional debridement centered on his most feared feeling of helpless rage toward his parents—rage made helpless for fear of its consequences and reinforced by his helplessness in response to his parents' excessive controls.

Debridement of his angry feelings came first. "I've read about children doing horrible things to parents, but I'd never hurt them physically because they never did anything like that to me," he said. "But what I would want to do is tie them to a chair and put their head in a vise so they couldn't move it because it felt like that's what they did to me. And then I'd give them homework and make them go over it again and again, and if they made a mistake I'd squeeze the vise tighter and tighter until they got it right and then make them write a report about what they had read and then go over and over and over it, and if they didn't dot all their 'i's' and cross their 't's' perfectly, I'd tighten the vise until they did," he said, oozing revenge from every pore.

"Your wish to do to them what they did to you is certainly understandable. I wasn't clear, though, what you meant when you said you would never hurt them physically. Squeezing their head in a vise doesn't qualify for physical hurt?" I asked.

"Oh no!" he said, astonished at my question. "I mean really hurt, like beating them."

Since this was the first time we had broken ground in exploring his raw hostility, I chose not to pursue right then the denial imbedded in his distinction between what he had said he would never do and what he actually did in his fantasies.

Debridement of these intense hostile feelings toward his parents continued over several sessions as he imagined turning the tables on them for their excessive controlling behavior.

His helpless feelings were less immediately accessible, but, after several sessions and many attempts to allow the feeling to arise, he said, "How does one talk about a feeling of being totally powerless. It seems like nothing I could say or do ever registered with my parents. Even now, when I try to think about talking back to them like Jerry did to Aunt Helen, it feels like nothing's there."

"How so?" I asked.

"No matter what reason I gave for not doing something," he responded, "they always gave me a better reason for why I should, and if I thought that something I might say would hurt them, my guilt would tear me to pieces. At some point, I just gave up. I used to think I would have to become a soldier or someone who just took orders because I could never think or say anything on my own if it disagreed with my superiors."

"What about 'just gave up'?" I asked.

"They had a way of acting hurt, like they were doing it all for my own good, and if I didn't do what they told me to, then I was just being unreasonable and doing something bad to them. I know that now I can say to you, and feel, the things I did about strapping them to a chair with their head in a vise and then tormenting them the way they did me, but that wasn't how it was when I was little. Then I felt so helpless I couldn't even think of anything to say, much less say it. This kind of sounds paradoxical because as a lawyer, I always talk back to an opponent or client if something needs to be said."

I responded, "It's as if there has been a lag time between what your intellect now knows and what your emotions haven't yet learned. Even though today you can, in fact, speak up with professional adversaries and clients and colleagues, the helpless feeling that made you take out your revenge on the judge has been stuck back when you were so helpless with your parents and couldn't say anything."

"I think I am only now learning that," he answered.

From this phase of self-knowledge work, he came to understand how his rage in reaction to the actual helplessness of his early years had caused him to develop his defense mechanism of quietly defying authorities. As he integrated that knowledge into his emotional structure, he found that the helpless feelings sabotaging his career and personal life had all been an illusion and had no basis in the reality of his highly capable and productive adulthood.

Once having overcome the fear of his rage and helpless feeling, as well as the need for the rage itself, Mr. Tucker could supplant the removed troublemakers with his proven, healthy strengths, and deal assertively with authorities, family, and colleagues, free of his passive-aggressive mechanisms. When he recognized that conforming to social and professional conventions was not the same as being helplessly demeaned and disgraced, he could cooperate willingly and freely with others. He also now realized that the times he felt shamed and humiliated were largely situations he had actively brought on himself, as when he was disciplined by the judge for his cavalier procrastination, and when the firm demanded he overcome his problem or be fired. Most important, he also now realized he could use his adult judgment rather than his self-defeating childhood emotions to manage his reactions in response to others.

Two weeks before concluding his self-knowledge

work, Mr. Tucker spoke of his growth. "If I've learned anything here, it's that most of what I felt in my early years came from how I saw things at the time. I see now how I learned to procrastinate because it gave me some sense of control when otherwise I would have felt absolutely help-less. And it was the same thing that got me in this mess with the judge and my firm. It was absurd to think that by meeting a court deadline I was being subjected to a judge who was determined to humiliate me, rather than my sim-ply following the normal procedures of my chosen career, something that I, not someone else, did to me. I was more headstrong in fighting this than with anything I ever re-member."

"Do you recall the turning point in understanding this, and what made it possible?" I asked.

He smiled gently.

"It happened during a session about a year after we started when we were working on why I regularly came late for my appointment and then gave you a bunch of bullshit reasons for it. I didn't realize it until later, and you may not remember it because in those early days I often came late, but that day I dragged in twenty or so minutes late for no real reason, and then tried to explain it by feed-ing you some noble crap. Then we talked about how my feelings toward people who try to control me had gotten transferred to you, and the most I could come up with to explain my being late was that you were arrogant and were trying to dictate what I talked about so you could turn me into someone Al Bailey wants. Then I realized that wasn't true about you at all, and I began to understand that I must have needed to see you that way for my own reasons."

Appearing relaxed, he leaned back in his chair and stretched out his six foot four frame, cupping his hands behind his head.

"That was the first time I'd ever seen how absurd my attitude was. Here I was doing something I wanted to do for my own benefit and of my own free will. I'd long since fulfilled the firm's and the Ethics Committee's require-ments. By then neither Bailey nor the judge were making me do this, and certainly not you, because you were never part of the gang that sentenced me to this, but I reacted to you as if you were making me do it for your reasons. And it hit me even more when you pointed out that you were my employee and that I was paying for a service and could fire you anytime I wanted to, not the other way around."

Suddenly becoming conscious that his lounging position had taken up half the room, he smiled, sat up, and retracted his legs to his usual sitting position.

"That realization changed my whole attitude about this work. I'd always been sincere about what we were doing, even if I sometimes didn't sound like it, but the problem was that I'd gotten my genuine desire to change all mixed up with feeling coerced by the firm to come here and change. After that, though, I was even more serious because I realized I was doing this for myself, and then I started getting so much more out of it, and it's gone further and faster than I ever imagined. I also suspect I didn't tell you this at the time I realized it because I still had enough of the same problem, and I would have felt humiliated, as if I would have been saying, 'Oh thank you dear Judge Landis and Al Bailey, you were so right,' and I sure as hell wasn't ready to do that."

In his last session Mr. Tucker reflected on how different his world looked. He shook his head and smiled. "What stands out most about my parents in this analysis is that since I've worked out my anger about being controlled and helpless and fearing my rage would alienate people who are important to me, what my parents did is not so important. I'm grown now, and I see things in a different way and can make intelligent choices and act on them in ways I never considered as a child. I'm just grateful I caught this before I destroyed myself by trying to frustrate or put down other people when I'd convinced myself I was perfectly innocent."

With a thoughtful expression, he looked outside several moments, then turned to face me as he, without self-consciousness, allowed tears to well up in his eyes.

"I know my parents loved me no matter what else I

said in the beginning of this work. Only parents who loved their child would have put up with all the shit I gave them, and any mother who'd drive her son 250 miles to a debate contest after he'd behaved like a jerk and missed the regular bus, has got to have a lot of love for him no matter what else she does." In a voice broken by tears streaming down his cheeks, he continued, "Whatever their flaws and however insensitive they were at times, my parents, like most parents, I think, did the best they could with what they had and thought was right."

In these observations Mr. Tucker was reflecting on how, during his self-knowledge work, he had been able to sort out the multiple, complex feelings and thoughts that belonged to his past, including his fundamental conflicts of love and hate, helplessness and strength, and gratitude and disappointment. He was particularly struck that now, having discovered his own internal sources of anger, he no longer felt toward Judge Landis, Mr. Bailey, his wife, and me, the rage and resentment he had felt as a child toward his parents.

Left entirely to self-centered emotions that lie at the heart of all our perceptions of ourselves, we cannot view our personal history with "immaculate perception" any more than a political historian can ponder human events with unbiased objectivity.

As Mr. Tucker discovered, our memories of early events, including those crucial to forming our emotional structure, are distorted by our phase of life at the time the events occurred, whether infancy, early childhood, or adolescence. As he also found, those distortions and the misshapen emotions and life problems they cause, can be rectified, so we can gain peace of mind and achieve our goals, only through the wisdom, strength, and maturity that come with self-knowledge.

Mr. Tucker took advantage of several court approved postponements in the case that had prompted his call to me so he could work through the problems that had almost ruined his career. By the time we completed our work, he no longer tortured his wife with his insensitive behavior, and they were were able to work out their normal differences through healthy discussions. The firm's managing partner, satisfied with Mr. Tucker's great progress and pleased that Mr. Tucker had given his client a favorable outcome, rescinded his threat. And while Judge Landis did not waver in executing the fine he imposed, Mr. Tucker said, with mixed bitterness and gratitude, "I have to acknowledge it was worth $10,000 for the son of a bitch to get my attention, something no one else had ever been able to do before."

4

Vodka Leaves No Odor

A slender, pleasant looking, plainly dressed lady, appearing to be in her early fifties, raised her eyebrows, smiled gently, and said, "Are you Dr. Stockton? I'm Patricia Poland."

"Yes," I answered with a smile, and extended my open palm toward the consultation room. After entering, she stood in front of her chair until I had reached mine, then, as soon as we sat, said, "I'm having some trouble, and my doctor suggested I call you," in a calm and serious tone.

"What kind of trouble?" I asked.

Taking a deep breath, she said, "Trouble at the office. I'm in awful bad debt and about to lose my business, and," her face became sad, "I'm afraid I'll lose Larry, my partner. He knows something's wrong, but he doesn't know how bad it really is, and I'm afraid to tell him."

"Did something in particular happen that brought this to a head?" I asked.

Looking confused, she replied, "Not exactly. Dr. Morgan, I think she's an internist, gave me your name after I talked with her a few minutes at a friend's party because, and Larry agrees with her, she thought I sounded depressed." Sitting up straight, Ms. Poland continued, "But before going on, I want to tell you about myself and why Dr. Morgan recommended you.

"Larry and I own a Temp Agency. He runs the outside operations while I manage the inside from our home office

91

near Philadelphia. We have several branches and about seven hundred full and part-time employees that serve the entire Northeast.

"The reason I want to see you in Washington is that I'm well-known around Philadelphia, and I'd feel self-conscious about seeing a psychiatrist there. Since I regularly come to the Washington area, mostly Northern Virginia, I thought I'd be more comfortable meeting someone here, so when I mentioned my worry to Dr. Morgan, she told me about you."

I responded, "I'm sure we can work out whatever is necessary—"

Interrupting me, she hurried on. "I called as soon as Dr. Morgan suggested because I wanted to get started as soon as possible."

I replied, "When you spoke a moment ago about Larry not knowing how bad things are, and that you were afraid you'd lose him, your face looked, and your voice sounded, depressed. Can you say what those expressions would have said if they could have talked?"

She half smiled and opened her mouth, as if she were about to speak, then her face suddenly lost all expression.

"I hadn't thought about it as clearly as you just said, but Larry knows that something's wrong at the office, and, because we're partners, whatever I do or don't do affects him as well as me. I know that when I don't tell him, he feels betrayed by me as well as financially threatened, since he's as responsible as I am for our liabilities, and his own security and life savings are at risk, too. He says I'm not paying attention to my work, and he's frantic because he knows there's something I'm keeping from him."

"Keeping what from him?" I asked.

She pressed her lips together. "Larry knows nothing about how much we owe the IRS [Internal Revenue Service] and that they're on the verge of freezing our assets, or about the fines we owe the regulatory agencies, and that all of this has our company, and us, on the brink of bankruptcy. And I'm sure he doesn't ask me what's wrong, except so indirectly that I can pretend I don't understand him, because he's afraid he'll hurt me or rock the boat of our relationship."

She delivered all this in such an unemotional manner I wondered if she were on drugs.

I asked, "You're afraid he can't help you solve the problem?"

"No, not at all. I'm sure he could, this is the kind of thing he does best. He likes hearing about problems because he's confident he can fix anything, and I know he would feel that way about all those debts and fines, too. I think what I'm worried about is how he'll feel about me. I know that he knows something's wrong, but he doesn't know what it is or how he can get me to tell him about it," she said, still without expression.

"Apart from your not telling him, I'm not yet clear how come he doesn't know about the debts and fines. Wouldn't he be aware of what's happening in the office as well as with you?" I asked.

Frowning, she again pressed her lips together, while she thought. "No," she responded, "he's out of the office most of the time and isn't there when the mail or government agents come, so he doesn't know about the IRS bill that came last month."

I let the silence grow for several moments, before saying, "You didn't say how much the bill was," with a question in my voice.

She hesitated. "It was for $600,000, $500,000 for unpaid taxes going back several years and $100,000 for penalties and interest."

Ms. Poland's matter-of-fact delivery remained unchanged, and, as I tried to put myself in her shoes, I wondered why she showed no anxiety about her predicament.

She continued, "And, before that, I hadn't told him about two other government agencies that had fined us a total of almost $100,000 for violations they say we committed. When you asked earlier what brought all this to a head, the first thing I thought about was this IRS notice, because I know that unless I deal with it soon, we could lose our business, and our home, and I could lose Larry, too."

"You said 'our' home. You and Larry live together?" I asked.

With a slight smile, she responded, "Yes, we have for several years, so what affects one of us, affects the other, too. Our relationship has always worked well, we love each other at home, but we keep that separate from our office work. I'm a few years older than he is and have had a lot more experience, so he usually defers to my business judgment, but if he knew about the mess I've gotten us in, and if we lost our company, I'm afraid he'd lose confidence in me, and worse, he might leave me. So, in the end, that's really why I'm here, and why I want to get these problems worked out."

She looked out the window, then turned back to me. "But I want to tell you more about my background so you'll know about my life before now. I haven't always had these problems. I have an MBA [Masters in Business Administration] from an Ivy League school, and I've worked as a high-level administrator in both government and industry. The trouble I'm in now is new for me."

Although knowledge of a patient's background is vital to the therapeutic process, the subtleties of when and how the person presents the information are extremely important in understanding her emotional struggles. Ms. Poland's interruption of herself to tell me about her impressive strengths suggested to me that I would have to be alert to her using her achievements to protect herself from the painful emotions she was not yet willing to face, those she had already described, and those she had not yet told me.

Since her most recent comment had been that her current troubles were new, I asked, "When did things start to go downhill?"

Looked annoyed, she pursed her lips. "I think they began two years ago when my office manager died suddenly. He took care of all the office details, including being solely responsible for handling IRS and other government matters, and he didn't train anyone to replace himself. Since I'd always left those matters to him, I wasn't prepared to deal with them when he died. I felt so overwhelmed by what I had to learn, I just gave up and ignored it all, and Larry says," she hesitated then looked skeptical, "that's when

I started drinking more."

The missing element I had sensed, but had not been able to define until this moment, had surfaced.

"Drinking 'more' than what?" I asked.

She looked at the wall. "Larry says I drink too much." Apparently startled at her own words, she glanced at me and quickly added, "But I'm not an alcoholic," with a touch of indignation.

"How much is 'too much'?" I asked.

"I've never thought that I drink too much; I only have a couple of drinks in the evening. Do you think that's too much?"

"I don't know yet," I answered. "Tell me more about what you mean."

"Well, I don't drink anything but vodka because," she hesitated slightly, then, eyeing me suspiciously, continued, "vodka leaves no odor, and people around me can't smell it," seeming confident of her response.

"Can you say more about 'a couple' of vodkas?" I asked.

She made a little moue of annoyance. "It means that I sip on a couple of drinks before dinner."

"How much vodka is in each of those drinks?" I pressed.

"Well," she scowled, "they're double, maybe sometimes triple, because I don't like to have to refill them all the time." She nodded slightly, seeming relieved and satisfied by her answer.

"What about with dinner?" I pressed.

"Oh, no," she retorted, "I don't drink vodka during dinner, only wine, unless it's a particularly long dinner, like when we have guests, or eat out, and then I have another glass or two of vodka. Usually Larry and I just have wine with dinner."

"How much wine would you say you drink on those occasions?" I asked.

"Just a fifth between the two of us," she answered.

"Larry also drinks?" I asked.

"Not really, he usually just sips on a half glass of wine—he especially likes a red Burgandy—to keep me company," Ms. Poland responded.

"Does that mean you drink the rest of the fifth your-self?" I asked.

Her face lost its expression again. "I guess so," she responded, "but sometimes I don't remember how much I've had."

"What about after dinner?" I pressed further.

She glared at the wall. "Well, I usually have a couple of more vodkas then, too. Larry says it's a lot more than two, although I don't usually remember how much I've had before I go to bed."

She frowned, as if she, herself, were beginning to hear what she was telling me about the amount she drank.

"You haven't said how much you drink earlier in the day," I continued.

Glowering at me, she responded, "I would've told you if you'd asked. I'm usually edgy when I wake up in the morning, so I take a big drink to calm my nerves as soon as I get out of bed, and then a few more as the day goes on. I drink mostly after work, when I'm home in the evening. Larry says that by the time I go to sleep I'll have finished a whole quart, and that the empty bottle is the only thing that stops me." She looked at me stone faced.

"Can you say what you remember about how alcohol affects you?" I asked.

Her face relaxed, and she almost smiled. "I'm lucky because it doesn't affect me like it does other people. I've never had a DWI [Driving While Intoxicated] or a car ac-cident."

Again I let the silence linger for several moments, then asked, "You didn't say anything about other kinds of acci-dents?"

"Well," her bland expression was back, "I have fallen at home a couple of times, if that's what you mean. Once I broke my arm, and another time Larry had to take me to the emergency room because I'd slipped and was knocked unconscious, although it never was clear whether I was out from the fall or from alcohol." With her last remark, she had begun to look confused.

"When you said earlier that your drinking didn't af-

fect you, did you mean you don't see any connection between your drinking and the 'big troubles' you're in at
work?" I asked.

Still looking confused, she shook her head. "I don't think
there's any connection. I don't know why there would be."

"You said you don't remember how much you drink
before you go to bed. Now that you recall that you also
drink in the daytime, could alcohol be causing some of the
office problems like not reporting and paying your taxes?"
I asked.

"Oh no. I'm at the office early every day, before I've
had hardly anything to drink, so in the middle of the morning, like now, I'm still perfectly clear." She looked outside as she concentrated her thoughts. "But now that you've
asked me, Larry did say he thinks I forget things at the
office, and some people who've known me a long time
have said, although not to me directly, that I don't run my
office like I used to." She looked thoughtful.

Drawing back into her business posture, she said, "But
even if drinking does interfere sometimes, I've established
office routines that take up the slack and maintain day-to-
day activities for just such instances."

She was nodding her head at her last comment when
she suddenly went still, then her body drooped. "But I
guess routines can't do everything. One of my big law
firm customers hasn't paid a $50,000 bill, and though I
need the money to pay my employees, I haven't done anything about it." She frowned. "More than a year ago Larry
thought I was depressed and insisted that I talk with a doctor, so I told my general practice doctor about feeling down,
and he gave me an antidepressant that I've taken ever since.
But it hasn't helped."

While I was not surprised to learn that drugs had not
helped her depression, which by now I knew was at least
complicated, if not caused, by alcohol, I was puzzled why
there had been no change in her treatment, since she had
taken the medicine for a year with no improvement. So, I
asked, "What has your general practitioner said about what
you've just told me?"

"He doesn't know; I haven't talked with him about it," she answered.

"How do you get prescriptions for the medicine?" I asked.

"I just get refills of the one he gave me. His nurse okays them," she responded.

"When the doctor gave you the medicine, what did he ask you about the depression?"

"He didn't ask me anything, I just told him my partner had said I was depressed, and he gave me the prescription and told me, 'Take this, it should help.'"

"Did he ask you anything about drinking?"

"No, that didn't come up. He didn't ask, so I didn't say anything about it," she said, still with no expression.

"Did he refer you to a psychiatrist or have you come back for a follow up?"

"No, not that I remember. I saw him a month or so ago for my yearly checkup, but neither of us said anything about my being depressed or the medicine he had given me the year before," she continued, almost in a monotone.

Since antidepressant drugs are designed to treat psychological melancholia, not depression due to toxic chemicals, the drug never had a chance to fulfill its claims. Ms. Poland's outrageously inadequate, but relatively common, stab at treatment resulted in her being left with an impaired mind that was physically incapable of recognizing her lack of improvement, and so she continued to take the drug, as well as a quart of Vodka and a fifth of wine, daily.

As this first consultation, that lasted two and a half hours, neared its end, I said, "I think the problem you face requires a two-pronged effort. You and I need to meet twice a week to sort out the issues involved, especially those concerning the real problems at work and at home that your drinking has created, and, even more important, it is vital that you attend Alcoholics Anonymous [AA] meetings, daily for a while, to deal more directly with your drinking problem. Then, and only then, when your brain is no longer weakened by the alcohol, and you have your full mental powers available, we can work to understand

and resolve the underlying emotions that have contributed to making you susceptible to excessive drinking."

Ms. Poland looked stunned; her eyes widened and her jaw dropped. Then she scowled with dark, angry eyes.

She looked at the wall several minutes and said nothing. Finally, still facing the wall, she said, "I can go along with some of the things you said, but I certainly don't accept your idea of going to AA. That would mean I'm an alcoholic. I'm not an alcoholic; I'm not a stumbling drunk like those people. If I have a problem, it's my fear of criticism and failure, and that's why I came to see you." Giving me a stern look, she said, "Why do you think I'm an alcoholic?"

I responded, "Do you drink?"

"Yes, of course, I've already told you I drink," she answered, looking irritated.

"Has your drinking harmed you or caused you problems," I asked.

"No," she replied.

I chose not to challenge her directly by using what she had already told me because even in the telling she had included enough ambiguity to allow her to deny what she was saying.

"Did you continue to drink after you broke you arm and fell unconscious from drinking?" I asked.

She glared at me for a full minute. "Yes, I still drink." Her glare hardened, as she added, "Sometimes," in a stern voice, while clearing her throat.

"I think you've answered your question," I said.

We were both silent several minutes, then I continued. "I have no doubt that you have deeper struggles, and since you know they relate to fears of criticism and inadequacy, those will be at the top of our agenda when your mind gets clear, but first we have to get alcohol out of your system."

After staring at me in stony silence, she rose to put on her jacket. "When do we meet next?" she asked, curtly, picking up her purse.

"We should meet tomorrow, and we can meet at this same time, if that works out for you."

"That will work for me," she responded brusquely. "I'll still be in town, but I can't see myself doing this AA crap, and if I ever do decide to go, I'm going to have to see it a lot different than I do now."

With a forced, polite smile, she said, "See you tomorrow," and I responded with a friendly nod.

The next day, Ms. Poland entered the consultation room looking pensive, neither speaking to, nor looking at, me and sat in silence for several minutes.

"I've thought a lot about what you said yesterday, and I resent your conclusion that I'm an alcoholic on the basis of all those glib, simpleminded questions. In any event, my drinking certainly isn't bad enough to have to go to Alcoholics Anonymous with all that riffraff. And I also resent your using everything I told you against me. You looked like you were sitting over there with your mouth watering and your adding machine, calculating every drink I ever had in my whole life, and you just couldn't wait to see how many you could make me confess.

"I once had a neighbor who went to AA, but he was a real drunk. His wife once called me to help her deal with him because he'd fallen on the floor and, we later found, had fractured his shoulder. When I got there, he sounded like a gibbering idiot, and then his wife told me he had just lost his job because he'd become so ineffective and unreliable. The poor lady was beside herself, and she didn't know what to do with him. So when you talk about AA, I remember him, and you would never get me to say I'm like he was. His life has really gone downhill."

I responded, "I understand your objection to the idea of being so seriously impaired, but you've already told me you're well on your way downhill. Your finding that such a picture of yourself is repugnant is very good, though, because we can take advantage of it in insuring you never have to face that kind of total ruin, at least due to alcohol. You did say that once you fell and broke your arm—translate that into shoulder—and another time hit your head and were knocked unconscious—translate that into lying on the floor—so common sense would tell you that it's just a matter of time before something like what happened to your neighbor will also happen to you."

"Except," she replied, "I told you that when I was knocked out, it never was clear whether it was caused by the fall or alcohol."

I said nothing, and she began looking self-conscious about her effort to rationalize away any connection between alcohol and her fall, then she added, "I suppose you think I'm making excuses," with a flat voice.

I nodded in silence.

Her relaxed expression quickly changed to a frown. "But none of this makes any difference. This is a free country, and I have the right to drink as much as I want to, and It's none of your, or anybody else's, business."

We both were silent a few moments to absorb what she had said.

"You're absolutely right," I responded. "I agree with you completely. You have every right in this country, or anywhere, since alcohol is not choosey about where or on whom it inflicts its deadly destruction, to lose your business, embarrass and disgrace yourself, get yourself arrested and jailed for drunken driving or vehicular homicide, die of liver cirrhosis, internal bleeding, or brain damage, wind up in the city morgue by getting yourself killed in countless ways, or, possibly worst of all, even if your body manages to survive, and you can get a good enough lawyer to keep you out of trouble, lose Larry, because he can no longer tolerate living with your drunken behavior. And the deadly list goes on, and on, and on. Yes, I agree with you, you have every right not to treat this fatal disease seriously."

She looked me straight in the eye, saying nothing, for several minutes.

Finally, she pulled herself up straight. "I've thought about stopping the booze, but that's as far as it ever goes. I get scared, and then I stop thinking about it."

"Say more about 'scared,'" I responded.

"I just can't imagine living without ever having a drink again," she said, in a dead voice. "I should be able to have *one* drink if I want to. I think I could quit for a year if I knew that at the end I could have just one drink. But an alcoholic friend of mine told me that people who really stop for good, say, 'You,' meaning alcoholics like themselves, 'are not like regular people, you have a disease, and you cannot drink "just one drink."'"

She gripped the arms of her chair, as if to restrain herself from leaping out of it and running away.

"In a movie I saw, an alcoholic said, 'One is too many, a million are not enough.' So when I said a moment ago, 'I should be able to have one drink,' I remembered all those things you listed that could happen to me if I did. But the thought of going forever without a drink is so dreadful, it seems like life wouldn't be worth living, or even worse, that it would be nothing but agony," she twisted the rings on one finger. "I think I would kill myself first."

I replied, "I'm sure you've heard the saying, 'One day at a time,' and people in alcohol and drug addiction recovery are especially familiar with what that means. It means you don't have to think about going forever without a drink, that you only have to hang in there for just one day, or hour, or minute, or even a second, and then you can decide at any time what you wish to do the next day, or hour, or minute, or second. And because it's so difficult to keep that principle firmly and constantly in mind, the people at AA, who are so grateful for their own recovery and good health, are willing, eager is a better word, to help you remember to do all the things necessary to maintain your sobriety.

"There's a true story about AA members that shows their devotion to helping others recover," I continued. "Bill Wilson was the recovering alcoholic and cofounder of AA whose name became a code word for AA members in referring to the organization. One time an alcoholic stranded at the Atlanta airport recognized a craving that put him at risk of breaking his six months sobriety, so he asked the airport telephone operator to announce on the loud speaker, 'Will the friend of Bill Wilson please meet him at the lobby information desk?' The information desk was only two hundred feet away, but when he reached it, eight friends of

Bill Wilson were already there to meet him."

Tears crept into her eyes, and she looked away.

"But there's something else, too," she said, then looked at me silently, as if wanting me to ask her what the "something else" was.

"What are you thinking?" I asked.

"I'd feel so humiliated if someone I know, especially a friend, saw me at an AA meeting. I'm so well known in the area where I live, it would be even worse than if they knew I was seeing a psychiatrist."

"I understand your concerns," I responded, "and, as you will find, so do alcoholics who go to AA, since that's why the second 'A' in AA means 'Anonymous.' But I think even then, it's not like you imagine. For example, you said how humiliated you'd feel if someone you knew saw you at a meeting, as if it doesn't occur to you that your friend would be there for exactly the same reason you would be. I think you'll find that rather than other people looking down on you from the outside, they'll be rejoicing with you from the inside for having the strength and courage to come to grips with your drinking, just as they rejoice with theirs."

Averting her eyes, she said, "I'll think about it. I would say I want to talk it over with Larry, but I'm afraid that if I did, it would open up this whole thing, and I can't do that, at least not yet."

"I'm glad you suggested the idea of talking with Larry," I responded, "because he's obviously supportive of anything that would be helpful to you, and can you think of a better place to begin than to share with him what you're doing about your alcohol problem, since you've already said he's terribly worried about how much you drink?"

She sat frowning in thought, then looked at the clock to confirm that our time was up. As she rose to leave, she glanced at me. "Well, I'll think about that, and about going to AA, too. I'll see you Monday," then, looking at the floor, she left.

Making a big deal of acknowledging something so obvious may seem puzzling to nondrinkers, but a major flaw of the alcoholic mind is its incapacity to believe that it is helpless to addiction. Many say, and believe, "I can stop any time I want," but accepting the fallacy of that notion is the pivotal step of recovery. Overcoming one's resistance to accepting that she or he is actually addicted is a fundamental concept of recovery, in AA it's called The First Step: "We admitted we were powerless over alcohol, and that our lives had become unmanageable."

I had strongly emphasized the importance of her attending AA meetings because while a small number of alcoholics can stop drinking on their own, most require help, first to stop drinking and endure withdrawal, then to have available the techniques AA uses to help addicts overcome their disease. Alcoholics and other addicts particularly need the unique help provided only by those who have "been there" and are recovering.

The most powerful source of resistance to alcoholic recovery, by far, is fear of the physical and emotional anguish that occurs when alcohol is withdrawn from one's physical body that has become dependent on it. While these withdrawal sensations are temporary, they are most painful in early recovery, when one is most vulnerable, and the withdrawal feelings seem as if they will last forever.

Over the next several weeks, our twice weekly sessions focused on overcoming Ms. Poland's resistance to acknowledging her alcoholic addiction, and to confiding in Larry, whose support would be indispensable for her emotionally demanding task. She came to see that while her lifelong fears of inadequacy and criticism had caused many of her difficulties, alcoholism was her most immediate problem, since she could neither work on nor resolve the underlying emotional problems as long as her brain was chemically impaired. Because her alcoholic fog would keep her from identifying, much less understanding, her troublesome emotions, her first job was to get sober.

This phase of Ms. Poland's work was greatly facilitated when she mustered the courage to tell Larry about our meetings so she could air the problem more fully with him and enlist his support in overcoming her alcoholic illness.

One day Ms. Poland entered appearing as if she had shed a great burden, an expression she had not shown before.

As soon as she sat down, she began. "Well, I finally did it. I talked with Larry," tears came to her eyes, "and he was totally supportive So I called an old friend, Lance." Again, her eyes filled with tears. "He's the alcoholic friend I mentioned once before, and he told me how happy he was that I wanted to go to AA and how honored he would be to take me to my first meeting. He also said he and all my friends had been worried about me for years, and that they all will feel relieved now that I'm ready to get sober."

She cried for several minutes as we sat in silence, and my eyes moistened as well.

Every human must cope with her mind's inherent, biologically based demons and defects—untamed raw anger, sexual euphoria, self-centeredness, greed, magical thinking, and many others—that we all have and seek to overcome. These demons, defects, and the mechanisms one uses to cope with them, are the principal issues in any therapy since they must be managed if the person is to achieve her goals.

Self-knowledge therapists seek to accomplish this without using "tough love" confrontations that almost certainly would create opposition to the work itself.

The treatment of addicts, however, allows for no such luxury. The alcoholic or other drug addict is not prepared to listen to reason, because her body physically demands the addictive chemical and because primitive defenses, particularly denial and rage, are so great, that nothing, N-O-T-H-I-N-G, especially something as easily ignored as sane, sound reasoning, is allowed to stand in the way of her next drink or fix. As a consequence, in order to break through the addict's denial, the treatment absolutely requires direct confrontations when the addict displays characteristics common to alcoholics and other addicts—inappropriate anger, loose sexual behavior, self-centeredness, personal entitlement, greed, yearnings for euphoria and bliss, need to control other people, use and abuse of others, lying, cheating, the need to numb unpleasant feelings, and even stealing, robbery, prostitution, and murder—when the next drink or fix is at stake. The drinking itself weakens the mind, and in so doing reinforces these attitudes that the alcoholic can and must change to maintain sobriety.

This is why AA meetings and therapeutic groups composed of alcoholics and addicts are far more successful in dealing with addiction than is individual self-knowledge therapy, although combining the two is most effective. Most self-knowledge therapists have not had training in "tough-love" techniques, and, even if the therapist knows and implements the techniques effectively, those techniques could fatally harm the therapist's neutrality necessary for a patient or client acquiring self-knowledge. Worse still, if these techniques are applied inappropriately by a therapist unskilled in working daily with recovering alcoholics or other addicts, the patient could become so embittered by what she feels is the harshness of "tough-love," she might chuck the whole process, alcoholic recovery as well as self-knowledge therapy.

When an alcoholic or addict in full-blown denial is faced with, for example, having told a "bald-faced lie," the confrontation is far more effective when done by fellow sufferers in recovery than when done by a more neutral self-knowledge therapist asking, "How can we understand the need to distort or misrepresent the truth?"

Therapy groups, especially those composed of members suffering similar problems, can confront lying and outrageous denial and still maintain the alcoholic or addict's trust; whereas if a self-knowledge therapist in individual treatment said exactly the same thing, it likely would be taken much more personally by the patient and risk ruining their therapeutic rapport.

Alcoholics and addicts in early recovery often feel bitter toward those who confront them. After achieving sustained sobriety, however, they usually feel grateful to, and develop respect for, their challengers. Yet growth is required to get there, since the lofty goals of sobriety have little appeal to an alcoholic facing painful therapeutic confrontations.

Bill Wilson called the alcoholic mind "cunning, baffling, and powerful." The experiences of those who have been down this rocky road are invaluable in helping the alcoholic combat the lies, tricks, and self-deceptions her mind uses to get another drink. AA meetings are especially helpful in the early stage of alcoholic recovery when the primary goal is to help the alcoholic "dry out" and stop drinking, so her mind can be available to solidify her recovery.

The combined personal stories of AA members reveal an understanding of the alcoholic mind that is far superior to psychoanalytic, self-knowledge, or general psychiatric knowledge of alcoholism and its treatment. Self-knowledge therapy is usually of little or no value if it is the sole form of recovery treatment. It can be worse than useless if it misleads the alcoholic into thinking she is doing something about her alcoholism when, in fact, she is not taking the hard steps necessary for recovery.

Ms. Poland began attending AA meetings regularly. Respecting her fear that her identity would be exposed, Lance had taken her to a meeting in a small town forty miles away. She soon learned that her anonymity was secure, and, within a few months, felt comfortable enough to attend meetings nearer her home. She found that people in AA know each other only by their first names, have a sole interest in their, and other's, sobriety and are unwaveringly loyal to the confidentiality of their fellow addicts. Excessive concern about anonymity is usually based on self-deception, since one's reputation as an alcoholic is already well known, and the only one the alcoholic keeps in the dark is herself.

Along with AA meetings, Ms. Poland took an additional step to support her recovery. She took a prescribed medication, *disulfiram* (Antabuse), that was not a tranquilizer, antidepressant, or drug that would directly reduce alcoholic craving; such a drug does not exist anyway. Rather, *disulfiram* helped her sobriety by being a constant reminder that any alcohol entering her body when she was on *disulfiram* would have very painful consequences. This threat, which she had deliberately created by taking the medication, would help motivate her to remain alcohol free long enough for her sound judgment to return and her recovery to remain intact.

[*Disulfiram*, when combined with alcohol in any form, even cough syrup containing alcohol, reacts in the bloodstream to make the person taking it feel dreadful with throbbing headaches, dizziness, nausea, vomiting, weakness, and fainting. In rare instances, severe reactions including convulsions, unconsciousness, and cardiac failure can occur. People with certain conditions, such as pregnancy, should never use *disulfiram*, and, whatever one's physical state, the drug must always be taken under medical supervision.

Although *disulfiram*'s effects on most people who ignore warnings and imbibe alcohol anyway are rarely lethal, drinkers who do defy this caution feel so sick they say they wish they were dead. Most people who take *disulfiram*, however, feel as did one grateful alcoholic who called *disulfiram* his "insurance" since he knew that as long as it was in his system, he would never drink. He discontinued the medication after three years, once he had gone several months with no desire for alcohol].

This additional security required only that Ms. Poland accept her vulnerability at unexpected and unpredictable moments, which she was willing to do. When someone half-seriously derided her for using the medication as a "crutch," she said, "Of course it's a crutch. I'm crippled, and until I get over my problem I need any help I can get. Wouldn't you use a crutch for a while if you had a broken leg?" After eight months she no longer felt an urge to drink and discontinued the *disulfiram*.

As the alcohol drained from her system, her body needed it less and less, and she discovered that the longer she endured withdrawal the easier her abstinence became and the less she needed external support. As her sobriety strengthened, so did her mind, and she could turn to her new strengths to help her recover.

One Monday, three months into our work, Ms. Poland walked in smiling.

"I've learned by now how easily I can lie to myself so I've crossed my fingers in saying this," she quickly began, "but I've been completely dry for six weeks, and, with the support of Larry, and Lance, and my fellow AA members, I feel so committed to my alcoholic recovery I think I don't need to use these sessions anymore for overcoming my resistance to getting sober. We talk about denial all the time at AA meetings, and denial has been the biggest part of my resistance. I feel like I'm ready now to work on the problems that have troubled me all along, like my fears of looking bad and people criticizing me, but that I couldn't think about until I got sober. And I also realize that 'sober' doesn't just mean 'un-drunk,' because even if I wasn't falling down like my neighbor, my mind was so fuzzy most of the time I couldn't think straight, certainly not enough to solve my mental problems."

The unique techniques of 12-Step programs—AA and its derivative organizations such as NA (Narcotics Anonymous) or DA (Debtors Anonymous)—provide tools for recovery and insight for living. Eighty to ninety percent of recovering alcoholics find, after achieving sustained sobriety, that their well-functioning emotional structures and recovery-based wisdom are enough to fulfill their needs and usually make their lives turn out better than average. Many alcoholics, like Ms. Poland, however, have goals that can be achieved only through the resolution of conflicts underlying the alcoholic's self-defeating behaviors.

After indicating, "I'm ready now to work on the problems that've troubled me all along," Ms. Poland looked contented, as though she had nothing else to say.

"What are you thinking?" I asked.

"Nothing," she smiled.

I said, "That's the first thought, let's see what occurs to you next."

Her smile faded, and she looked out the window. It was a pretty spring day outside, trees leafing out and squirrels scrambling over branches, but she was focused inside and saw none of it.

"What's coming to mind?" I asked.

She turned back to me. "I'm thinking I've been afraid of criticism and people hurting me my whole life. In high school and college I made sure my friends were less intelligent or attractive than I was so I wouldn't feel so inferior, and I chose courses that I knew would make me look good. It didn't always work, but I know that's why I picked them."

She smiled as she went on. "Last night at my AA meeting the topic was, *How I Started Drinking*, and that made me think of Lance." Her smile began to wane. "I guess I haven't talked much about Lance. I started drinking with him when I was in my early twenties. He said when he took me to my first AA meeting how ironic it was that he gave me my first drink and now he's helping me stop. That was about thirty years ago, and he was in his mid forties. I dated mostly older men in those years," she said, looking out the window again. "I needed someone who felt good about me so I could feel good about myself. Lance really fit the part because I knew he admired me and wanted me sexually, and he made me look good because he looked good, and I felt good with him, for a while. But he introduced me to alcohol, which I'd hardly touched before."

She looked at me and continued, "My drinking with him started innocently. At first I drank only occasionally when Lance and I were together, but within a few months I was drinking alone, and every night. By then I had discovered that alcohol could numb my bad feelings, especially since I always felt like a failure when I compared myself to him."

She shifted around, as though she could not find a comfortable position. "I liked Lance, but I felt so inferior with him, I really got mixed up about how I thought of myself, and that's when I started drinking more to make it all go away," she said, finally settling into her chair, and looking thoughtful. "But my confusion and inadequacy were still there when I woke up the next morning, and my drinking increased. I know now from AA meetings that my body had become addicted, and my tolerance was so great I had to drink more and more to keep from having those terrible withdrawal feelings.

"A couple of years later, Lance and I drifted apart." She blotted her eyes with a tissue. "Once I started my heavy drinking, I lost any sexual feelings for him, and I knew we had no future, but I stayed with him for a while because he was an interesting and pleasant companion, and I had no one else." She brushed away more tears. "I knew I wanted a meaningful relationship, but I didn't know with whom, and I'm sure Lance knew he wanted to be with someone who really wanted to be with him, too."

She hesitated, appearing unsure of herself. "I feel embarrassed to tell you this, but by the time I was thirty I was drinking a pint of Vodka every day and couldn't quit. I gradually drank more and more for another twenty years, and then, as you know, I started neglecting my work, and it was downhill after that."

She cried for several minutes, then took a deep breath and continued.

"Larry and I have been together fifteen years, and I don't really understand what he saw in me that made him willing to accept me. I think that in the beginning he denied my drinking just like I did, and, although he and everyone else who knew me became aware of my downward spiral, they were as helpless as I was to break through my wall of denial." Her voice was strong, but she shook her head slightly, as if troubled by what she was hearing from herself. "When I first met Larry, I wondered if he would reject me because of my drinking, and that was the first time I even had a sliver of suspicion I might have an alcohol problem. But I guess I didn't do anything about it because I was drinking all the time."

Then she smiled, and her eyes became soft.

"Larry said he loved me because I have a good heart, and that I'm warm, and friendly, and even-tempered, and he enjoys being with me. I think my employees like me,

too. Larry and I love being together, but, and people sometimes ask us about this, neither of us has ever wanted to
get married or have children. We like what we have just
the way it is.

"But sometimes the pleasure I get from helping someone who needs me has made me vulnerable to people who
take advantage of me." She made a wry face. "Like the
time a young man asked me to help him get started in a
business that ended up failing and costing me $20,000."

She paused, looking thoughtful. "I just remembered
something I wanted to tell you earlier.

"Since I'm sober, and can finally think again, I see
what happened. My fears never went away, and I'm right
back where I was before I started drinking." In spite of
her weary expression, her voice was full of determination.

"Can you say more about the fears?" I asked.

She smiled mechanically, looking at me in silence.

"What are you thinking?" I continued.

"I don't seem to be thinking anything," she replied.

I said, "Does it seem to you, as it does to me, that you
are free to think clearly about most things, especially past
events, but, just as you numbed your mind with alcohol
when you felt inferior and inadequate with Lance, you may
also blank your mind when you have painful feelings?"

She gazed out the window, sighed, then turned back.
"That sounds right. I've always known I can't stand feeling like a failure, and that that was why I starting drinking
heavily, but I hadn't realized until just now that making
my mind go blank does the same thing." Her face brightened at her discovery. "What I don't understand about
this is how I can know something and still not actually
know it until I hear someone say it the way you just did.

"I think there's another way I try to get away from
these feelings. I've always known how much I hate other
people's cutting words and patronizing attitudes, but the
more we talk about this, the more I'm aware that it's not
really other people's words or attitudes I'm afraid of, it's
more how I *feel* about what they say, or what I say to myself that's so painful. I remember you said that once, but I

think I really learned it at AA where I hear it all the time."

Ms. Poland's observation that her fears were not of others' "cutting words" but of how the words caused her to feel, told me that, in spite of numbing her feelings and blanking her mind, she was still aware of what she was experiencing inside. Only this kind of honesty about oneself allows a person to overcome the pain of emotional conflict and self-defeating behaviors. Ms. Poland's efforts were facilitated by the honesty and wisdom she had gained in AA meetings and alcoholic recovery.

"Can you say more, then, about the *feeling* that comes when you hear someone say cutting words about you?" I asked.

Wearing a deep frown, she did not answer for a full minute. "It's there, and then it's not there. It goes away too quickly to describe it, and that's the way it always is. It stays only a second, but that's long enough to know I can't bear it. I can talk about it with no problem, because that's like thinking about it from a distance, it's *feeling* it that I can't stand." She paused. "It's gone away for now. When I have the feeling again I'll tell you."

The pressure of expectation often adds to the difficulty of retrieving an idea or feeling, so to help her approach the question, I asked about it indirectly, "How did you become aware of what you said about fearing the feeling rather than the cutting words themselves?"

She knit her brow. "It was when I remembered how I used to be afraid of looking bad when I worked in the government. Back then, I wouldn't say what I thought because I was afraid my superiors would dismiss me and just use their own ideas. I was afraid they'd hurt me, not because they might disagree with me, but because if they did, it would feel like they were putting me down. Whatever reasons they gave me when we disagreed, I always heard, 'You're wrong, you're bad, you're unlovable, and you always will be.'" Her jaw muscles tightened as if she were trying not to cry.

"Say more about how, 'You're wrong, you're bad, you're unlovable' feels?" I asked.

She grimaced, and quickly replied, "It feels like I'm dirt. But dirt's not bad enough to tell you how it feels. This is much worse, like I'm despicable, and there's nothing good about me, not like I was dumb or something like that, but that there was something so bad about me that no one could ever like me or love me. And I don't know what it is, or what's wrong about me, it's just that I'm the most worthless person in the world."

Bursting into tears, she cried hard for several minutes.

After composing herself and drying her tears, she continued. "Listening to this, you might think I'm saying my government superiors were terrible people, but whenever I felt safe enough to speak my mind, they were always grateful for my ideas, and often used what I said to guide their decisions. But no matter how much I told myself I was wrong about the way I heard them, it didn't matter. I was so afraid of them putting me down, I rarely took chances."

She looked at me and smiled. "When we first started, I felt wary of you, especially when you told me all the terrible things that would happen to me if I continued drinking. But pretty soon I felt safe in a way I never did in my government job, and I'm sure that's because I usually feel safe with older men, and can say things to you I couldn't to others."

While she had momentarily eased off her unbearable "dirt" feelings, there was an unspoken assumption between us that she would return to them when she felt ready.

I asked, "Where do you think the safety with me comes from?"

"I'm sure it comes from Dad. He was never critical, he was always loving and kind and supportive. I always enjoyed being with him and talking to him. His only failure was that he was so passive he would let Mother dominate and control him and the family with her criticisms. I was thirteen when he died suddenly of a heart attack." Tears came to her eyes. "I feel so sad when I remember that I never had the opportunity to know him after I grew up."

She looked out the window in thought for several minutes.

"Let's see what you're thinking," I said.

"I'm thinking about Mother and the way she acts."

"Acts how?" I asked.

"Like I said a moment ago," she scowled, "she was hard, and unreachable, and I feel like I'm frozen in that world. When I think of home, I hardly think of Dad. All I remember is Mother's constant criticism of me, my attitudes, my behavior, my schoolwork, my friends. I felt like I couldn't do anything right. Even as an adult, I never brought a man home that she didn't criticize, often to his face."

I said, "These qualities in your mother sound very similar to the hard, critical ones you turn on yourself, like when you were afraid your government superiors would dismiss you, or you'd fail, and to the way you can't reach yourself with reason."

She moved her foot in circles a minute or two, then, with tears creeping into her eyes, responded, "I know that when that happens, it's like I'm back at home again with her, and my feeling like dirt comes up all over again. There's no way to describe how bad that felt." Tears poured down her cheeks. "I couldn't do anything right, and I wouldn't know what I'd done wrong. When I tried to ask her why everything I did was wrong, she never answered, and finally I just gave up and stopped trying." She burst into tears again. "It was like she knew I was the worst person in the world, and that nothing I could do or say would make any difference. And I just couldn't bear feeling like dirt, but no matter where I went or what I did, it was always with me."

When her crying eased, she wiped her eyes with a tissue, and, after a few moments of silence, added, "I know our time's up today, but I want to talk more about this when we meet on Monday. It's terrible feeling this way all the time."

She began the next session, saying, "When I left last time I knew I was going to have to get to the heart of these feelings of being bad and unlovable that I've dreaded so much. My whole life, I've lived in fear of being criticized and told I'm a failure, but yesterday was the first time I ever really thought about the difference between what little value I put on myself and how others see me. I don't talk about it much, but most people in my life like me and think well of me." She smoothed back a lock of hair that had not been out of place.

I said, "You said a few moments ago that the feelings of being criticized came from the way your mother treated you, and that no matter how much you tell yourself that what you're hearing from others is coming from inside you, rather than from them, the feelings that you're wrong and bad are still there. Is this a way of saying that this pattern is carved so deeply into your emotions, that reasoning with yourself, like we all try to do at times, has no effect on the feeling?"

She looked at the wall, then turned back to me and said, "I hadn't looked at it that way, but that helps me see it more clearly."

I replied, "I know you've already described the feeling, but can you immerse yourself in it even more fully and help us understand what makes it seem unbearable?"

Several moments passed while she looked at the floor. "It's the helplessness, the absolute, utter helplessness, and there's nothing I can say or do to change Mother's, or anyone else's, mind. When she criticized everything I did, I was devastated. It was like I was a nothing, or if I did exist I was rotten to the core." Shifting her eyes to the floor in the corner of the office slightly to her left, she continued, "It seemed like the only way out was just to curl up in a corner and die," in a dull, barely audible voice.

"When you said, 'curl up in a corner and die,' your tone and inflection, and your eye movements, suggested you may have a mental picture that goes with this feeling?" I asked.

Looking puzzled, she thought a moment. "I'd never questioned it before because it seemed so natural, but I guess so."

"Can you describe the picture more fully?" I asked.

She glanced quickly at the corner, then looked away.

"Well, I'm all curled up in a dark corner, crying, and pleading, 'Please don't be mad at me, I'm sorry, I didn't mean to do anything wrong.'"

"There's someone else in the picture, too?" I asked.

"Yes," she said, as she looked back at the floor in the corner. With tears in her eyes, she continued. "It's my mother. But I don't know where the image comes from. Her criticism always hurt me, but I never curled up in a corner like I was afraid she'd do something to me physically."

"What more occurs to you about the picture?" I asked.

She thought a while, then half-smiled and shook her head. "You know where I think that comes from? From Cinderella. I imagined I was Cinderella, and I was pleading with my stepmother, or stepsisters as if they were going to beat me. I know I kept hoping that Cinderella's real mother would come back, like I kept hoping my real mother would come back."

"Your real mother would come back?"

She shook her head again. "Boy, that's really something. My mother was my real mother, and I never really thought otherwise, and I certainly was never afraid she'd beat me."

"You said, 'I never *really* thought otherwise, referring to whether you thought she was your real mother," I responded.

She smiled slightly. "I guess I meant *really* really, because I remember that for a while, I think when I was about five or six, I kept hoping my real mother would come back because I thought my real mother wouldn't criticize me the way Mother did. I guess that's the way kids think, but somehow that has stuck with me all this time."

I said, "You seem to be saying that you can't reach yourself with reason when you fear you'll be beaten down with criticism because imbedded deep within the feeling is a wish, the wish that your real mother will come back and be good and loving to you, and that you're stuck in the feeling because you've never given up hope that she'll return. This sounds similar to when the feeling has worked for you by helping you reach your high achievements. When you fear people will criticize and dismiss you, like your mother did, your determination keeps you hanging in there to make things come out right. And they usually have."

She sat in silence for several minutes. "That's the story of my life," she said quietly, then remained silent until the session ended a few minutes later.

She rose, gently smiled, and said, "I'll see you tomorrow," then left.

No single insight in a single session provides the recovery that allows one to "live happily ever after." But while work on Ms. Poland's unbearable feelings would continue for many months, the awareness of her driving wish to regain her real mother, whom she felt she had lost, provided a strong base from which we could, step by step, demystify and resolve the cause of her dreaded feelings, a process self-knowledge therapists call "working through."

One session, several months after Ms. Poland had begun immersing herself into feelings about her mother, she started by saying, "I think the only reason I can finally accept these bad feelings is that deep inside I also have the feeling that it wasn't always that way. I know I've always felt betrayed when Mother criticized me, like she'd broken a promise from some time I couldn't remember. I've seen her be so sweet and tender with little babies, so I know she can be, and when I do, I always feel envious, and hurt, like, 'Why wasn't she that way with me.'" She looked away for a moment, then added, "But maybe she was."

"She gets stern, even cold, with older children, like she did with me, and that's what I remember. I once read that some mothers can be very loving until their children become independent, but then don't know what to do with them after that.

"Maybe that's what happened with Mother and me. I can't prove it of course, and I know I couldn't talk with her about it, but all my deep feelings tell me it's right.

"There's something odd about this, though, because even though it's dreadful remembering how she criticized me, I still feel kind of close with her. I know that after my father died, I didn't resent her so much, I guess because she was all I had. I often did things, like bring home a boy I knew she wouldn't like, that would make her criticize me because I kept hoping, every time, that she wouldn't be so critical, but she's never changed." As Ms. Poland spoke, tears formed, and she quickly brushed them away. Then, she shook her head, as if to clear her mind.

"I thought I saw you shake your head in a way as if to wipe some idea out of your mind," I said with a question in my voice.

"Yes, but it was nothing," she replied.

"I know it may seem like nothing, and it may be, but often important feelings conceal themselves behind what appear to be insignificant ideas," I persisted.

"Well, I'll tell you, if you insist, but it's really nothing, or, more than that, it's wrong," she declared.

I nodded my head to suggest she continue.

"Actually, I was thinking two things. The first one was that I remembered something you said about how similar my criticisms of myself are to Mother's criticisms of me, and I wondered if I learned to do that to myself first so it wouldn't hurt so much when she did it to me. And I think that's right, because I remember saying to myself, many times, 'Now Mother is going to criticize you for this when you get home, so say it to yourself now, so that when she says it, it won't surprise or hurt you so much'." She looked at me with a defiant, severe frown.

"Did something stop you from saying the second thought?" I asked.

"No, nothing stopped me," she snapped. "I already told you it's not important."

"I appreciate that, but why don't we let our understanding of your thought decide whether it's important rather than prejudging it," I said.

She stared at the wall, then sighed. "What I thought was that I may feel close with Mother when I criticize myself, not just to protect myself, like I told you, but to feel really close," she said, with a sad smile.

"Say more about 'really close,'" I asked.

"It was like, if I couldn't have her the way I wanted, maybe I could have her another way." Tears pooled in her eyes. "I thought maybe she was right about me, and that if I said those things to myself, maybe I could please her. I was always so afraid I'd lose her when she criticized me. It was as if I became like her and thought bad things about me the way she did, then I could feel close with her, and keep her with me all the time, and then I'd really know she wouldn't ever go away." She looked at the floor, tears streaming down her cheeks.

The clock said our time was up, and we both had other commitments, but the moment said the world would have to wait until she felt ready to leave.

The next day, she entered the consultation room, smiled gently, then sat and looked out the window for several minutes.

I asked, "Can you think out loud?"

"Yesterday was a turning point. Knowing that I criticized myself so I can be like Mother and always have her close to me is like most of the other things we talk about here. Somewhere inside I've always known them, but it's like I know and don't know all at the same time, and," she smiled, "that must be why sometimes it takes a kind of arm-twisting, what you once called, 'dental psychiatry,' to get to it.

"I think the reason I already knew it is because, particularly as I look back on it, I never really knew how much of the criticism was actually coming from her and how much was coming from me. And maybe the reason I didn't want to see it, was because I didn't want anything to happen to the way I had found to be close to her."

She breathed a deep, heavy sigh.

"Yesterday was such a relief, and what I've been thinking most about since yesterday is that one of the main reasons I love Larry so much is that although he's different from my mother he's also the loving person I've always wanted Mother to be and never could have when I was little, even by criticizing myself like she did. One thing about yesterday that really struck me was that, although criticizing myself has given me a feeling of being close with her, it hasn't made things between her and me come out the way I hoped.

"My love for Larry isn't primarily physical. I feel at

home and secure with him. He's the best of all worlds. I guess it's what they call chemistry. He loves me, he's gentle and uncritical like my father, and he enjoys, as I do, just being together and sharing our feelings and ideas. And because he's also strong and has high standards and expectations, his approval somehow makes up for my mother's criticisms, and it tells me that I really am a good person, no matter what Mother said or did."

"It sounds like you're saying," I responded, "that you love Larry most because his uncritical love and caring makes you not have to feel those old feelings of failure and badness that came from your mother."

"If you hadn't said that, I would have, because I recognized what I was saying while I was still saying it," she replied.

We had to revisit her feelings of being bad, wrong, and unlovable, many times—for instance when her dealings with the IRS reminded her of her lost years due to alcohol, and when she would visit her mother, who still saw something in Patricia to find fault with, but each instance provided an additional crucial element that deepened and broadened her mastery of her most dreaded feeling.

Ms. Poland came to understand how her drive to make things come out right with her mother had led her to create events that would bring about the very feeling of failure she dreaded. In her effort to regain the sense of value and security she had had with her mother as a small child, Ms. Poland constantly created situations her subconscious mind hoped would recapture her very early days when she had felt loved by her mother. Patricia's attempts never worked out right, though, as when she brought home suitors she knew her mother would disapprove of, or when she strove to do her best at work but always assumed her superiors thought the worst about her.

In a session near the end of our work, Ms. Poland said, "I think the most important thing I've learned in this work has been that my fear of being criticized didn't belong with my friends and coworkers, or, in the end, even to Mother. Everything I've ever said about how critical she was, and still is, is true, but my fear of being criticized came from inside me because the way I kept her close to me was by being like her and criticizing myself the way she did. Those feelings have all gone away now, and it's such a relief to know I can accept Mother for who she is, carping and all, and love her for all she gave me and did for me when I was little and that I don't have to keep repeating those futile attempts to make things come out right with her, which they never have anyway."

After Ms. Poland had overcome her drinking and fears of criticism, her life of sobriety fell easily into place. With an alcohol-free brain and a mind unencumbered with fears and self-defeating protective mechanisms, she brought order out of the chaos her drinking had created. She faced business and personal problems head-on, she resolved disputes with the IRS and regulatory agencies, her business thrived, and she felt physically and mentally better than at any time she could remember.

While she had been drinking, Ms. Poland had attributed her problems to others—as alcoholics almost invariably do. A striking example had occurred when she explained a law firm client's failure to pay its bill as having being due to the law firm's office manager's resentment about some unknown or unexplained problem with one of the temps. After Ms. Poland and I worked on the issue, she spoke with the office manager, who reminded Ms. Poland that the law firm had never received a bill because the office manager and Ms. Poland had agreed that the law firm could defer their payments a few months due to the law firm's temporary cash flow problems. Ms. Poland had no memory of any of these transactions since she had been in an alcoholic fog at the time.

While we were discussing this, she smiled knowingly, and I asked, "You just had a thought, can you tell me about it?"

She responded, "I remembered reading something about Wilbur Mills [former Chairman of the House Ways and Means Committee of the United States House of Representatives] some years ago that's always stuck with me.

Even before I got sober, the story felt familiar. The article said that after he started recovering from alcoholism, he told of having once read in The Washington Post that, the day before, he had spent two hours in the Oval Office with the President discussing matters critical to the nation's economy, and that he, Mills, had absolutely no memory of it." She shook her head in bewilderment. "I wondered at the time if that—what we in AA call 'blackouts'—might be happening to me, but I just attributed my memory lapses to age and didn't think any more about them." After a moment's thought, she added, "But that did happen to me," nodding her head, as if to reinforce her words.

When Ms. Poland called me recently to refer a friend, she said, "I never told you about this because I didn't think it was a big problem, but another benefit of my sobriety and of this therapy has been that I'm not afraid of being on escalators and in high places anymore. None of that happens now, and I know alcohol caused those fears because I never had them before I drank and I haven't had them since I stopped. The most meaningful part of my new life, though, has been my freedom to be open and honest with Larry. Since I'm not stuck in that alcoholic isolation and secrecy any more, we can show our love for each other in ways I never dreamed before. Larry is so loving and devoted and uncritical, I really do have someone who has made things come out right."

Ms. Poland was fortunate. The shock of the IRS notice, the looming prospect of business and personal bankruptcy, and the threat of losing her loved one had scared her into obtaining help to overcome her addiction. But many people are not so lucky; their drugged minds and emotional denial prevent them from perceiving and acting on warning signs to fix their problems. Wasting one's assets, career, and relationships, and destroying one's life is always tragic, but it is especially regrettable when resources for overcoming internal saboteurs are available but not used.

With alcoholics, only the inability to acknowledge their powerlessness over alcohol and its disastrous consequences stands in the way of their recovery. Likewise, with those whose demons and defective mechanisms sabotage their lives, only their resistance to overcoming a self-identity measured by an ideal of excessive independence prevents them from accepting the self-understanding they need to use their full strengths in fulfilling their goals.

❦

When this book's editor studied this chapter, she felt it seemed less empathic than the others. Although I had not recognized any lack of empathy while writing it, I immediately understood her observation. What she sensed was not lack of empathy, for I feel the agony of those suffering from alcohol and other drug addictions, just as I do of those whose pain is due to other mental-emotional conditions. Rather, she accurately perceived my description and elaboration of the therapeutic mode necessary to help recovering alcoholics and drug users when they are struggling to overcome the addicts' particular demons and defects.

The bullheaded self-righteous outrage most drinking alcoholics and drug addicts use to justify their defiant resistance to attempts by others to save an addict from killing herself, which the desperate alcoholic or drug addict interprets as taking away her lifeblood, requires that therapeutic efforts be expressed in "tough love" techniques rather than the more conventional expressions of empathic care familiar in normal relationships and in self knowledge therapy. Those who know the horrors and perils of addictive drinking and drug use, as well as its potential for creating human heartbreak, also know that compassionate, honest, firm confrontations about the horrendous realities of alcoholic addiction are the only real way one can help those suffering from the deadly poison.

While the hearts of addiction therapists and counselors reach out bounteously to help people in the clutches of chemical addictions, the therapists' attitude must be absolutely objective and firm. Since an addict is constantly at risk of taking the next drink or drug, his chemically impaired brain will exploit even the tiniest opportunity, such as misinterpreting compassion or gentleness for approval, to break his sobriety.

5

It's All My Fault She's Sick

At first I didn't think much about it, I'd lived with worry and fears all my life, but this fear was different. It had a sense of hopeless doom, too vague to know what it portended. I couldn't account for it, understand it, or fight it.

I was seventeen, and the clock showed almost noon on a beautiful south Texas day in late March of 1947. I routinely had lunch at a small cafe near my work as a freight line dispatcher, but that day I wasn't thinking about eating. My insides were screaming, "Something's terribly wrong, and I'm scared." I felt a vast emptiness inside inhabited by only pain, as if my stomach were being cut with a dull knife, and while I struggled with this dread, a giant magnet pulled me home where I thought I'd feel safe and the bad feeling would go away.

I phoned Momma and didn't tell her I was afraid when I said I wanted to come home for lunch, but she must have picked up something in my voice when I asked, "Is anyone else there?"

The moment I reached the front stoop I knew she understood. The smell of Mexican food greeted me, and I felt, "God, am I lucky to have a Momma who loves me and will always be with me and take care of me." She met me at the door, then said with her customary eager-to-please smile, "Son, I made enchiladas, and they're all ready." She

125

always fixed food I liked, and today, aware her boy felt needy, she wanted to fix something special. Her greeting also told me she knew something was wrong. No one ever met a family member at the door; it stayed unlocked most of the time, and we just walked in.

Momma was by herself. Daddy had gone to the hardware store to get packing material for their move, Maurice, my five years younger brother, was in school, and Betty, my five years older sister, had married and moved away. As much as I loved Daddy and Maurice, today I needed the security of being alone with Momma. Her open arms and hands were even more reassuring than her words; they were a warm sanctuary, like I remembered from my early childhood. Rather than shying from her hugs, as I had since becoming a teenager, I felt grateful for any relief from my foreboding. In contrast to my usual excessive self-sufficiency, I didn't resist when she tried to find any way she could to ease me.

Momma's plain demeanor suited her. She wore a neatly pressed dress printed with Texas bluebonnets, her coal black hair had begun, at fifty-one, to show some gray, and she carried, as in my lifetime she always had, thirty to forty extra pounds on her five-foot-eight-inch frame. Her vision was slightly impaired due to a crossed left eye she had had from birth, and a detached retina in her right eye from complications during Maurice's birth, but her uncomplaining nature and innocent lack of self-consciousness added to her appealing nature.

As we walked to the kitchen Momma said in hushed tones, "Reverend Jones came by this morning to say he's sorry we're moving and hopes we'll enjoy our new church, and that he'll write our new minister in Chickasha to introduce us." And then, with great excitement, she added, "We got a letter today from our new landlord saying we can move in next week."

I felt the hole in my stomach growing as she spoke.

Daddy had gratefully accepted a job from the Chickasha Cotton Oil Mill in Chickasha, Oklahoma, offered by the Mill's superintendent who, almost twenty years earlier, had been Dad's apprentice and now wanted to re-pay the trust and kindness he had received from Dad. Chickasha was five hundred miles north of San Antonio, Texas, our present home, so Dad, Momma, and Maurice would move to Chickasha, while I, with a secure job and uncertain future plans, would remain, alone.

Daddy's new job was a godsend. Born in 1876, Daddy was fifty-three when, in 1929, he lost his job after, simul-taneously, the Wall Street crash triggered the nation's Great Depression, and the forces of nature brought the Dust Bowl drought that wiped out the cotton industry.

Having begun work at fourteen to support his family after his father died, Daddy had worked solely in the cot-ton industry for almost forty years and knew only the skill of a cotton linter inspector. Except for the three-and-a-half years of World War Two, from December, 1941 to August, 1945, when everyone was needed for the war effort, Daddy had had only occasional day labor for eighteen years.

By the spring of 1947, the war effort had restored the economy, God had brought back the rain, the cotton in-dustry flourished anew, and on the day after Easter Daddy's beloved career would be reborn. When the Chickasha Cot-ton Oil Mill, in Chickasha, Oklahoma offered Daddy, then seventy-one, a job as cotton linter inspector, Momma called it "truly a gift from heaven."

I liked the small kitchen where Momma and I sat and talked; it concentrated the good aroma of onions, toma-toes, kidney beans and browned ground beef, all wrapped in corn tortillas and smothered with chili and cheese. Usu-ally I salivated and tasted the enchiladas long before I took the first bite, but today even Momma's food didn't tempt me.

Forcing myself to talk, I said, "Momma, you make the best enchiladas in the whole world," and then added, "when I told Juan, the chef at Casa Grande, how good you fix them, he told me to ask you if you'd teach him."

With an amused smile she responded, as she had many times, "You're just like your Irish ancestors who kissed that Blarney Stone."

Momma served from the cooking pan on the stove; the small table covered with a rose printed oilcloth had room only for plates, utensils, glasses, and a side dish of tortillas. Any other food would have interfered with the enchiladas my heart and taste buds would ordinarily have been set on.

While we ate, Momma asked, "Can you get some large boxes for the packing? We have enough small ones, but I need some really big ones for sheets and quilts."

I said, "Sure, I'll get them this afternoon and bring them home tonight," then added, "we need to finish packing over the weekend. The movers said they would pick up the load next Tuesday and have it all in Chickasha by Thursday."

My making arrangements with the moving company came naturally from my work in the freight line business and my role as the family breadwinner. During Daddy's unemployment for the two post-war years, I had been the family's sole financial support and would pay for the move.

The pain in my stomach eased while Momma and I talked about the food and packing material; when the topic changed to details of the actual move, though, the wrenching in my gut came back.

Continuing to make myself talk, I said, "I made reservations for a room at the Y [YMCA] beginning Tuesday. I'll take off work most of that day, and then, after the movers leave, which should be around three, and you catch the bus for Chickasha at five, I'll move my things in down at the Y." With conscious, labored, enthusiasm, I went on. "I'm really looking forward to staying there. I've never lived away from home before, so it'll be a step up in the world." I hoped the humor would take the edge off my sense of impending doom. "I'll be completely on my own, and with you and Dad and Maurice secure, I can start looking into college." The roiling around inside got worse, now greater than ever.

No doubt seeing anxiety in my face, Momma immediately tried to reassure me, "Son, you're as white as a sheet. I hope you aren't upset. It's hard to go off and leave you here, but I know you'll be all right. You're such a good boy, and you've always been so responsible. You have a good job at the freight line, and the Y is a safe place to live."

And then it hit. Raw terror seized my mind with indescribable, helpless, hopeless fears of death and eternal nonexistence. My insides ripped apart, and my heart raced out of control, as I imagined, "I'll be in the ground, trapped in a casket forever. My body will disintegrate. and I'll never be alive again. I won't even exist. There's no way out of this and there's nothing I can do about it. I can't bear this." Sweat dripped from every pore. I tried to get relief by asking myself, "What happens after I die? Is there life after death? Is there a heaven? Where is it? Can I ever come back? How long is eternity? What happens after eternity?" But my questions were unanswerable, and each brought a new round of anxiety and fear. All these thoughts, in all their clarity, flashed through my mind in a matter of seconds.

I put down my fork, my appetite gone, and stared into space, no longer aware of Momma, the food, or the kitchen. I couldn't even say, "Sho am good," like in the old days.

Momma asked, "Why did you stop eating, son? I thought you loved enchiladas. Is something wrong with them?"

Unable to answer her question, and wanting not to hurt her, I said, "No, I just had a little gas and had to wait a minute until it went away," and then put a bite in my mouth and swallowed. The food no longer tasted good, and nothing mattered. Everything felt dismal, especially the future. The thought of death, the picture of being buried, or worse, cremated, were real and terrifying, and I saw no escape.

"How's Daddy today?" I asked, my mind still preoccupied with terror.

Momma's face lit up, as she answered, "He feels better than I've seen him in years. His new job has made him feel he's been given a new life, and he acts more like he's thirty-one than seventy-one."

"What does Maurice say about the move?" I asked, as I tried to fill the rest of the lunch hour with routine questions.

"It may be most difficult for him," she answered. "He likes his friends and teachers here and doesn't know what to expect up there."

"Does Betty talk about the move?" I asked.

"Not really," Momma responded. "She's happy for Daddy and us, but she's too involved with her own family to say much."

Clearly Momma, Daddy, Maurice, and Betty, with her own family, were in their own worlds, all different from mine.

My home, where I had come for sanctuary, had become a prison and I desperately had to get out. Fortunately, by then, I had finished lunch and had to return to work. "Maybe this will go away when I go back to work and talk with other people," I thought.

Fearing Momma might be hurt by my sudden, unexplained gloominess, when we walked to the door, I said, "Momma, your Mexican food is always so good. Please save the leftovers so I can have them tonight." She smiled and seemed reassured, but I could tell she knew something was wrong.

Momma did not press me, and I never told her what happened that day to change my uneasy mood to deadly somberness. I thought, "How could I explain to a normal person the logic of being terrified by feelings most people don't even think about, especially someone with religious faith like Momma?" I also knew that if I told her about my terror, she would worry about me. Most of all, the vividness and realness of my fears about non-existence after death made me afraid that if I told her about them, then she, too, would be terrified.

Panic in the face of some immediate and overwhelming threat, like murder or rape, is understandable, but I panicked sitting alone with my Momma, a simple lady who only loved me and felt not an iota of harm toward me. Until then, the adversities I had faced had been real life situations that I could size up and overcome: mowing yards on a steep hill required merely stamina and perseverance; filling the family's empty coffers needed only cash I could earn. I could not have been prepared for this strange feeling; its power and unreality were unlike anything I had ever known, except in nightmares.

Driving back to work in a company truck, I thought, "There's no way out of this. I'm terrified to live and I'm terrified to die. Living means being terrified of dying, and dying is more terrifying than living." In shock, I had no idea of how to go about getting relief from these unbearable thoughts. Common sense told me other people didn't feel the way I did, so I knew I should talk to someone who understood death and eternity more than I did, except I couldn't imagine anyone changing immutable reality. Meantime, I would have to endure with whatever I could muster inside, so no matter how bad I felt at the moment, I had to return to my duties at the freight line.

The police were waiting for me when I got back. No one could find Chester, one of our pick up and delivery men, and everyone had assumed that I, his dispatcher, would know where he was. The night before, Chester, apparently, had nearly killed some fellow in a drunken barroom brawl. Fortunately, I did not have to lie to the officers; having been away at lunch, I actually did not know, unlike the other workers who knew but would not tell the cops. Chester was hiding under the loading dock the police were standing on.

After the police left, another driver, aware of my late return and preoccupied with sex, as is truckers' wont, winked and smiled knowingly as he said, "Where have you been so long? Mary Sue must be really good in bed." Mary Sue, a flirtatious office clerk and the object of much sexual machismo, had, coincidentally and unknown to me, also taken an unusually long lunch break. For a wide-eyed teenager, being around truck drivers was a truly enlightening experience. All they talked about was sex, their many conquests, the best sexual positions, the best woman they ever had, the kind of baloney that was usually amusing. That day, though, it was just words I hardly heard.

As I entered the building, Fred, my replacement, who couldn't go to lunch until I returned, met me with gripes about my having been gone "forever." My boiling brain did not miss the irony of our different perspectives: I felt panicked about the forever of hopeless non-existence for trillions of years, while Fred felt put upon by the forever of hunger pangs for forty-five minutes.

All afternoon I deliberately focused my thoughts and actions on warding off the constant fear and torment trying to muscle in, and by evening my terror had eased. While I could not have known that this had been only the first of what would become many similar attacks, I did know the dread felt so real and so hopeless that it was inconceivable I could ever see death and eternity any other way.

During my boyhood I had been told that "love conquers all," and I assumed it worked for everything. When Momma kissed my skinned knee, she healed it instantly, and when at church we sang *God Will Take Care of You*, I knew He would, but when I had gone home for Momma's loving, caring arms and enchiladas, and found terror instead, I learned the healing power of love alone did not magically cure my mind run amok.

Two o'clock the next morning, my insomniac wandering around the house woke Momma, who called out, "Are you all right, Billy?" and Daddy, who added, "Is anything wrong, son?"

I answered, "I'm OK, everything's fine," to reassure them, as I paced and paced. As the night deepened, my terror increased until exhaustion eventually overcame my physical brain and I dozed a little.

At daybreak I caught the small city bus, a ten passenger broken-down jitney, already twenty years old by the mid 1940's, that made its rounds only during early and late hours and stopped less than a block from our house. Still in shock from the day before, I rode to work sleepy from insomnia and wide awake from anxiety.

When the bus passed Hargrove's Funeral Home, I thought of burial preparations for dead bodies, and another round of terror hit me: "I'll be embalmed with formaldehyde, and I can never come back to life; and then, I'll just disintegrate into chemical elements and be absorbed by the earth and never exist again."

As the bus turned south on Austin Street a tall, wide, cylindrical structure I'd seen many times before, came into view. I had heard it called a "crematorium" and, until my panic attack, I hadn't thought much about it, but this time I could only think about the horror of its use. "I'll be burned up, and nothing'll be left of me." When I thought of being reduced to ashes, my childhood notion that somehow I could continue to exist on earth after I died went up in smoke.

As I walked into work, I immediately saw ancient, eighty year old Mr. Head, our chief salesman and a stark reminder of the finiteness of life and the imminence of death.

During my morning coffee break, I glanced at the newspaper. The headlines leaped out: "Hospital for The Dying Closes" and "Scientists Think Earth Fifteen Billion Years Old." The triggers of terror were everywhere.

During my noon break, I ordinarily enjoyed a two mile walk, preferably alone so I could think and plan, followed by a chili with ketchup and crackers lunch. Today, though, I longed for a conversational distraction. I tried to make my dreads go away by posing questions to myself and expecting answers to magically form in my mind and give me relief. "What's the purpose of life if we live only to die? Why exist at all if we have to face the futility and horror of death and eternal non-existence?" I had no answers.

Riding home on the afternoon bus, I ordinarily loved the smell of burning coal and oil when we passed the railroad roundhouse where dozens of trains collected, but my tormented thoughts and images ruined this pleasure today. The good smells were emanations of fossil fuels formed in the earth from animal and plant remains hundreds of millions of years ago, and they set off a flood of anxious questions about limitless time and space. "When did time begin and what existed before? When will time end and what will happen then? What happens after the sun burns up in five billion years? Where is the beginning, and end, of space, and what lies beyond?" Again, no answers.

After supper I sought diversion in a movie about Mark Twain. The final scene dramatized his death at seventy-five by its synchrony with the passing of Halley's comet, the celestial body whose seventy-five year cycle has been observed since 466 B.C. My mind eased when I discovered that Halley's comet has a measurable future of only several hundred more centuries, not five billion years or infinite time.

Three days later our family attended church together one final time at Harlandale Presbyterian Church. While the minister preached about "Faith in Everyday Life," I sat preoccupied with questions about my fate in the hereafter. Half expressing my sense of futility, half seeking a comforting answer, I thought about the Christian concept of an afterlife. "Where is Heaven? What does one do in Heaven? Will I see my family? Can I look down upon others on Earth? Could I return to Earth?"

I thought, "I'm doing this to myself," although I did not know what to do with that awareness. In spite of my pain I could not stop the torturous thoughts and questions. I wanted to believe that if I could find answers they would give me relief, but what I found instead were empty abstract concepts, and no peace.

Worst of all, each time the fears were set in motion, they were relentless. Nothing I did would make them go away, or even diminish them. Every attempt I made to deflect my attention succeeded only a moment, and then left me terrified that I'd be in the grip of panic forever.

Regular sleep became impossible. At night I lay awake thinking, "Why isn't everyone afraid of death and eternity? My fears are so real, why doesn't everyone feel the way I do? When people learn what death and eternity really mean, they'll be terrified too, and that will be even worse because it will truly mean that no one has an answer to my fears." I gained relief and nodded off only when reminders of death were absent long enough for the panic to subside, or my mind collapsed from fatigue.

When nothing worked, and I felt depleted, I hoped resignation to my fate would help. Remembering a line spoken by an elderly uncle, "Death comes to us all. It's a normal part of the life cycle," I concluded, "If God intended death, it must be right. Countless others have lived without being terrified, so there must be nothing to fear." But I found no comfort from that either.

Any possible option short of death itself would have been preferable to this demon. Looking into the jaws of an uncaged hungry tiger seemed an inviting alternative; at least I would have a fighting chance.

Death and taxes were said to be the only things certain in life, yet as clearly as I knew a smart tax attorney could find loopholes for the rich, I knew of no escape from my terror. Death and eternity were absolute, inevitable, and inescapable.

The movers came on Tuesday, and at first the churning in my stomach made it seem that watching my family leave would push the terror beyond unbearable. But Providence intervened as a Texas spring shower brought back sweet memories of Momma and me in my childhood Paris, Texas home, standing at the east bedroom window watching it rain and seeing the cows take cover under the bois d'arc tree in Old Man Pickens' pasture. This memory, my pleasure in helping Momma and Daddy finish packing, and our excitement about Daddy's new job and their new life in Chickasha took me away from my anxious fears.

By mid-afternoon the truckers had finished their loading and had taken off for Oklahoma. I drove Momma, Daddy, and Maurice to the bus station in a company car, we said goodbye, and they left for their new home.

I had dreaded for the entire previous week this moment of their leaving, anticipating my world would come to an end, though I never connected my terror about death and eternity with my family moving. My mind worked overtime reassuring me that my family would be merely an overnight bus ride away, and I would see them again soon, and gradually my turmoil receded.

Despite being weighed down by the dreads, I felt a glimmer of excitement when I thought of starting my new life as an independent adult living at the Y. Still, I knew that the terror, like a dozing crocodile, was only waiting for the right moment to strike again.

As I ate dinner alone that night and reflected on the day, I was encouraged knowing I had survived my family's leaving. I had helped make my family's departure a happy occasion in spite of my terror, just as I had worked each day the week before in spite of my panic.

But the terror returned the next morning and continued relentlessly, invading everything I thought or did. The following Saturday afternoon I stood up for a high school friend at his wedding, and when the bride and groom said, "till death do us part," panic struck again. I didn't think about two people in a loving life together on earth, I imagined life after death and myself alone in amorphous outer space forever unconnected with others.

The next weekend I attended the funeral of Mr. Brooks, an eighty-three year old former neighbor, triggering a new round of terror.

Mr. Brook's obituary spoke of his "body" being available for viewing at the funeral home, but, like "remains," this callous reference to his body, as if it were not Mr. Brooks himself, just a piece of meaningless, inert matter, confronted me with my future non-existence.

At the open grave, I stood listening to the minister reassure the family, "In sure and certain hope of the resurrection to eternal life, through our Lord Jesus Christ, we commend to almighty God our brother, Clayton Brooks, and we commit his body to the ground, earth to earth, ashes to ashes, dust to dust."

Hearing a man of God speak such words of "reassurance" horrified me. Earth to earth meant a dungeon for my dead body; ashes to ashes said there would be only mineral leftovers of my cremated body, the rest of me becoming gaseous carbon dioxide with no palpable form; dust to dust reminded me that someday my body would become fully decomposed. Resurrection meant entry into infinity. But to where? For how long? And eternal life meant eternal terror. I faced the terror of eternity wherever I turned. My insides screamed, I sweated profusely, and my heart pounded like mad, as if I were the person being buried and as though I would know what was happening to me.

In my daily life, other people spoke of their uncertainty about the unknown, or losing life and loved ones, with the calm assurance they would be all right whatever happened. They had found solace or peace in the reassurances about life after death, rewards of eternal bliss, and union with God and loved ones central to most religions. I knew no such peace, yet I also knew my survival depended on finding answers to my seemingly impossible questions.

As a seventeen year old, poor south Texas boy with only a high-school education and an unpromising low-level white collar job, I knew only religion to turn to as a source for answers.

I feverishly prayed, "Dear God, please give me peace. Please help me know what others know to make them not afraid," not really believing my dread of eternity could be seen any other way.

My Protestant Southwest breeding taught me that genuine faith in God could heal the sick, move mountains, and in matters of death and the hereafter, relieve all anxiety. Any doubts about the hereafter not relieved by faith meant one did not truly believe.

Sunday school had taught me the Bible's wisdom in facing life's tribulations, how people who felt impossibly defeated had found hope for a better tomorrow, as had the Israelites in their exodus from bondage in Egypt to new life in the Promised Land. I repeated to myself, "Yea, though I walk through the valley of the shadow of death, I shall fear no evil; for thou art with me," words from the 23rd Psalm that often comforted those facing their darkest hours. My Presbyterian upbringing assured me that the Resurrection of Jesus Christ would always give me hope, just as would John 3:16, "For God so loved the world that He gave His only begotten Son, that whosoever believeth in Him shall not perish but have everlasting life."

But I found the passage from Psalms too abstract to be meaningful or helpful in my struggle with anxiety. I knew of no "evil" causing my fears. Had I known, I would have been grateful, because I could have done something about them. Nor did I sense God "with me," since my all-consuming terror left no intellectual or emotional room for faith. "Shall not perish" and "everlasting life" were promises involving eternity, concepts that reinforced my dread.

The image of Heaven did not help either. I could not picture where it was, how I would get from here to there, or what form my existence would take if I were there. Because I could not imagine Heaven, I could not visualize being there with Momma and Daddy, the ones I feared losing most. And if there were a Heaven and I were with God and Momma and Daddy, being there would be for eternity, and by then my fear had extended to eternity under any condition, with or without Momma and Daddy. The promise of heaven was more terrifying than relieving.

My parents' move and the onset of my terror symptom in the spring of 1947 occurred a year after I graduated from high school. I continued to live and work in San Antonio one more year before beginning college at the University of Oklahoma in Norman, forty-five miles northeast of Chickasha.

One weekend during my first semester, while visiting my parents in Chickasha, I asked Reverend Mitchell, our minister, "When we are in Heaven, will we know about and see things happening back here on earth?" I knew the hope of being connected to my loved ones on earth would lessen my fears. The Reverend assured me we would, then dashed my hopes by adding, "But you won't be in direct communication with them. Only through spiritual faith will people back home know you are looking on." I was back to the bottom line of my fears. When I died I would lose life on earth with Momma and Daddy, and I knew of no way even God could change that.

When Reverend Mitchell asked me if I were afraid of going to Hell, I was puzzled. The idea of Hell never crossed my mind; its portrayal by fundamentalist Christians and Medieval writers made it even harder to imagine than Heaven. My religious upbringing had never emphasized punishment for sins by everlasting suffering, nor did I recall ever hearing any Presbyterian minister threaten his sinful parishioners with eternal damnation.

Even if I had had concrete evidence of its existence, the concept of Heaven would have seemed like a meaningless mirage in an empty desert. The term Heaven's "eternal bliss" was an oxymoron, how could eternal be blissful? "These are false reassurances," I thought, "we're helpless to change our inevitable eternal non-existence any way we look at it, and I will not allow myself to be lulled into some fool's paradise by an illusion that our terrifying fate is not real."

Having found no help from theology, I sought answers in philosophy. Although philosophy did not try to explain the supernatural, its speculations about human truth suggested it as a source of great wisdom. But what I found was that where theologians at least sought to provide refuge for humanity's fear of the unknown, philosophers made no bones about our condemned future:

"... death is a state of nothingness and utter unconsciousness....", said Plato, c 428-348 B.C., in his *Apology*.

Euripides, c 485-406 B.C., offered still more bleakness, "Today's today. Tomorrow, we may be ourselves gone down the drain of Eternity."

Later writers were equally ungenerous.

Pascal, 1623-1662, apparently struggling with his own version of my fears, wrote, "The eternal silence of these infinite spaces [the heavens] terrifies me."

And Vladimir Nabokov, 1899-1977, "The cradle rocks above an abyss, and common sense tells us that our existence is but a brief crack of light between two eternities of darkness."

Even painters. "Life is hardly more than a fraction of a second. Such a little time to prepare oneself for eternity!!!" Paul Gauguin.

Before reading *The Razors Edge*, I had hoped W. Somerset Maugham, 1874-1965, in his account of the protagonist's internal turmoil and global pursuit of the meaning of life, would reveal some special knowledge to help me alleviate my fears. Maugham's question was as futile as mine, although, I hoped, not as terrifying to him.

Wherever I sought wisdom, one fact repeatedly and inescapably appeared: no solution could avoid the reality of eternity. Peter Ustinoff, the renowned actor, when asked in a television interview if he feared death, admitted, "Yes, I do, but I don't like the alternative of living forever either." I readily agreed, although for me the idea of being a 900 or 9,000,000 year old Methuselah with all his loved ones and friends long gone sounded not just bleak, as Ustinoff implied, but terrifying.

These attempts to find solutions to my problem had not been entirely fruitless; they had helped me take a step in clarifying one element of my fears: other people struggled theologically and philosophically with the same ideas, but they were not consumed with terror about the notions, as I was. Others dealt with the ideas as concepts to think about, but not as causes for terror.

After my fruitless efforts with theology and philosophy, I gave up trying to find help for my fears from conventional sources. I knew there had to be a rational explanation for my fears, even if I did not yet know what it was, and, no matter how desperately I wanted an answer, I knew it had to make sense. Unsubstantiated beliefs had always scared me, since they felt like self-deceptions. I could never remember a time when I was willing to blindly accept "just trust me" or "have faith" reassurances. My "why?" questions helped me learn very early that Santa Claus and the Easter Bunny were not exactly what they were portrayed to be. My questions also made me slightly unpopular at times as when, in the third grade, I asked my Sunday School teacher, "How do we know that two thousand years from now people won't be laughing at us for believing in Jesus like we laugh today at the Greeks for believing in all their gods?"

Though I envied and yearned for the way others comforted themselves with theology, I feared that if I relied on supernatural solutions, I would be blindsided by inescapable doom. I was not clear what the answer would be, or how or when I would find it, but I did know that the knowledge had to be out there somewhere, and I knew my life depended on my discovering it.

I had to make do in the meantime with whatever I could muster to cope with my fears. From March, 1947, when my terror episodes began, until January, 1958, when at last I was able to pursue the self-knowledge work that would relieve my fears, I had frequent bouts of severe terror interlaced with occasions of relief. My reprieves from terror came when the good feelings from momentous events in my life pushed the terror into the background. In 1952, I entered the University of Oklahoma Medical School; in 1953, Irma Louise Ford and I married; our first daughter, Becky, was born in 1955; I graduated medical school in May, 1956; Kathy, our second daughter, was born in December, 1956; Debbie, our third daughter, was born in 1959; and, following graduation from medical school, I served a general internship and psychiatric residency at Walter Reed General Hospital in Washington, D. C. from 1956 through 1960.

Though those events eased my symptoms at the time, I was never truly free of terror and panic or of the threat of their appearance. In an attempt to prevent panic episodes, I avoided flying, crossing high bridges, entering caverns, nearing precipices, reading obituaries or articles about endless time and space, and watching eerie, otherworldly movies or television programs like *The Twilight Zone*. While these avoidance mechanisms helped me prevent panic attacks, the limitations they placed on my family and my professional life exacted a heavy toll, so my long-term goal of finding the cause of my terror made me constantly alert to any possibility for discovering that knowledge.

During the course of my medical school studies, I finally learned of the science of understanding how the mind works, though at the time my meager means, my growing family, and my academic duties would not permit me to act on that knowledge.

Finally, in January of 1958, one week after beginning my psychiatric residency, the time was ripe and I met with Dr. Franks, a Washington, D.C. psychoanalyst, to begin the process of discovering and overcoming the mysterious emotions and mechanisms causing the terror that had tortured me for almost eleven years.

The self-knowledge I gained from this work changed my life forever. It not only relieved my terror and crippling inhibitions, it opened ways of understanding the human condition and its countless forms of expression, such as in literature, history, the humanities, art, education, politics, and the judicial system, unknown to me before I had learned how the mind works.

As I sat in Dr. Franks' waiting room before my first appointment, profoundly aware this was the moment I had waited so long for, my stomach felt empty and my heart raced. Dr. Franks, a chubby, cherubic man of medium height, calmed my apprehension when he opened the door, then shook my hand while introducing himself. His expression betrayed no evidence of his having noticed my sweaty palms. He smiled and furrowed his brow, as he affirmed, "You're Dr. Stockton?" As I nodded, he invited me into the consultation room and gestured, palm open, to the chair where I would sit.

While we were still walking to our seats, he asked, "When we spoke on the phone yesterday, you said Dr. Lyon referred you to me. How did you know him?" His friendly manner continued to ease my tension.

"Dr. Marcus Barker, my medical school professor of psychiatry at Oklahoma Medical School, gave me his name," I answered.

Pulling his ottoman close to his chair, he asked, "You said on the phone that you'd had episodes of terror for many years. Can you tell me about them?"

"Where should I begin?" I responded, feeling eager, yet apprehensive in this new experience.

"Wherever you feel comfortable, and we can take it from there," he said with a gentle smile, opening his palms and extending his arms toward me, "but perhaps a good place would be to tell me about the terror."

After pausing several moments to collect my thoughts,

I spent the rest of that session, and the next several, telling him the details of my story related earlier in these pages: my terror's spontaneous explosive onset followed by what was now almost eleven years of feeling hopeless doom with unaccountable periodic acute eruptions of the terror and an ongoing sense of helplessness.

Ironically, even though terror was the very feeling I had sought self-knowledge to overcome, my fear of the terror led me to use any defense mechanism available to avoid thinking and talking about the terror for several months following those initial sessions. My favorite device was to talk at length about the universal human apprehension of death and peoples' use of religious assurances to protect themselves from their terror of death and afterlife, and how people "whistle past the graveyard," to guard against the cemetery's reminder of death, since these well-recognized traditions "proved" there was nothing irrational about my feelings.

By now I had begun my own psychiatric practice, so another ploy I used was to avoid looking at my problem by talking about my own patients' problems instead. By speaking intellectually about their issues, I could avoid my feelings, particularly my terror. Many years later I realized that I had regularly, especially during the twelve years I had been relatively free of symptoms, used my intellect not only as a constructive instrument for learning, but also as a defense against my terrifying emotions.

Several months into the work, Dr. Franks began one session by saying, "At the end of yesterday's session, you wondered, almost in passing, when were we going to get to the roots of your fears." Then he asked, "Do you think your comment may be your feelings' way of saying you feel more ready to learn about the causes of your terror from your earlier life?"

I was silent several moments, uncertain what to say.

"Let's see what's occurring to you?" he gently prodded.

"I was thinking about how the terror hadn't come as a total surprise, because I'd had fears almost all my life, although they were never as bad as the terror," I responded.

"Tell me about the fears?" he asked.

I hesitated, wondering which fear to mention first. "I don't know why I'm thinking about this, and I'm sure it has nothing to do with my terror, but Momma was awfully depressed during all those years Daddy couldn't get a job, which was my whole childhood. When she was really down, she'd say, especially late in the evening, 'I just wish I could crawl into a hole and pull it in after me.'" My whole body stiffened as I described the memory, though I didn't know why.

"And this probably has nothing to do with it either, but when I was five I said something to Momma that was so bad it still rips me to shreds whenever I think of it," I said, with a sudden empty feeling in my stomach.

Still too ashamed and afraid to repeat what I had said to Momma, I hesitated several moments.

Dr. Franks waited for me to continue, then, after a time, asked, "It's too upsetting to say?"

"I'd do anything to take back what I said, and I don't want to tell you because that just makes it more real," I responded, beginning to sweat.

"Say more about real?" he asked.

"Just thinking about it makes me feel so guilty I don't want to remember it, just like I used to feel when I carried it around in my mind all the time," I said, my stomach now churning and feeling empty at the same time.

"Can you sense what you're afraid would happen if you talked about it?" he asked.

"I'm not afraid of anything happening, it's just that I feel so guilty I'd rather die than have to live with what I said, and there's nothing I can do to take it back. I'd cut my tongue out if it could make what I said not have happened. Every time Momma got depressed, I'd think 'It's all my fault she's sick,' and I think it's because of what I said. I've never told anyone about it before." I covered my eyes with my hands as if to make it all go away.

"Guilty of what?" he asked.

For several moments I shifted around in the chair as I tried to form an answer that would not make me feel so bad. But when I found no way to avoid the pain, I knew the only way I could say it would be just to blurt it out.

"One time I was so mad at Momma, I told her, 'I wish there was no such thing as mothers.'" My heart raced, and I felt dead inside.

"Can you say more about what made the guilty feeling unbearable?" he asked, with no indication of surprise or criticism.

I sat in shock for a moment, stunned by his straightforward question. "I'll try," I responded, "but, before I do, I want to tell you that I find incomprehensible what you just did."

Before I could elaborate, he asked, "Found what incomprehensible?

I stared at him wide-eyed. "You didn't even wince when I told you what I'd said to Momma, and when you asked what made the guilty feeling so unbearable, as though it wasn't perfectly obvious, you sounded like you understood why I felt so guilty, but that it wasn't the worst thing in the world."

"What about 'perfectly obvious'?" he asked.

"I don't know," I said, shaking my head. "I've always felt so guilty about what I said that it's always seemed like there's no other way to look at it, but you make it seem like there's more to it than that, and I don't really know what it could be."

"Well, let's see what comes into your mind?" Dr. Franks asked.

Feeling unsettled about what I was going to say, I squirmed in my seat trying to get comfortable. "This comes purely from logic and doesn't change how I feel. Momma took what I said like any sensitive parent would in understanding a small child who was upset, but what's puzzling is that it still didn't keep me from feeling guilty, because it seemed like what I said to her was the worst thing in the world. I would've done anything to take it back, and I still would, and I told her again and again, 'Momma, I'm so sorry for what I said.' But no matter how much I apologized, or she reassured me, which she always did, I couldn't unsay what I'd said. That's when my guilt and fears started."

I shook my head, feeling my lifelong sorrow and helplessness. "I understood later that Momma was depressed even before I was five, and maybe her feeling sad was why I felt so guilty, but I don't know if that was why I felt guilty, all I knew is how sorry I was for what I'd said." I shook my head again, wanting to make it all go away.

"What do you mean about when your 'guilt and fears started'?" Dr. Franks asked.

"They've been with me ever since then. At first I was just afraid that I'd hurt her, but then I started blaming myself for making her feel so bad and crying all the time. And then when I remembered what happened to her when Maurice was born . . ."

An onslaught of feelings overcame me as I tried to shut out the memory of the scene of Maurice's birth.

"You stopped yourself when you thought of what happened to Momma when Maurice was born?" Dr. Franks asked, his soft tone saying he recognized my difficulty in speaking the unspeakable.

After several moments of silence, I continued. "She nearly died. And I saw it. I can see it right now as though it were happening this very moment. Maurice was born at home, two months after my fifth birthday. Betty had stayed home from school, and she and I were squatting on the front lawn trying to figure out what was happening inside our house. Several neighbor ladies were screaming, so Betty and I knew something was wrong with Momma, and then, even outside, we could hear Momma make loud, snoring-like noises, and we were afraid they were doing something horrible to her.

"Then I got so scared I couldn't stand not knowing what was happening to her, so I barged in past the women who were trying to keep me out, I guess so I wouldn't see Momma. Her face was swollen so bad, Dad later said, 'as big as a horse's face,' that I didn't recognize her at first, although I knew enough to be afraid. She was having convulsions and making really deep, doomful groans, and Dr.

Hammonds was frantic, and yelled, 'Somebody get me a clothespin or a spoon, I've got to hold her tongue down or she'll swallow it and choke.' I was so scared, I didn't know what to do. I didn't learn until later that Maurice had just been born, and Momma had almost died of uremic poisoning."

When I thought of Momma almost dying, I had to stop for several moments.

"Seeing Momma and hearing the doctor made me afraid I'd lose her forever, and that I'd never, ever see her again. And that if she died, I would know that somehow I had caused it."

I sank into desolation at the memory of these events, despairing of hope and my body sapped of spirit, as if by remembering, all those terrible things were happening all over again, and I was still five years old.

I needed several moments to shift from feeling hopeless to finding the strength to tell Dr. Franks what happened next.

"I felt so relieved and happy the next day when they let me in to see her. When I bent over to kiss Momma my eyes were so much on her that she had to say, 'Look out for the baby,' who was lying next to her on the same side I was leaning from, because she was worried I would hurt Maurice. I was bewildered since my only concerns were about Momma, and, as far as I can remember, I had no idea that a baby was part of the goings on.

"It all left me with an eerie feeling. I'd grown up feeling good about that front bedroom. Doctor Hammonds called it 'The Delivery Room' because he had delivered Betty and me there, and Momma and Daddy had always smiled when they talked about it. But after Momma almost died there, the room felt gloomy and scary, like it was haunted."

Dr. Franks glanced at the clock, and I recognized our time was up, so I stood, mustered a perfunctory smile, and, feeling disappointed, said, "These sessions go so fast they always end at the wrong time. But it can wait till next time, so I'll see you then." We both nodded and I left.

The next session I began as soon as we both had sat down. "What I wanted to say at the end of last time was that it was only a little while after Momma almost died that I screamed at her, 'I wish there was no such thing as mothers,' so those times seem to be mixed together. I know that Momma was sad and cried an awful lot after that, and I lived in constant dread that something awful would happen to her, and I'd lose her. That's also when I started being aware of her moods, so I could do something to make her feel better and to reassure myself she was all right."

Dr Franks said, "You've always thought that the guilt and fears began when you screamed at her, but since it didn't seem to bother her, and since your screaming at her and her almost dying seemed to get mixed together, let's see what more we can learn about where the guilt and fears got their power?" he asked.

After an initial shock, I felt the beginning of relief from his words since the implication of his question let me hope, for the first time, that there was a way of understanding, that I had not known before, the grip my guilt and fears held on me.

"That question never occurred to me," I responded, "because I've always assumed that it was what I'd said to her that made me feel guilty and afraid I'd lose her. But you're saying maybe part of those feelings came from someplace else?"

Dr. Franks nodded. "You had just been saying how guilty and afraid you felt when she nearly died, and that if she had died you would have caused it, so you were already carrying those feelings before you screamed at her."

I needed to go over in my mind his clarifying what I had actually said, but not realized that I had said, that my guilty feelings had in fact preceded my hateful curse. Once I felt I understood it, I said, "I remember being so happy when I was little, but that all seemed to change when Maurice was born. Momma once said, and so did a neighbor lady I called 'Aunt Essie,' even though we weren't related, that I got mad easily and was unhappy a lot after Maurice came. When Aunt Essie said that, I remember thinking, 'You'd be mad, too, if your mother brought home a new baby and left you out all the time.' I'd been the youngest until then, so I guess I hated her for making me lose out to Maurice." I looked at Dr. Franks with a sheepish smile, and said, "I guess I thought I was Momma's 'Golden Boy'—my sister Betty called me that enough times.

"I don't know how long I hated her, but I do know that I yelled at her and started being afraid I'd lose her during that period."

I leaned over and held my head in my hands for a few moments, then sat up and continued.

"Maybe feeling bad about what I'd said was why I stopped hating her, because I remember thinking when she nearly died when Maurice was born, that my hating her had almost caused her to die, so then when I yelled at her about wishing there was no such thing as mothers, I got afraid that what I'd said was like a deadly curse that might come true, and she might actually die. My guilt and fear about what I said have never left me, although after my terror about death and eternity started, the terror bothered me so much I didn't think any more about those earlier feelings."

Dr. Franks said, "You seem to be saying that there's a connection between the rage toward Momma for having Maurice, the guilt you felt about screaming at her, and the fear of losing her, in those early years, on the one hand, and your terror about death and eternity later, on the other."

At that moment, an April rainstorm produced a loud thunderclap that shook the room, and though sometimes I might have welcomed the distraction, the strength I was starting to feel from understanding what had always defied reason held me fast to Dr. Frank's question.

Continuing the work would have to wait, though, since we were already overtime.

The next time, I began, "I've been thinking about your observation at the end of last time, and it feels right, especially the part about my terror actually starting with my rage at Momma. There must be more to it, though, because I've worried about death completely apart from my fear Momma would die."

"What about worrying about death?" he asked.

I hadn't noticed any fear when I had just said, "I've worried about death . . .", but Dr. Franks' asking, "What about worrying about death?" somehow made the idea more real, and my stomach began churning and my heart started racing, though these body reactions were much less intense than at any time since my fears of death and eternity had started, more than eleven years before.

"About a year before Maurice was born," I responded, "Momma's daddy, Grandpa Landers, came to live with us. Grandma Landers had died shortly before that, and everyone said he was lonely and wanted to be near Momma, who was so nice and loved him more than any of his other children. Then, less than a year after Momma almost died, just before my sixth birthday, Grandpa died, and when I saw Momma cry so much about him dying, I felt guilty all over again about yelling at Momma what I did."

I was silent a few moments while picturing the scene of what I was about to say, and my racing heart told me I was scared to go there.

"Watching them bury Grandpa was the first time I'd seen a dead person or thought about eternity. When the pallbearers lowered him into the grave, and the family threw dirt on his casket, I knew I'd never see him again. I imagined him floating underground, forever, on a great body of water, like a big lake, and for a long time after he died I wondered if that was what happened to people when they die, and if that would happen to me. When I studied Greek mythology in college, I was really struck by how similar that image was to the Ancient Greeks' belief that the River Styx was the entrance to the underworld.

"Sometime later, Aunt Essie told me something I hadn't remembered, that Grandpa must have sensed the end coming because a week before he died he wanted Momma and Daddy to take him back to the family's old home place in Roxton twenty miles away, and Aunt Essie took care of me. She said that while Momma and Daddy were away, I stood at the front room window and stared for hours, looking up Neathery Street in the direction they had left when

Uncle Gill came and took them and Grandpa to Roxton. Aunt Essie said she couldn't get me away from that window no matter what she did, that I just stood there, not saying a word or answering a question, just looking out the window, like my whole life had gone away, and I was waiting for it to come back."

Remembering what Aunt Essie had told me made me sad, but not afraid like I had felt when I'd had thought about Grandpa dying, or as I did now when I pictured what I was going to talk about next.

"Something else also happened about that time," I continued. "Bruno Hauptmann, the man who kidnapped and murdered Charles Lindbergh's son, was executed. The media hyped the case because the whole country was still in awe of Lindbergh from his transatlantic flight several years before. Even though I was in just the first grade, I read well enough to become possessed by the step-by-step detailed description of Hauptmann's electrocution, of his walking in chains to the execution chamber, of the prison guards strapping him into the chair and putting the blindfold over his head, and the warden pulling the 2,000 volt switch that killed him."

"What did you mean about 'becoming possessed'?" Dr. Franks asked.

I had to reflect a minute before *I* knew what I had meant.

"I meant I became possessed with what I thought Hauptmann must have been thinking when I imagined myself in his shoes, every step of the way, from the time I left my cell in chains to when I sat strapped in the electric chair, knowing that at any second 2,000 volts would be going through my body, and then I'd be dead. I was preoccupied with whether I'd be awake long enough to know what was happening to me, and, if so, what would it feel like. That was like later on when I thought about the Royalists, during the French Revolution, walking step by step up the scaffold to the guillotine, then lying on the board and the blade coming down and cutting off my head, and then I got to worrying that if that happened to me, how long would my mind be conscious after my head was cut off, and would my now dismembered brain see itself falling into the bucket below."

Only after I finished what I had meant by being "possessed" did I realize that I was sweating gallons, and my heart was pounding out of my chest.

"It sounds like you're saying," Dr. Franks observed, "that when other people suffer or face death, you so strongly want to understand their pain that you put yourself into their shoes, and then you feel what seems to be their suffering, and fear, and death, including what happens to them after death, so that their and your fear and death become fused and confused."

I sat back and looked at him for a moment. "That's going to take a while to digest," I responded, "but it sounds right. The first thing I think about that, is that when they buried Grandpa I was so occupied by what was happening I didn't realize how my picture of Grandpa being on an underground lake forever was like my image, that I'd forgotten until now, of what would happen to Momma if she died, and that that was what would happen to me, too.

"After I read about them killing Hauptmann, my fears about what happened to Grandpa, and what could have happened to Momma, turned into terror when I imagined myself in Hauptman's shoes, totally helpless to do anything to stop my being executed and then buried forever. It felt even worse when I read about convicts who were electrocuted, or hanged, or gassed, or shot, because it didn't help them to confess and repent their crime. Being punished rather than forgiven, when someone is truly sorry for what he did, seemed like the worst possible betrayal, and that's what I worried about all the time after I started feeling guilty for yelling at Momma that I wished there was no such thing as mothers."

I shook my head a dozen times because there seemed to be no way of escaping the worst possible punishment when you've done or said something bad.

"And then Old Man Pickens died about the same time. I knew him because he owned the dairy up Neathery Street, and I talked to him a lot when I went to watch him milk his cows. I worried about how he died, too. He got up at five one morning, as usual, fed his cows and bull, lay back down to rest, and died in his sleep. What bothered me most was his helplessness, that when he lay down, he didn't know he was going to die, nor did he have the remotest chance to struggle against whatever killed him. Hauptmann at least could fight back even if it didn't do him any good, but Old Man Pickens never knew what happened to him. I put myself in his place of being so helpless in sleep that he didn't even know he was helpless. When I learned how he died, I resolved absolutely never to go back to bed after getting up in the morning, and I didn't for years, even when I was sick."

I leaned back and closed my eyes, but it didn't help. When I opened them a few moments later, Old Man Pickens was still dead, and I still imagined myself in his shoes.

"I don't remember anyone dying for a long time after that, but five months after they electrocuted Hauptmann, I started second grade and began having headaches that made me vomit every day when I walked home from school. I also got those headaches when I read something or saw a movie involving a tragedy, especially if the story included someone knowingly facing death. When Joe Rushing, Jimmy Dick Hurt, and I saw the movie, *The Public Enemy*, in which the final scene showed prison executioners overpowering and then electrocuting James Cagney, Joe and Jimmy Dick went home telling jokes, and I went home with a headache and vomited all night.

"Momma took me to the pediatrician, Dr. Gilmore, to find out what was causing my headaches. He sent me to a free eye clinic where the doctor said my headaches were due to astigmatism, and arranged a pair of glasses for me through the clinic. I never doubted that I had some kind of eye problem, but I never believed it was causing my headaches. I could read a little better after I got glasses, but my headaches and vomiting lasted for years.

"I'm sure you remember how in those days a lot of people, like my parents, thought that many illnesses were caused by some inexplicable gastrointestinal 'poison'?"

Dr. Franks nodded.

"Momma used to treat me with two tablespoons of Milk of Magnesia anytime I had a headache. My headaches eventually did go away, but that was much later on, and I never really thought it was because I took Magnesia."

I was grateful for having to be thorough in telling Dr. Franks about my headaches and vomiting, since that topic was free of the dread and anxiety I connected to death, eternity, helplessness, guilt, loss, and terror.

When I stood to leave after that Friday session, I said, "I'm thinking about what happened after that, but I'll remember it for next time. See you then." We nodded, and I left.

I was bombarded all that weekend by thoughts about the next session, but when I got there the next week, it took a minute or two to sort out what to say first.

After a few moments, Dr. Franks asked, "Is something hard to say?"

"No, not hard," I responded, "just confusing, because there's so much, and I didn't know where to start. Well, maybe it is hard in a way. I was thinking about our move from Paris a year so after all those deaths, and how terrible it was."

"Say more about the terrible move?" Dr. Franks asked.

"We haven't talked about this yet," I responded, "but in 1938, when I was eight and in the spring term of the third grade, we moved from Paris to a suburb of San Antonio called Harlandale, and I've often felt that that move was the worst, and, I think, most crucial, event of my life."

"How so?" Dr. Franks asked.

"Leaving Paris was painful, as I guess moving away from where you've grown up is for anyone. I could have endured that, though, because people in Harlandale were just as nice as people in Paris. What was so dreadful, was . . . ." The pain of the memory stopped me cold.

"You stopped yourself in mid-sentence," Dr. Franks said, with a question in his voice.

After a long pause, during which I felt sad about what

I knew I had to talk about, and restless because I knew it would be upsetting, I responded, "I was just going to add, that it was what made us move, and then what happened after we moved, that was so terrible."

"What about what made you move, and what happened after you moved?" Dr. Franks pressed.

Shaking my head in disbelief even after all these years, I said, "It's hard to imagine today, but we had to move because we lost our house that Daddy had built with his own hands, and that's still there today, because we didn't have $300 to pay off a loan Momma and Daddy had used the house as collateral for."

I always knew how upset I was by how frequently I crossed and recrossed my legs, and I could tell from my constant movement this time that talking about losing our Paris home was more upsetting than I had allowed myself to realize.

"The Depression hit everybody hard, but it hit us worse than most people because the Dust Bowl drought hit at the same time and dried up the cotton industry that Daddy had worked in for forty years. It destroyed the only trade he knew, and, by then, he was fifty-two and couldn't get a job anywhere. That's when the bank foreclosed on the loan, and we lost our house."

I shook my head in despair, not only about what had happened to us, but about all the poor people who suffered those terrible days and lost their homes, security, dignity, hope, and even lives.

"Since you're older than I am, I know that you know about those times, but people who didn't live through them can't comprehend how bad they were. I think the closest most people come to it is when they read *The Grapes of Wrath*. Steinbeck could have been writing about us just as well because that's really what it was like. Paris was only eight miles from Oklahoma, so when we lost our home and had to move to San Antonio, it was the same as the 'Okies' having to give up their farms and lives in Oklahoma and move to California.

"We chose San Antonio because Daddy's nephew, Ernest, convinced Momma and Daddy that we'd be better off there, where Ernest and his family lived, since everyone knew the war was coming, and San Antonio had a lot of military bases where Daddy could get a job. But nothing was any better there than it had been in Paris, at least until the war started three years later. In fact, from my standpoint . . . ."

I wasn't aware I had stopped talking and been silent for several moments, until Dr. Franks asked, "From what you said earlier about why you stopped yourself, does your hesitation tell us that talking about the move is more difficult than you'd expected?"

Surprised by his question, I replied, "I don't know, my mind was just blank." After pondering it some, I continued. "My mind went blank when I thought that the next thing I have to do is talk about what happened after the move. That's what I thought about a few minutes ago, when I didn't finish my sentence."

I forced myself to go on.

"Being poor was hard, but it was *nothing* compared to Momma's depression after we got to Harlandale. That's what made the move so terrible. Momma and Maurice had come by train, and Betty and I had ridden in the cab of the moving truck with the driver and his helper. When we got to San Antonio, we went to Ernest's house first, and then he took us to an old, dilapidated, brick building surrounded by weeds. I looked around for our house, but there wasn't a house. Our house turned out to be the old brick building, and then I knew it was what I'd heard Daddy call an 'abandoned ice house.'

"Momma didn't say anything at first, but then she started crying, and I had this horrible feeling that things had gotten worse, not better. I was scared of what would happen to us, and that Momma's crying meant something terrible would happen to her.

"That first evening was unreal. I'd never known anything like it. There was dirt an inch thick on the concrete floor, and we had to clean it up before we could take anything inside, even something to sleep on. Momma cried the whole time she swept up what had to have been years of collected grime, and then she cried all night. Betty and I helped Momma clean up the mess, but there wasn't anything we could do to stop her crying. I felt so afraid and helpless.

"And then I got a bad headache and started vomiting, and I did that every night for months."

In talking about that first evening at the ice house, I felt like a zombie, aware I was just going through the motions.

On my way to the next appointment, as I walked from the parking lot to Dr. Franks office, my stomach was in knots, like it had been that day in San Antonio when panic hit me the first time, since I knew I would have to continue with the events and feelings that followed the move.

I began immediately. "We had wound up way out in the boonies on a dirt road they called Mission Road. It had been an old trail named for a Spanish mission two blocks away. I need to tell you about the ice house, though, because it was so run down. It really was. There were just two rooms and a closet-like area they called an ice vault where they had stored the ice before selling it to customers. The only light was a single forty watt bulb screwed into the socket of an extension cord hanging from a bent nail in a wooden rafter. The other room had a socket but no bulb in it, and we didn't have any money so we couldn't buy one. We didn't have any indoor plumbing, or even an outhouse, so we used the toilet at a filling station a block away by sneaking in and out and hoping the manager wouldn't catch us. We had to bathe in a tub with water we hand-carried from the filling station. Daddy told me later that the rent was three dollars a month.

"But I don't really believe that what I'm telling you is the problem, because even as I paint this dismal picture of the ice house, I didn't really pay much attention to it, and I could not have cared less about what the place was actually like. All I saw and heard, and all I thought about was Momma's crying.

"And everything was like that from then on, for years. Since we'd moved in March, I had to start school right away, and one of the worst things I remember happened just a few days later. My third grade class was planning an Easter egg hunt, and the teacher told us to bring a basket from home. But since we didn't have any money and couldn't afford a regular Easter basket, Momma tried to improvise with a wicker flower basket that had a great big handle, I'm sure it was three feet in diameter, and was obviously makeshift and told the whole world how poor we were. And when I balked at taking it to school, I felt, and I still feel, guilty when I saw the helpless pain in Momma's eyes and the tears pouring down her cheeks.

"She could tell I was upset, and I could see how guilty, and helpless, and futile she felt. If I took the basket and felt embarrassed, she would feel she had failed me, and if I didn't take it, she'd be hurt because she had tried to help me and couldn't. I felt guilty for putting her in such an impossible position, and it brought back all my guilt for having yelled at her, 'I wish there was no such thing as mothers.'"

I cried as I talked, but my tears were only a drop in an ocean of tears I had felt for years.

"I took the basket to school, and nothing bad happened. No one was cruel to me, and only one of the kids said anything, and that was in passing. Almost everybody was poor, so most of them understood. Some of them had no basket at all. But I've felt guilty about hurting Momma ever since.

"We had three months left in the school year, and I dreaded every day of it. My grades were terrible. I was afraid to leave Momma at home depressed and crying, and when I got to school all I did was worry about her.

"Worrying about Momma must have made me more aware of how much other people suffer, too. One day I heard some kids snickering behind me, and, when I turned around to look, I saw a little girl who was terribly mortified for having peed in her seat and made a puddle underneath her desk. I felt so embarrassed and ashamed for her, but in some screwy way my having realized how much she was hurting kind of eased how bad I felt."

Aware that Dr. Franks had been silent for several minutes, I asked, "You haven't said anything for a long time,
and when that happens I get to wondering if what I'm saying is boring?"

"I haven't said anything because you were so involved
in that terribly painful period you were reliving. I was very
much aware of your sadness, so I thought that anything I
might say would only interrupt you and wouldn't be helpful to our understanding, and your overcoming, your
struggle with the terror," he responded. "You don't usually feel that what you say is unworthy of my interest,
though, so can you sense what was in what you were saying that might bore me?"

I thought about his question a few moments. "I think
my question is not really about whether I'm boring you,
but that I'm afraid all of this may be as depressing to you
as it is to me."

"Are you saying that as you talk about Momma's depression, you become depressed with her," Dr. Franks responded, "and that, as you tell me about it, you're afraid I
will become depressed with you, as you did with her?"

I thought a moment about what he said, then answered,
"That sounds right. And I guess I asked you about it when
I did because I was starting to tell you about one of
Momma's most depressing times.

"After we'd been in the ice house for three months,
Daddy found us a real house. It cost fifteen dollars a month,
but I guess that somehow he had found enough work to
pay for it. We were all excited about moving, but it didn't
last very long. The really bad part of Momma's depression
started all over again because one day, about two months
after the move, I came home from school and found her
crying as bad as ever. She was crumpled half on the floor
and half on the bed holding a telegram and crying that
Tom, who was her favorite brother and the one she always
relied on the most, had died. He'd had a grocery store, and
was the one person she knew she could rely on when everything else failed. He'd had a lung hemorrhage while he
was recovering from TB, and his death was a terrible shock

to the whole family. It devastated Momma, though. She cried every day after that, sometimes all day, so I was afraid all the time that something terrible would happen to her.

"From then on she cried practically all the time. Anything that reminded her of losing Uncle Tom, or any of her brothers and sisters, if you can believe this she had sixteen of them, or our poverty, made her cry. She cried at church when we sang "The Old Rugged Cross," it was her mother's favorite hymn, and she cried when a group of church ladies brought us several large sacks of groceries during an especially hard time."

I stared at the floor as I talked, not wanting to remember what I was hearing myself say.

"Momma's crying about our poverty always devastated me. I enjoyed the few things I had, and knew deep inside that someday I'd have a lot more. But when she cried, which was most of the time, all I could think about was how guilty I felt about all the times I'd hurt her or failed her because when I suffered like she did I didn't feel so afraid of losing her."

As we neared the time for ending the session, I asked, "Since this is a government holiday [Washington's Birthday], is it possible you have a cancellation after this hour, and we can continue for a double session, like we've done sometimes before? It is so hard to get into these feelings about the move, and I feel so immersed in them now, I'd like to strike while the iron is hot, if I can."

"As it turns out, I do, and we can," Dr. Franks replied, "but I'd like to take a five minute break first to use the bathroom and make a phone call."

While I waited for Dr. Franks to return, I reflected how the necessity of talking about and working through the background of my terror confronted me with the relentless depressive events of those years, an awareness I had not had earlier, because I had become so accustomed to them.

Yet, paradoxically, this extremely painful phase of my work was resulting in lessening my fears and the limitations they placed on me. I was now in the third and final year of my psychiatric training, and was becoming more able, at last, to attend professional meetings in places I had previously avoided. In the past, flying to a meeting in San Francisco, for example, would not have been possible because getting there by air would have triggered my panic. Similarly, I was beginning to feel more free to vacation with my family wherever we pleased, even if it meant driving across the Chesapeake Bay Bridge.

When Dr. Franks returned a few minutes later, I continued.

"Between the time we moved to Harlandale, in March, 1938, and when the country started gearing up for World War II, in early 1942, Daddy still couldn't find work, so he took any odd job he could find. Sometimes I'd walk with him as he went door-to-door offering to sharpen scissors for five cents a pair. Most people didn't have even five pennies to spare, and one time we made twenty-five cents all day." Tears were streaming down my face. "Daddy never complained or said how he felt, but I felt so sorry for him because I thought he must have felt awfully defeated and humiliated because there was so little he could do to feed his family.

"Another time, Daddy and I were at the grocery store, and I saw the man behind the butcher counter shake his head to a question Daddy had asked. When we got outside, I asked Daddy what had happened, and he told me he'd asked the grocer for a pound of hamburger on credit until the end of the month, and the grocer had said, 'No, times are hard for me too; I just can't do it.'"

I could not hold back my tears as I recalled those memories of seeing the humbling, dispiriting dejection in his eyes.

"Daddy tried anything he could to help us get by. He learned to repair clocks, but he couldn't make any more than he did sharpening scissors. When nothing seemed to work, he sometimes just lay in bed. He always answered when I talked with him, but he never started a conversation. Momma cried all the time, but Daddy just got quieter and quieter. I never realized till later that he'd been depressed, too.

"Mostly, though, I thought about Momma's crying, and it made my stomach twist into knots. I was constantly afraid of losing her, and I always felt guilty about what I might have done to make her cry. School didn't mean anything. I couldn't pay attention during class because I was always worried about Momma at home. Whenever a student monitor came into the room with a note for the teacher, I was terrified Momma might have died or had to go the hospital, and that I had said or done something to have caused it."

Dr. Franks said, "I understand how painful your guilt was, but maybe, without your awareness, it also helped you not feel so totally helpless, since the guilt was about your behavior, that you could do something about, when there seemed to be so little you could actually do about Momma's depression."

I pulled myself up straight in the chair, and responded, "When you put it that way, I remember several things I did to try to help her not feel so bad.

"When she was especially upset, her voice would get so weak and hoarse she could hardly talk, and that frightened me more than her crying. I was frantic to do something, until I discovered a magical treatment that worked every time. She loved ice cream, and it always made her voice come back," I said, feeling warm and secure about how I had been able to help her. "Double dip cones in those days cost only a nickel, and, even when we didn't have any money for food, I somehow could manage to scrounge, beg, borrow, or bargain my soul to find five pennies and run to the ice-cream parlor to get Momma her wonder drug. Every time, like magic, her hoarseness would go away and she would stop crying, and then I wouldn't feel afraid of losing her anymore." I looked at Dr. Franks a moment, then said, "I knew this was something I could do, and I've thought since that the good feelings I had about my ice cream cure for Momma's hoarseness were what led me to become a doctor.

"I found other ways, too, so I wouldn't feel so desperate about losing Momma. I became a hard worker, just like she was. I haven't mentioned this before, but she was an excellent dressmaker, and she had kept us afloat when Daddy couldn't find any work, in spite of how bad she felt. In fact many of the hours she spent crying were while she was at the sewing machine making dresses for other ladies. Her dressmaking often paid the rent and bought us groceries, as well as paying the doctor bills, like when she bartered her dressmaking for Dr. Gilmore's wife in return for his medical care for us. She was so pleased when I made money by mowing lawns for neighbors, or sold Colliers and Life magazines, or collected rags and old newspapers for recycling and the war effort. And the day I got into medical school was one of the happiest of her life."

As I began talking about what I had learned that I could do to help Momma's depression, I was aware I felt much stronger than when we had been talking about my helplessness.

"I felt most reassured I wouldn't lose her when I could connect to her by being sensitive to her moods or what she said. Not long after we began, I told you that, especially late in the evening, she would often moan, 'I just wish I could crawl in a hole and pull it in after me.' When she said that, I got so scared I tried to picture what she meant, so that if she did 'crawl into a hole' I could crawl in with her."

Dr. Franks asked, "What do you see when you picture you and her in the hole?"

I responded immediately, "I imagined her and me together in a burrow, like a tunnel, or a grave, lying side by side just like I'd seen her and Daddy do many times when they took a nap together. It seemed so loving and secure, and I would have her all to myself."

"How did it feel in the grave with her?" Dr. Franks asked.

"Oohhhh, I felt very secure," I immediately responded, "because I knew we were there together and she would never go away, and I would never lose her."

Dr. Franks must have picked up something in my tone, because he asked, "Do I hear anything else in your voice?"

I had to think before I answered. "Yes there is something else, though I don't know what it is." Then I continued to think about his question.

"Can you sense how 'something else' feels?" he asked.

"Not really, but I can tell it's a kind of uneasy feeling I
can't put into words."

"Say more about 'uneasy'?" he pressed.

"Well, I know I didn't think about this when I first
started wanting to be in the grave with her when I was five
or six, because then it just felt so good and secure to think
I would be with her forever. I think the older I got, though,
the more I realized, and it was very gradual, what being in
that grave for eternity would be like, and the more I learned
about what 'forever' meant, the more I felt what I just called
'uneasy.' That's what that uneasy feeling is, and, at some
point, maybe twelve or so, when I tried to think about being buried for eternity, I got so terrified of being trapped in
that grave, I put the picture, and everything connected to
it, out of my mind."

I was restless at the thought of describing the terror I
had pushed out of my mind at twelve.

"Even as I talk about it now, I can sense some of those
terror feelings, not nearly like they used to be, because
we've worked on them so much, but they're there a little,
including my heart beating fast and my body sweating right
now."

"Momma being with you in the grave didn't keep you
from being scared?" Dr Franks asked.

"I've never thought about that question, or at least more
than a split second," I responded, then paused.

"How so?" he asked.

"Because it's too frightening," I answered.

"What's 'too frightening'?" he pressed.

"She wasn't in the grave with me, and I think that's
when my trouble started," I said. "I wasn't panicked when
I first thought about it, I was around twelve, because it
didn't last long, but being alone in that grave without
Momma is what I later called my terror of eternity."

"Can you sense what made you start to think about her

not being there?" he asked.

"I'm sure it must have been that I wanted to feel like I was big and independent, because about the same time, I don't remember exactly when, I found out that people aren't buried together, especially a grown boy with his mother, and I think that's what really caused the terror, because I wasn't just trapped in that grave, I was in it all by myself, and that brought back all those feelings of losing Momma, and being alone without her, starting with the time she nearly died.

"Things were going well at home by then, though, and I could push those frightening images out of my mind. Daddy finally had a job because of the war, so Momma wasn't depressed, and I was working and doing things with my friends, so I didn't even think about terror again until it hit when they moved to Oklahoma five years later."

Not long after that session, in a hour near the end of the therapeutic work, Dr. Franks asked, "Knowing what we do now, what can you sense there was about your family's move to Oklahoma that made the terror hit at that time?"

"I couldn't have answered that question before, but I understand it now. That move was the first time I would be permanently separated from her, so I couldn't be with her and be certain she would be all right like I always had before. In the past I could always make her feel good when she was depressed, not only because I loved her, but so I wouldn't feel guilty and afraid of losing her, but now there would be nothing I could do to know she would be all right." I could feel tears forming, though I knew that this time, they were more from relief at my discovery than the pain of my memories. "So although I didn't realize it at the time, I reflexively wanted to be in the 'hole in the ground' with her, and, by that time, I was seventeen and knew that that meant being alone, and so the terror I started to have when I was twelve and realized what 'eternity' meant, came back, only now I couldn't push the terror out of my mind because she was really going away, and not only was I actually alone without her, but with her that far away there was nothing I could do to be sure she would be all right.

"It was all so bizarre," I continued. "There I was, an alive person with a live mind preoccupied with a subconscious wish to be in a grave with Momma for eternity, where, instead of being dead, I'd be alive and aware that I'd be in that grave alone, forever. I know this sounds certifiably insane."

In our final session, Dr. Franks summed up the major issues underlying my terror. "What you've told us is that being in that 'hole in the ground' with Momma fulfilled two needs. That the rage you felt toward Momma for betraying you by having your baby brother, made you feel guilty as though you had hurt and almost killed her and afraid you would lose her approval and love, both at the time of Maurice's birth and when you later told her, 'I wish there was no such thing as mothers.' You've also told us that you could make those bad feelings go away by working hard and by tuning yourself to the wavelengths of her moods, mechanisms that later became invaluable strengths in your therapeutic work with patients."

After a short pause to allow me time to digest what he had said, Dr. Franks continued. "Although the original basis of these feelings, your murderous rage at Momma, had long since faded, you were stuck with the guilt and fear that had grown out of the rage. So when Momma moved to Oklahoma, and you knew your permanent separation from her would mean you could no longer stay connected to her, you subconsciously wished to, and in your feelings did, crawl into that hole to be with her for eternity, both to atone for your guilt by suffering with her in her depression, and to reassure yourself you had not lost her. Only then did you realize the long range consequences of that solution: trapped alive in a grave, alone without Momma, and terrified for eternity."

I nodded in agreement, as he spelled out in simple, clear words what I now understood had been my mind's attempts to cope with my deepest conflicted emotions that had tortured me for years.

Each of us must come to our own view of the mysteries of death and eternity, whether based on religion, agnosticism, atheism, or other beliefs. Central to my view, though, is that once I clearly saw how my early life's tortured imaginings had distorted the lens through which I saw those mysteries, I became able to think about them as most people do—abstract concepts for which I have no definitive answers, but of which am no longer terrified.

I also came to understand why my early pursuits of theology, spirituality, and philosophy as sources of relief were doomed from the outset. The explanations for my dreads had nothing to do with the supernatural, and the persistence of my terror had nothing to do with failed faith; thoughts and feelings in my subconscious mind had been as unavailable to transcendental reassurances and philosophic reasoning as are suppressed guilty feelings to the reassurances of forgiveness by a father confessor.

Since overcoming my terror and its underlying causes, I have had an exceedingly fulfilling career and personal life.

No longer tormented by anxiety or inhibited by fear of anxiety, I have determined my life by my judgment, sensitivities, and priorities. I travel, fly, and visit places—caves, bridges, precipices—whenever and wherever I choose, and I cannot imagine being unable to think about any topic—death, eternity, time, space—or to talk with anyone about any idea, including the innumerable potentially raw nerve issues arising in self-knowledge therapeutic work and meaningful personal relationships.

The primary negative residue of my early troubles has been an excessive sense of duty and work ethic that has frequently led me to overcommit myself to my professional life, taking time away from other important responsibilities and pleasures, particularly those of husband and father. This was more of a problem in my early adult and professional years before common sense and maturity allowed me to get my priorities straight and taught me to distinguish between what I could and could not reasonably do.

The process of understanding my own mind has also allowed me to recognize, appreciate, and enjoy the depths and breadths of others' minds and experiences—not only in my work with patients and clients, but in the works of writers and other artists who share with us their sensitivity to the human soul.

When, after becoming free of terror, I first saw the Giuseppe Verdi opera, *Aida*, I was spellbound. In the final scene, two lovers are condemned to death, sealed alive in an underground room together, forever. No longer conflicted and troubled with fear, I could feel the lovers' rapture as they sang their glorious love duet and anticipated spending eternity together in such a cozy, secure place.

6

Ooooh, My God

Feelings of euphoria can occur as ecstasy, bliss, grandeur, rapture, rhapsody, headiness, elation, exhilaration, a high, a rush, a glow, and as part of many different experiences that give their owner extremely pleasurable sensations. Like other strong emotions, though, euphoria is a double-edged sword, and its perils are ubiquitous.

Because the appeal of a "high" is so strong, pursuit of euphoria often accompanies, and is the motive for seeking, exciting occupations such as fire fighting, law enforcement, and rescue and emergency medical work. It also may be the first step in alcohol, drug, sexual, eating, gambling, and spending addictions. Euphoric feelings frequently go hand in hand with the commission of crimes, particularly arson and sexual offenses that range from simple touching to serial murders.

Though mild to moderate transitory euphoria supported by reality may form the good feeling base of healthy self-esteem, self-confidence, and the pleasures of love, achievement, and other fulfillments, excessive euphoria is our most underrated troublemaker. Its problems begin with lies: lies of eternal bliss and the value of pleasure we tell ourselves in a moment of passion, lies of power we feel when we are in positions of importance, and lies of greatness we daydream when we try to escape disappointment or failure.

169

Most people enjoy moments of wholesome euphoria that allow them to feel, in the proper time and place, the grandeur of a sunset, the ecstasy of being in love, and the thrill of an orgasm. Excessive euphoria, however, promises a never-ending exhilaration suffused with a heavenly glow that everything associated with those sensations is perfect and always will be. These states often lead one to behave as if he were invincible, and to believe, subconsciously if not consciously, he is above the laws of nature, common sense, and society, and that the feelings of others, including loved ones, do not matter. People in high places regularly sabotage their lives when they fall prey to this deadly emotion, just as do those who succumb to the illusory promises of the full range of addictions.

Euphoric feelings come from the promises of our infantile illusions, those moments when, even in the most painful childhood, and even if not remembered, the world was our oyster. For many, the temptation to return to these feelings is irresistible, only to learn in the end that their feelings have lured them into a Faustian bargain that can have sad and, frequently, tragic consequences.

Since euphoria is so intoxicating, any idea or emotion experienced through its prism becomes part of a grand illusion, no matter how self-destructive it might actually be. Story writers, movie makers, and young lovers rhapsodize about the heady bliss of being "in love," even though the American divorce rate of fifty percent tells us that this is a grossly flawed notion. When one has found, or seeks, romantic ecstasy, one thinks only of its pleasures; its potential pitfalls are either not considered or are quickly dismissed, even when repeated bitter disappointments and heartaches have told one otherwise. Since the glow of rapturous love feels total and timeless, love affairs limited to as little as two hours a week or month seem as though they will last forever, yet generally do not endure when put to the test of a committed marriage. Relationships built on such illusory feelings cannot bear the reasonably expected conflicts, trauma, and scars that inevitably occur when two people live out their lives together. The vulnerability to this emotional state lies in us all: saints, teetotalers, and the morally upright, as well as sinners, drunks, and crooks, are all vulnerable to being duped by the promise that those who drink the nectar of being "in love" will live happily ever after. This state usually continues, however, only as long as one forbids through denial the introduction of contradictory reality or conflicting emotions.

John Stetson was a victim of this promise, and his quest for euphoria took the form of a desperate pursuit of sexual ecstasy.

As I entered the waiting room, a good looking, slightly graying man, appearing to be in his early forties and dressed in a dark blue suit, light blue shirt, and bright red tie, promptly stood, smiled, and greeted me eagerly.

"Hi, I'm John Stetson."

His hail-fellow-well-met beaming smile was so infectious that when I responded, "I'm Dr. Stockton, it's very good meet you," my own smile was wider than usual. He walked briskly ahead of me as we entered the consultation room, then I gestured toward the chair where he would sit.

He began talking before I said a word.

"I had a great family, a good wife and four wonderful children, for eighteen years, and then I had an affair and ruined it all."

As he spoke, his bright smile changed to a look of profound sadness.

"Tell me more about what happened?" I asked.

"I'm forty-three and have a good reputation as a computer systems engineer, but I've destroyed my marriage and I don't know how to repair the damage I've done. My affair with Floretta didn't turn out the way I thought it would, and my wife, Sarah, actually my former wife, is involved with someone else, and I can't get her back. Now I don't have anyone, and I don't know what to do," he said, sinking into gloom.

"This is hard to talk about?" I asked.

He stared at nothing for a moment, then sat up and said, "My friend Marvin Jackson suggested I call you because he said his work with you was all that saved his marriage."

Half-smiling, he added, "He told me I needed to see you for my sanity, if nothing else."

"Say more?" I asked.

He peered out the picture window, then leaned forward so he could see the sky.

"It looks bad out, the clouds are getting dark and the weatherman said it's going to storm."

"Yes, it does look gloomy out, perhaps like it feels inside?" I asked.

Pausing to refocus his thoughts, he grinned slightly. "I finally realized I didn't know what I was doing or what I wanted. I want Sarah back, but I know I've got to get over Floretta first, and I also don't ever want to make the same mistake again. I left Sarah because she wasn't the woman I was sure I had to have, and I lost Floretta because she wasn't who I thought she was."

He shook his head and frowned.

"Say more about not knowing what you wanted?" I asked.

"When Floretta and I first met she needed me as much as I needed her, and we couldn't get enough of each other." His face flushed. "In the beginning, it felt like what we had was made in Heaven, and when we made love I got so crazy with passion, I was certain she and I would last forever. When she said she had never known such pleasure before, I was sure she'd never want to be without me. Everything was so right there were no words to describe it." He looked directly at me and paused a moment. "I guess the feeling was like a drug addict's 'rush' I've read about, except that a drug high sounds like a thrill or excitement, and mine was just pure bliss," he said, with a faraway look.

"Tell me more about 'pure bliss'?" I asked.

With a deep frown, he replied, "When I felt that bliss, we seemed to have no problems at all, but the truth was we lived in two different worlds, and I had to bite my tongue so I didn't say what I really thought because I was afraid I'd upset what we had together. I had to lie to myself a lot about how perfect all of it was."

"What about lying to yourself?" I asked.

"For more than a year, we called each other several times a day, and somehow managed to make love regularly. But then she changed, and she'd only call once a week or even less. We would talk or just be together, but then," he opened his palms and shrugged his shoulders, "she'd just vanish until the next time, and I'd be crushed." Looking puzzled, he shook his head.

"You feel confused about what happened?" I asked.

"I never understood why Floretta changed, but when I look back, I guess I knew even then that it was all built on sand." He sighed, as his hands dropped into his lap. "She told me she didn't want to be together because it made her feel bad about herself and weak for giving in to her urge. Something about what she said didn't feel right, or maybe," he grimaced, "I just didn't want to believe it. After she pulled away she'd call me when she had an urge to make love, but, before long, I stopped calling her because after we'd make good love her rejections would hurt too much. Sometimes she'd call just because she'd had a dream about me, and then, after we talked or were together, she'd pull back until the urge hit her again. It was as though she needed just to reach out and touch me, and then, once she was reassured I was there, she'd vanish again. I was devastated when she'd go away, but, every time she called I was convinced, deluded is the right word, that this time she wouldn't go away."

He leaned back in his chair and looked through me for a full minute.

"The need to believe she'd never go away was very strong," I repeated for emphasis.

"I wanted to believe that she adored me and loved me and wanted to be with me forever. The hardest thing I've ever had to do was to accept the reality that we never had a real relationship, and that what I'd assumed we had between us, just wasn't to be. When she pulled back, it had to have been her way of telling me what she meant when she said, 'I'm not the person you want to believe I am.' I just never wanted to acknowledge it." He shook his head slowly.

"You may find this hard to believe, but I fell in love with her smile. It said she was all mine. I was exhilarated!"

he exclaimed, still shaking his head. He paused to think for a moment, then shook his head again. "Her smile was like a promise of eternal bliss. She tried to tell me from the very beginning she wasn't who I thought she was, but her smile and what we had sexually were absolutely irresistible." His face glowed even as he continued shaking his head.

"Her smile made you believe she was who you thought she was, rather than who she actually was?" I asked.

"The answer to that has to be 'yes,' and that's what she kept telling me. When we kissed the first time we were alone together, I told her 'I love you,' and she told me later that she'd thought, 'How can you say you love me, you don't even know me?' More than once," he said with an edge of despair, "she said, 'You love who you think I am, or who you want me to be, but it's not really me.'"

He ran his hands through his hair as tears came to his eyes.

"Soon after we met, I'd say to her, 'I love you more than I've ever loved anyone in my life,' and I wanted her to say the same thing to me. But instead, she'd say, 'I love you in a way I haven't loved anyone before', and then I'd be crushed," he said, wiping his tears.

He paused, and a look of resignation settled on his face.

"If your expression could talk, can you sense what it would say?" I asked.

"I suppose it would say I know our affair was doomed from the beginning," he sighed. "We both actually had good marriages and were usually sensible people, and, believe it or not, had good values. But I got so swept up in my feelings about her, they took over my life." He sighed again.

Over the next several weeks, Mr. Stetson began to realize that his strong feelings of the moment did not tell the whole story.

"Floretta used to say," he began one day, "'What we have together is good, but leading two lives is too hard on me. I want my life to be all under one roof.' She and David, her estranged husband, hadn't lived together for five years when we met, but she felt guilty about being disloyal to him anyway." He began shaking his head. "It's clear to me now that almost from the beginning she had more sense than I did, but I wanted her so much I didn't understand what she was saying, and I still don't want to accept it."

He screwed up his face, as though holding back help-less rage.

"You look like you're angry at something. Are you aware of the feeling?" I asked.

"When Floretta would disappear she'd stay busy with work and see her friends, but all I had was my daydream that she would call and tell me she truly loved me more than she had ever loved anyone, and that she missed me so much she couldn't live without me and would never go away again. It was all so crazy," he said, shaking his head. "When she didn't call I was afraid she'd gone away forever, and when she did call, my brains turned to mush, and each time I was sure that this time she'd never go away again. When I was clinging to my fantasy, it was as if I had hold of an electric cable I couldn't let go of," he said, as his fists gripped an imaginary cable.

His hands relaxed their grip, and his eyes wandered around the room then out the picture window to watch the falling autumn leaves before turning back to look at me.

"What about not being able to let go?" I asked.

"I was crazy jealous when she wanted to be with any-one but me, and I'm angry even now when I remember see-ing her with Martin, her boss, because I knew she liked him more than anyone. I wasn't upset when she was with her clients, or even when she talked to David, but," he clenched his fist, "when I saw her with Martin, I could have killed them both. And I hated her almost as bad when she wanted to be with her colleagues or friends more than with me if her work or personal business didn't require it!"

Wide eyed and breathing heavily, he paused, then took a long breath.

"Floretta was twenty when she married David, his last name is Corelli, and he was in his early thirties," he went on, in a dull tone. "She said she needed companionship and intimacy much more than David did, and that's why meet-ing me was a godsend for her. She said that she was so lonely she'd sometimes follow David around the house just to have a conversation."

Mr. Stetson's fury had been palpable when he talked about seeing Floretta with Martin, so when he shifted topics to Floretta's marital problems, I had to consider whether to ask if his turning to Floretta and her husband's history helped him avoid his rage about feeling betrayed by her feelings for her boss. Since this occurred so early in our work, I knew that my learning about Mr. Stetson's problem as he saw it was more important, so I tagged for future work my awareness of his fear of his rage, and chose to facilitate his telling me about his response to Floretta's need for his companionship and intimacy.

"That's why her meeting you was so meaningful to her and exhilarating for you?" I responded.

"That's what I always thought. She and David had separated after ten years, but didn't divorce because they were Roman Catholic, and during that five years before we met, they had kept up a kind of close-but-not-too-close relationship. She didn't get involved with anyone, and David, who didn't socialize much, seemed content to live alone and work as an accountant. They talked by phone, but she needed more, and when she saw how I responded to her smile, our chemistry was instant." He smiled grimly. "And I assumed it was forever."

"Floretta said that before she married David, she had been unsuccessful with men, and that she had been mixed and uncertain about marrying David in the first place. She told me she'd never had feelings for any man like she did for me," he smiled, "and that she'd never had a sexual awakening before me. When she said those things," his smile became a grin, "I WAS IN HEAVEN, because I thought it meant she'd love me forever. She said David was a good man and she admired him, but he didn't spark her passion or let her be close to him like I did. I guess she felt with him the same way I did with Sarah. But when she said things like that I believed they meant she was so devoted to me she'd never even think of leaving."

After the session I thought about the many people I have

worked with who break up their marriages and look for another sexual partner because they feel their spouse is not passionate enough. Such individuals often feel a God-given right to have, through some kind of intimate relationship, the euphoric bliss they had in early childhood but inevitably lost as part of growing up. When they deny this inescapable loss, and hold accountable their spouse, who has her own normal individual needs, for not recovering it, the relationship often suffers irreparably.

The next appointment, Mr. Stetson continued where he had left off the previous session.

"As soon as I left last time, I realized I hadn't told you that instead of her telling me that she wanted to be with me forever, she said, 'Now that I've found love and had a sexual awakening, I'm ready to die.' I asked her what she meant, and she said, 'With you I've fulfilled my greatest dream, so I'm ready to die happy.'" He looked stunned. "I couldn't believe she would say that, I guess she thought she was saying something nice to me, but I was devastated. For me life was just beginning, and I wanted for us never to be apart."

Composing himself, he summoned the strength to continue.

"In her heart Floretta was loyal to David. She said she loved him, and, the way she described him, I understood why. He was a responsible man, he worked hard, he made a good living, he was good around the house, he did things for her, and she thought their common Italian heritage gave them a special bond. She said she wanted their marriage to work, but that he could not give her the intimacy she needed. She never said it outright, but I think her devotion to David was the main reason she wouldn't leave him for me, and I also think that she herself, not just David, might have a problem with long-term intimacy, like people who are afraid of commitments, although I don't really know."

I took advantage of Mr. Stetson's comments about David and Floretta's relationship to introduce observations about marriage realities that are usually ignored, as Mr. Stetson had, when one is under the spell of being "in love."

I replied, "The strength of passion and bliss often blur and overpower all other considerations, especially when one doesn't recognize that people express their love and devotion in many different ways, like through mutually shared values, companionability, loyalty, fidelity, responsibility, and reliability, that favor in-depth and lasting relationships.

"Resolving this impasse requires maturity since it involves forsaking wishes we feel entitled to, and requires the willingness of both partners to sacrifice some of their own yearnings in order to fulfill each other's needs. So when one wants to preserve a marriage as you do with Sarah, that's where someone like myself comes in to help resolve the need for intimacy short of breaking up an otherwise good relationship and marriage."

He crossed his arms, slumped in his seat, and thought for several minutes.

Shaking his head, he said, "We couldn't let go. She couldn't let go, I couldn't let go. Even when I knew it was all over, and she'd call me to talk about things I wasn't interested in, like complaints about slights by her colleagues and clients, I'd still listen and pretend to be interested." He lifted his hands, then dropped them. "She acted like we were in the same place, but by then I was so hurt I'd lost everything I ever felt for her. But I kept seeing her for months, and I'm still confused about why. I don't know how much of why I didn't go ahead and break it off was out of fear of hurting her, or how much was that I couldn't bear it myself."

He had largely disregarded what I had said. When such a response occurs in self-knowledge therapy, a therapist must decide whether to treat the person's apparent avoidance as a defense and interpret his wish not to think about what the therapist said, or should the therapist accept that his comment was poorly timed and then wait for a more appropriate opportunity to explore the topic. In this instance I decided it was the latter, and chose to follow Mr. Stetson in his more immediate concerns.

"Can you say more about the fear that you couldn't bear it yourself?" I asked.

"When I wanted to break with her and couldn't, I kept remembering that glow I had when she was so loving, and I felt so close with her. I couldn't imagine living without it. Her smile gave me such a thrill I just knew it still had to be in there somewhere, and I kept believing she was the person who had smiled at me and not the person who would just vanish and leave me hanging.

"She kept calling and withdrawing for a long time after I knew it was all over between us, but it eventually became so painful I really had to end it." He scowled, "but I have to admit that even then I couldn't resist putting my life on hold, and in the back of my mind I was hoping, *waiting* for her to call again." He shook his head as if astonished by what he had said. "How could I have been such a idiot?!"

"The power of the glow you felt was so strong," I responded, "it overrode being able to remember that her smile, as sincere as it was, came from only one part of her, and that her other feelings and behaviors that devastated you, like her vanishing, were far more prevalent than the smile that gave you the glow."

"When she smiled, and I felt so great, I couldn't think of anything else." He turned and stared out the window.

As Mr. Stetson talked, I was reminded of another patient, who had had difficulty breaking with her abusive husband, because she clung to a tiny sliver of his total personality, the one moment he had been a gentle and tender man caring for an injured little bird.

Mr. Stetson uncrossed his legs and sat up.

"When I finally couldn't stand it any longer, I left a message on her voice mail that Sarah and I were getting back together. It wasn't actually true, but it was what I hoped would happen, because by then I wanted Sarah back and our marriage to work, and I knew that the message I left was the only explanation both of us would really accept. Floretta had made it easier by abandoning me and hurting me so much, but, uh . . . uh," he wiped away a tear, "having to swallow that my balloon with her had burst, and that I no longer cared for her was really hard. Only someone who was brain dead would have tried to go on at that point."

"You hesitated before you added that having to accept that you no longer cared for Floretta was really hard," I commented.

He chewed the inside of his cheek as he thought.

"I was thinking that I've made the break with her, but I know I still haven't completely lost my feelings for her," he said, looking at the floor. Lifting his head, he went on. "I've got to get over thinking about her so much, it runs me crazy. I've also got to stop getting turned on so much by just a woman's smile, it makes me act like an imbecile. I sure as hell don't ever want to be drawn to another woman for the wrong reason, this time was enough."

"I never felt the sexual magic with Sarah that I did with Floretta, but I didn't have the sense to know there was more to life than sexual magic. I really loved Sarah and enjoyed being with her, but she wasn't passionate and didn't arouse me." He yawned. "I have a feeling that a lot of people have the same kind of disappointments they never get over and are unhappy without ever knowing why."

"What about the passion and sexual magic not being there with Sarah?" I asked.

He closed his eyes and rubbed his forehead.

"I felt the magic with Sarah our first several years, but she was matter-of-fact about sex like she was about everything else. After a while I couldn't get aroused by her. I was impotent most of the time, and we rarely made love for many years before the divorce."

Glancing out the window, he spied a titmouse standing on the sill.

When his attention had not returned after a few minutes, I asked, "Perhaps looking at that bird is less upsetting than thinking about impotence?"

He looked at me and nodded his head slightly.

"Maybe so, because I was thinking that every time I was impotent with Sarah, I felt like such a failure I was desperate for someone who would turn me on. I think that's why I loved Floretta's smile and why I was ecstatic when we made love—I didn't feel like a failure any more, and that's what made being with her so magical." He had a wistful smile.

In the days before our next appointment, I thought how often I had worked with men suffering from impotence caused by their reactions to unmet needs and disappointed wishes. Hurts and resentments inevitably occur when two people live together, and, unless the partners accept each other's individuality and work out their differences, these hurts and resentments remain as unhealed wounds that frequently impair the feelings of intimacy necessary for making love.

The inability to grow in this way is a major reason partners often lose interest in making love together, why they drift apart, and why they turn to sexual affairs with others with whom they share no scars. Many also, especially men, preserve their marriage by masturbating to tailor-made sexual fantasies free of emotional trauma.

When one is young, the physical sexual drive alone can override almost all emotional differences, but, since the hormonal drive lessens as the body ages, intimate feelings for one's partner become increasingly vital in ensuring that lovemaking works physically.

When I greeted Mr. Stetson in the waiting room for the next session, his smile and "Hello," were grim.

He began immediately. "I've looked forward to us meeting today because I want to pick up where we left off last time about my feelings of failure and when my impotence began. I didn't have sexual problems with Sarah our first several years. I never had trouble getting hard, but when I started feeling bitter about her lack of interest, I couldn't get aroused enough to have sex anymore." He leaned forward with his hands on his knees. "I knew that about myself long before I came here," he said, in a dark voice. "Before I met Floretta I saw a urologist who obviously didn't understand what was causing my impotence. He wanted to prescribe some drug or one of those contraptions to give me an erection, which I didn't even try because I knew the only thing that could help me was the special feeling like I got from Floretta's smile."

"This was even before Sarah left you?" I asked.

He sat back with a look of despondency. "Yes. When Sarah divorced me, she told me she loved me, but she wasn't going to put up with me as long as I cared for someone else. She didn't understand how desperate I felt about being impotent, but, of course, there was nothing she could do if she didn't know anything, and I didn't want to tell her because she would just feel hurt, and there was nothing she could do about it anyway because she couldn't be someone she's not. For a while I tried to get her to take me back, but she said she knew I still had feelings for Floretta, and she didn't want me as long as that was true. She told me to grow up and get my head straight, and if she was still around, we could talk then, unless she married someone else in the meantime. In my heart I feel she loves me and will wait for me as long as she can, but she's sensible and principled and strong minded, and I know she won't take me back if I don't straighten out." He shook his head, as he added, "I really screwed up."

"Say more about feeling desperate?" I asked.

He paused a moment. "It was because I couldn't get an erection, and I was terrified I couldn't get one again with Sarah. But I didn't have anyone to talk to about it, especially not Sarah, and that urologist didn't have the slightest idea of what my problem was. Losing sexual interest in Sarah would have made sense and losing her would been easier if she were a bad person, but she wasn't. I liked her, she was attractive, she wasn't unpleasant, or critical, or anything else that would justify breaking up my marriage for Floretta." He stopped abruptly and looked at the floor.

"You're reflecting on what you said?" I asked.

He nodded at me. "I just realized I sound like I don't know that problems go with marriage, or that I, too, didn't have problems that disappointed Sarah, or that I don't recognize all her good qualities. I acted like unless she had the exact magical qualities that would turn me on, then life wasn't worth living."

He thought for several seconds.

"And those were only half my problems. What I understand even less about myself was that when Floretta sometimes acted like she needed me, but then kept going away, why couldn't I accept that she didn't feel about me the way I did about her?" He shook his head again.

"And there was more. When I felt hurt about her withdrawing, she said, 'It's always the one who loves the most, and puts the most on the line, who gets hurt the most.' But I still couldn't hear that she was telling me she cared less for me than I did for her, and worse, that she didn't care how what she said made me feel."

Shaking his head in disbelief, John sat in thought. "I can see now how much I had to deny the way she treated me in order to feel I loved her."

I said, "You seem to be saying that your desperate fear of becoming impotent with Floretta blinded and deafened you to anything that would suggest you might lose her."

He slowly nodded, looking subdued. Then, glancing at the clock that showed we were already overtime, he rose from his chair, mumbled "See you tomorrow," and left.

The next session, his greeting was as subdued as his parting had been the time before.

"All I've thought about since last time was how far I went to deny all those things Floretta used to do and say, because they meant that she didn't care for me the way I needed her to, and that my feeling about how much she cared for me really came from me. It obviously didn't come from her or any real devotion she felt toward me, but from what I read into what I thought was her admiring smile. I made myself dumb and blind so I wouldn't see that her withdrawals and hurtful words really did mean what they said. It was all just an illusion so I wouldn't have to be afraid of being impotent."

He sat pensively a full minute.

"I think I've acted like she and I were one and the same, that we both shared my heavenly glow together. It's taken a long time to recognize this, because it's so difficult to sort out, and I know what I'm saying must sound obvious to you, but I'm just now seeing that Floretta and I are separate people; she's not just an extension of me, she's a person all in her own right. She has her own needs, and they fit with some of mine, but it's not as if we were emotional twins or clones who shared the exact same feelings together." He shook his head. "This must be what she meant when she said, 'You love who you think I am, or who you want me to be, but not who I really am.' When I felt in that glow with her, though, it was as if she and I were one and the same, rather than her being someone completely different from me."

By dwelling on all its facets, he seemed to be coming to grips with his newly recognized reality.

"There's another thing I didn't understand, in fact I didn't even think about, until recently. I've always wished for someone like Floretta, but until I met her, I never felt I absolutely had to have her, whoever she was. And I still don't know why now, or last year, I became so desperate for her. You started me thinking about this when you pointed out how my desperation blinded me to a lot of things about Floretta that I didn't like and didn't want as part of my life."

"Say more what you're thinking about this?" I asked.

"Several years ago I had a short, actually just flirting, romance with my secretary, Evelyn. A year or so after she started working for me, I noticed her smile, and I had the same wonderful feeling with her that I did later when Floretta smiled. That little quasi-affair with Evelyn didn't last long, though. I think her husband suspected something because he asked for a transfer to the West Coast soon after that, and he didn't tell her why." Mr Stetson's face relaxed. "She went with him of course, and I realize as I'm talking, that that must be why I never became desperate for her; I didn't have time to get hooked on her the way I did to Floretta."

He stared at me wide-eyed. "Figuring this out has helped me see something about myself I never saw before. I thought it was Evelyn and Floretta I loved, but it really was that their smiles gave me such a wonderful feeling I thought I couldn't live without them."

This insight gave him a sense of peace I hadn't seen before.

"You seem to be saying that the 'heavenly glow' inside has made you feel like an addict in search of his drug. Say more about how you became aware of this?" I asked.

"Our talking about Evelyn got me to thinking about all of this in a way I never did before. What I'm seeing is that this feeling of wanting a woman like Evelyn and Floretta has been with me my whole life. It's always been there, just under the surface, although its only really strong at certain times, like when they smile. I'm more aware of it now that I'm concentrating on it because of what we're doing here. But, except for the times with Evelyn and Floretta, I don't usually think about it. Actually, I'm aware of the feeling right now, although it's not strong enough to make me want to go out looking for a woman." Then he grinned, and added, "Unless she smiled."

In spite of Mr. Stetson's new insights that Floretta's smile was only one part of her and that it was that smile that gave him the wonderful feeling he felt he could not live without, the magnetism of this euphoria still led him to cling to the illusion that, if he wished passionately enough, Floretta would return and their basic incompatibility would not exist, and that his illusion of grandeur with her would protect him from his fears of inadequacy and failure, sexually as well as other ways.

As he reflected on how he had used euphoria with Floretta to overcome failure feelings, Mr. Stetson said, "When I was little and something bad happened, like a friend being mad at me or a teacher giving me a bad grade, I always made myself feel good by thinking that my mother and Ruth, my older sister, loved me." With a wistful smile, he added, "Actually what I did was picture Ruth's smile, and that made me feel warm all over.

"I often did the same thing as an adult, too, until I couldn't make it work any longer. And I think that's when my problem started." He took a ball-point pen from his shirt pocket and tried several times, in vain, to make its faulty mechanism work properly, then frowned with a slightly embarrassed look. "As a grown man I'd feel silly trying to make myself feel better by remembering my big sister's face, and when I tried to think of Sarah's face, her smile just wasn't there. I first started feeling disappointed with Sarah when I was afraid I didn't have the grades to get into graduate school, and I needed a woman to smile at me. Sarah was a good everyday companion, but that didn't help. She didn't smile then any more than she does now. As it turned out—"

He stopped in mid-sentence, wide-eyed, and his face grew ashen.

"What stopped you?" I asked.

"I never realized until now how these are connected, that when I was afraid of failing, I got desperate for a woman's smile to give me confidence, and then when I got it, I felt strong and confident, so since Floretta had given it to me, then the good feeling I had meant that she loved me and that I loved her."

He stared at nothing for several minutes.

"What you just said really struck you," I observed.

"This is like an epiphany. I never realized before why I couldn't let go of Floretta, or felt compelled to cling to her."

He slipped the open palms of his hands under his belt, anchoring them with his thumbs.

"Now that I think about it, this answers the question that bothered me earlier. I started noticing Floretta's smile when I was trying to install a really difficult computer system, and I was afraid that if I didn't do it right, I'd lose my job.

"And that's also what made me jump at Evelyn's smile. She'd been around for a year, but I hadn't paid much attention to her until my company started laying off people, and I was afraid I'd be next."

He relaxed, stretched out his legs, and looked at me.

"But even when I didn't need a smile out of fear I'd fail at something, I always needed it when I made love with Sarah. And since she didn't smile much I eventually lost interest—I couldn't get an erection even when I wanted to do it. So I felt like a failure all the time because I thought I should be able to get it up no matter what."

"You somehow translated Sarah's lack of smile into your being a failure?" I asked.

He looked forlorn. Then, squinting in the bright sun shining through the window, he noticed one squirrel chasing another, smiled, and looked back at me. "After I met

Floretta I tried making love again with Sarah by imagining Floretta's smile, and that worked for a while, but gradually even that wouldn't do it for me. Then I started having sex with Floretta, and Sarah's and my marriage was lost after that. I see now that it wasn't me personally Floretta wanted, she just needed someone with the right chemistry for her, but I couldn't see that then."

"Say more about 'chemistry'?" I asked.

He raised his brow, and looked directly at me. "I've heard about chemistry as long as I can remember, but I don't have a clue what it means."

I responded, "Let's start with what comes to mind about your chemistry."

He looked puzzled. "Well, I guess it's not the same for everyone, but for me it means whatever it is that gives me that good feeling and makes me confident and right with the world."

"What about 'right with the world'?" I asked.

"Like I'm at home!" he answered, with hushed excitement.

"What about 'at home'?" I encouraged him.

With a contented smile, he replied, "It's not just being at home, it's being with Ruth—" He again stopped himself in mid-sentence, looking pale and wide-eyed. "This is something else I never realized before, that my chemistry for Floretta and Evelyn is like it was for Ruth, and maybe Mother, too, but especially for Ruth."

Wiping his eyes with his handkerchief, he sat and collected his thoughts.

With a deep breath, he continued. "Ruth was seven years older and took care of me most of the time because mother had some kind of back problem and had to stay in bed a lot until she had an operation. I always felt so happy with Ruth."

"What about feeling happy with Ruth?" I asked.

John smiled, caught up in his memory. "I have a picture of me at two that shows me running to Ruth. She was beaming at me, and I can see in my own smile that I was feeling the same glow with her that I came to have with Floretta." With an embarrassed smile, he said, "I remember that when

I was twelve or thirteen, I secretly wished Ruth would let me have intercourse with her as part of my 'sexual education.' She was off in college by then, but the image was very exciting, and I thought about it when I learned to masturbate a couple of years later. I don't go around with that feeling about Ruth any more, and I certainly don't think about sex with her, but I can tell that those feelings are still inside me, and I really think that's where my chemistry for Floretta comes from." He looked thoughtful.

John's overidealization of Ruth's, and later Floretta's, smiles gave him an elation and self-confidence that protected him from feelings of inadequacy and failure, and his dependency on this mechanism had become deeply engraved in his emotions by the time he began puberty. During his teenage years, this euphoric self-assurance he felt from a woman's admiring smile then fused with his sexual urges, and the blend of these emotions became vital for his sexual arousal and lovemaking. This combination, that felt so secure and pleasurable, became a sanctuary whenever he feared failure.

Mr. Stetson had not learned he could accept the normal failures of life without turning to euphoria. Although he was well respected in his work as someone who could handle tough jobs, he always had a smiling woman in the back of his mind, the eager-to-please receptionist down the hall or just a friendly stranger who greeted him in passing on the street.

People who become addicted to elation usually think it is absurd to suggest that good feelings can cause problems, so identifying excessive euphoria as a problem can be difficult for many to accept. We recognize that heavy despair and tormenting fears are problems when they make us feel so bad we cannot work or enjoy living, but elation and euphoria feel good, and the wish to feel good is natural. In one session, John said, "I once said to Floretta, 'When we make love, I feel like I'm soaring to heaven,'" then, speaking to me, added, only partly in jest, "if God had not intended me to be this way, He would not have made my heavenly glow feel so good."

A seventy year old man I saw as a patient had felt rhapsodically in love with his twenty-eight year old secretary. He said, "Who in their right mind wouldn't want to feel good, you'd have to be crazy not to." Although his marriage and his business were at stake, and the young woman herself thought he was nuts, he was unconcerned. When I asked him about his resistance to working on the problem he said, "Doctor, you don't understand. Most of your patients come to see you because they're in some kind of trouble that makes them feel bad. I don't feel bad, my feelings for Diane [the young woman] make me feel good. I came to see you because my wife wanted me to, not because I think I need to be here."

The origin of such enchantments, often referred to as "chemistry," lies in the long forgotten, early life emotional attachments discussed at the beginning of this chapter, emotions an adult is usually unaware of when trying to account for this "chemistry" in later life.

A married Chicago defense attorney I saw came to understand the "in love" chemistry he felt for Sally, a prostitute. He consulted me not because he thought being in love with a prostitute, with whom he never had, nor expected, sex, was a dubious pursuit, but because he felt devastated when, in the middle of their times together, she would answer her cell phone and be off to turn a trick with another john.

As a child, the attorney had felt a profound sense of loss when his mother became depressed and distant, and he had learned to overcome this loss by sitting with her and feeling reassured by her presence. Although Sally was cheerful on the surface, her sunken eyes, forlorn expression, and subtle qualities of loneliness were the key to her appeal. Sally's sadness so evoked the pain the attorney felt about his mother's remoteness, he was in rapture when Sally allowed him just to be near her, so he could relive the comforting reassurance he had felt when he sat near his depressed, emotionally unavailable but physically present mother.

A clergyman I saw as a patient had a similar experience. He began his first session by saying, "I enjoy a well-turned ankle as well as any man," as if his behavior were as innocent as noticing a teenager's brightly colored bobby socks. He told me only later that his earlier statement was a paraphrase of, "I feel like I've died and gone to Heaven when I see a full breasted woman, and I can't resist getting my hands on her."

A fear of isolation and aloneness was etched in the minister's deep emotions during most of his childhood when his mother's multiple sclerosis and father's remoteness had made both parents unavailable. His aunt, who stepped in to care for him and his younger brother, comforted him when he cried by lying in bed next to him so he could feel the solace of her warm body. She stopped this practice when he was eleven, after she had become aware of his erections and heavy breathing as he pressed his face on her breasts and put his hands on her buttocks.

As an adult, having learned as a boy with his aunt the ecstasy of, literally, "reaching out and touching" a woman sexually, he easily seduced several admiring, trusting, vulnerable women church members who felt trapped into accommodating their honored pastor. The congregation discovered his behavior when a number of the women learned of each other's experience through a mutual confidante, though not until his secret philandering had ruined several of the women's marriages, disillusioned parishioners who had sincerely believed in the sanctity of their man of God, and caused his denomination to defrock him, as well as his wife to leave him.

My consultation with these men showed, in each instance, that their pursuit of grandeur had developed to protect them from a lonely, empty depression that lay underneath. Had they not uncovered and resolved their underlying depression and fear that they could not endure life without the joy and headiness of temporary sexual unions, they would have continued to be caught between two equally unacceptable states of mind, melancholic emptiness and self-destructive grandeur.

Mr. Stetson's self-knowledge work required that he resolve his two major troublesome emotions: the excessive euphoric ecstasy he used as a defense mechanism, and the fear of inadequacy and failure his excessive euphoria defended him from. His excessive euphoria was the more difficult to overcome because, until it had caused him to lose his wife and family, it had felt so good he had wanted to preserve it at almost any cost. Resolving his fear of failure encountered less resistance because it felt bad and he was eager to be rid of it.

He began one session by saying, "Pursuing this euphoria causes me more trouble than I've been aware of." He slumped in his seat, his eyes wandering around the room.

After a few moments, I said, "How so?"

He responded, "Before we began, I thought I'd just wrecked my life by leaving Sarah and then trying to find in Floretta what I was missing. It never occurred to me that I feel heady in other ways, too, and that that feeling carries a lot of baggage."

"Say more about 'other ways' and 'baggage'?" I asked.

"I think about the baggage first because even though I've talked openly with you about all this, I never let anyone else know the real reason Sarah and I divorced. I didn't tell Sarah because I didn't want to hurt her, and I didn't tell anyone else because they'd think I was silly if I said I had an affair with Floretta because her smile made me feel like a million dollars, or that I got a divorce from Sarah because she didn't smile enough to give me an erection. So when people ask why Sarah and I divorced, I say things like, 'It just didn't work out.'" He averted his eyes.

"I'm not yet sure what you are saying, since most people aren't eager to reveal their private emotions in public," I said.

"Yeah, that makes sense, and it's no big deal, but that's not all. My pride gets involved when I expect too much, and then it's hard to accept even normal disappointments. A perfect example of something that happens all the time took place here yesterday, although I didn't recognize it until later in the day. As I walked out, I thought, 'Boy, that sure was a good session,' but what I didn't realize at the time was that I was feeling so excited and heady about the insights I'd had, that I was afraid I'd look crazy if I told you how high I felt about it and then couldn't come back and do as well today."

"What about 'excited and heady about the insights here'?" I asked.

He smiled. "Up to now I've called the feeling 'heavenly bliss' or 'glow', but it's more than that. It's thrilling, like I'm on top of the world, and I can do anything. When I say 'do anything,' and I know you're going to ask me what that means, it means I can do really well whatever I'm doing at the moment, like when I made love to Floretta." His smile slowly faded. "The feeling doesn't last long, but it gives me so much confidence while it lasts, and it's a lot better than feeling like a failure. If I don't have that confident feeling, I see everything, like Sarah's not smiling, as a put down, and my impotence as a failure, and then I can't do anything," he said with a mournful sigh.

"You said, 'The feeling doesn't last long.' Is that part of what you meant about being afraid you couldn't come back and do well today?" I asked.

He twisted his lips in concentration.

"I think I meant that after the feeling goes away I feel down and don't have the spirit to do anything. I always felt down after I was with Floretta, and what was peculiar was that the more sexually successful and ecstatic I felt, the more depressed I'd feel afterward."

"What about feeling depressed?" I asked.

His shoulders sank.

"At those times, I felt like a total failure and that life wasn't worth living. I used to think of it as something that just happened, but now I can see that it occurred too regularly after I felt high for me not to know they were connected. I guess I got depressed because I felt like I'd finally found the most important thing in my life, and then it was gone. And so then I kept trying to get back my euphoria."

I responded, "It's as if your emotions said that the price of divorce and depression you paid for euphoria were less painful than feeling inadequate and a failure. That when you didn't get aroused with Sarah and felt you were a sexual failure with her, you turned to the euphoria of an affair with Floretta so you wouldn't be impotent, but then found that that remedy was worse than the disease, and you wound up both depressed and without a wife."

He stared into space, shaking his head. "I never looked at it that way, but that is the choice I've made, even though I didn't know it until now. It's crazy, because feeling inadequate is nowhere near as bad as feeling depressed after a high, or losing my wife and family." He rested his chin on his folded hands for several moments, then drew himself up, narrowed his eyes, and said, "I guess the biggest problem with euphoria really is that it leads me into these ridiculous expectations. When I thought I was in love with Floretta, I truly thought it was going to be like that forever, but all it actually did was lead me from one crash to another."

The next session, he began as soon as he sat down.

"I want to start where we left off last time, about choosing divorce and depression rather than feeling inadequate or a failure, but I'm not sure where to begin." He gave me a questioning look.

"What comes to mind about inadequate and failure feelings?" I asked.

He nodded, "That's what's been on my mind since last time, and the more I think about it, I'm not even sure I've used the right words. I know I said, 'inadequate and failure,' but that's not how I really feel. Even without the euphoric feeling, I actually feel confident when I'm doing something that's within my reach, like setting up a computer system. What I've called being inadequate is how I feel when I've wanted to do something and couldn't, or wasn't allowed to, and felt helpless to do anything about it. That's what happened when I was afraid I couldn't get into graduate school and didn't have Sarah's smile, or when I was afraid my company would lay me off, and I wanted Evelyn to make me feel better."

He clasped his hands in his lap.

"I don't know where this comes from, but I do know the more we talk about this, the more I think that what I am talking about is feeling helpless."

"Helpless?" I asked.

"Helpless to growing up with three older sisters. They all were bigger and could do things I couldn't," he said, looking slightly puzzled. "But, the truth is none of them ever made me feel inferior or a failure when I was little." He frowned. "Everyone teased me in a loving way about being the baby of the family," he forced a sardonic smile, "but no one ever made fun of me for being smaller or behind everyone else."

"I'm not clear yet what you felt helpless to. What did you mean about 'growing up with three older sisters'?" I asked.

He pushed his jaw forward and pursed his lips.

"Helpless to wanting to be older, or bigger, or do what they did, or even hold my own with them. I did well in the first grade, but I wanted to be in the third grade like Janice because she could read and do arithmetic better than I could, and then I felt helpless, like a failure, because they wouldn't let me. Ruth made me feel better when she smiled and told me I was a big boy and that my time would come." With a lopsided smile, he said, "I guess her smile stuck, but her wisdom didn't."

"You haven't mentioned feelings about Janice before. Say more?" I asked.

"Janice was two years older. Ruth was seven years older, and Sandra was five years older. Janice was the one who did so many things I wanted to do but couldn't, because I was too little. She was, and still is, really nice, and I've always loved her. When I got upset because I couldn't be in the third, and fourth, and fifth grades, like she was, she'd teach me what she'd learned, like how to write longhand, and geography, and history. We played together, too, since we were so close in age. She and Ruth and I are still very close."

"You didn't say anything about you and Sandra, and sometimes the things we leave out are more important than the one's we mention," I commented with a questioning tone.

He frowned and was silent for three or four minutes. Then, in controlled, calm tones, he said, "I didn't intend to, but I lied to you a few minutes ago when I said, 'No one ever made me feel inferior or like a failure because I was little.' They all teased me about being the 'baby,' but everyone was good-natured about it except Sandra. She was mean, and made fun of me all the time. She'd say terrible things to me and make me cry, and then make fun of me for being 'Mommy's little cry baby,' and for being smaller and behind everyone else. When I'd ask Janice a question about school, Sandra would wait until no one else was around, and then say, 'See there, you're just a stupid little brat, you don't know anything.' One day when she said that to me, I cried, and said, 'Someday I'll be big like you, and you won't say those things to me,' and she said, 'Oh no you won't, because I'm five years older than you are, and no matter how old you are, I'll always be five years older than you.'"

His voice sounded harsh and demeaning as he quoted Sandra.

He looked at the wall as he waited for the roar of a low-flying plane to pass and appeared grateful for the respite.

"The worst thing she ever did to me happened, or started, when I was eight, and she was thirteen." He shook his head in utter dismay. "The damn bitch. I can't imagine I didn't remember this."

"Remember what?" I asked.

He scowled, clenching his jaw and staring at the wall.

"One day when no one else was at home, she asked me, 'How would you like to touch my naked breasts?' I realized later that she'd said it with a smirk, but at the time, I was too excited to notice. She could tell from my face how much I wanted to, so she opened her blouse, and took off her bra, and I couldn't wait to get my hands on them. Ooooh, my God," he said, in hushed, rhapsodic tones, remembering the moment, "I'd never had a feeling like that before, I was so thrilled I thought I could take off and fly. I still don't know what made her ask me, she must have been very proud of her breasts, since they had just started growing, but I felt so big to be playing with a girl's bare tits."

His face lighted up for several moments in his remembered rhapsody.

"But she still said cutting things like she always did. Even when I put my whole hand on her breast, she'd say,

'See there, I have something you don't, and you can't play with them unless I tell you you can. You just remember that.' When I listen to myself tell you about this, it may sound like what she said was kind of good-natured, but that's not the way she said it. She was cruel and made fun of me for wanting to touch her and that she had the power not to let me, and I felt so helpless when she would lead me on and then wouldn't let me touch her. It felt so crazy for her to be treating me both ways at the same time, first she'd let me play with her tits and make me feel like a million dollars, and then she'd rub my nose in being the littlest person in the world who couldn't do anything unless she said I could."

"Say more about helpless?" I asked.

"I got so mad at her when she would dangle her bait in front of me like that and then take it away, I wanted to hit her and really hurt her, but I was so little, and couldn't."

"This went on for about a year when we were by ourselves at home, and every time she'd let me touch her, I'd soar sky-high. It was the greatest feeling I could imagine. But then she hurt me more than she ever had." He looked as if he had been kicked in the stomach. "All of a sudden she stopped letting me feel her tits, and told me I couldn't do it anymore. She didn't say why, and I never knew for sure. It had felt so great to put my hands on her bare breasts, I thought it would last forever. I was so crushed. I hated her. But I didn't say anything about it to her because I kept hoping she'd change her mind and let me do it again."

"Say more about hating her?" I asked.

"I never knew if she'd stopped just to be mean. She knew I loved it so much, she had to have known how much it hurt me when she stopped letting me do it. I just hated her," he roared with anger, "and I hated her even more when she started dating boys soon after that and I knew those boys were putting their hands all over her tits, and maybe all over her body, and I hated those boys, too. When they came around, which they did all the time, I couldn't bear it. I wanted to kill them, so I just left the house until I knew they were gone.

"Now that I look at this thirty-five years later, I guess

she stopped with me because she was older and had gradu- ated to older boys, but just saying that makes me so furious, I could kill her even today," he fumed, in a deep rage.

"And in a crazy way, too, the more I hated her, the more I needed to get her back. Even before she'd let me put my hands on her breasts I wanted her to love me like Ruth and Janice did, and I was always so hurt when she said mean things to me. So when she let me touch her and made me feel so good, I thought that now she was finally going to love me, and, no matter how many bad things she said to me, as long as she let me put my hands on her I felt like she loved me. But then when she stopped, I not only lost that wonderful feeling of touching her, I felt like I'd lost her, too, and I was afraid that if she thought I was mad at her then I'd lose any chance of ever getting her back."

"What happened to your feelings after that?" I asked.

"They just dried up," he shrugged his shoulders, "and, eventually, I just stopped wanting her. Things between us just faded away. She grew up, and so did I. When we see each other now, we're cordial, and act like those days never happened. I still ache in my heart, though, not just because I long for those days, but because things never worked out between her and me, even in a normal brother-sister way.

"I've never told anyone about what she and I did to- gether. At the time I was afraid I'd get into trouble and they wouldn't let us be alone together any more. You're prob- ably the only one other than Sandra and me who knows about it because I assume she's never told anyone either.

"When I played with her breasts, it was so exciting I didn't think much about Ruth and Janice. But when she stopped letting me touch her, and I was really feeling bad, I started noticing Ruth's smile again, and Janice and I started playing together again."

He looked into space, seeming lost in thought, for two or three minutes.

"As you've told me this story, does anything sound fa- miliar to you?" I asked.

He thought several moments. "Only the long-lost memory of those special times with Sandra when she'd let me put my hands on her breasts. But I don't let myself think much about what happened anymore, because after we stopped I was so sad I didn't want to think about all the good feelings I had about it because I'd just get sad again."

"Is anything else about those feelings familiar?" I asked.

"No, I never had any experience like that before or since. I never did anything like that with Ruth, although I wanted to, or with Janice, or any girl in those years. In fact, I never had a girlfriend that I did things with like I did with Sandra."

"What about the part of the story where you felt inferior, and then a special woman made you feel big, and you soared with elation when she gave you unbelievably ecstatic sexual pleasures, and you thought it would last forever, and then she rejected you, and you were devastated and couldn't believe it, and you held on in the hope she would come back, but she never did, and never told you why?" I asked.

His eyes slowly widened, as he stared at me, then his expression became somber as he again looked into space several minutes.

"Jesus," he said, "all the time I was talking about Sandra, I used the very word, 'familiar,' to myself that you did a moment ago. I thought, 'this sounds familiar,' but it never occurred to me that what I was saying about Sandra was almost exactly the same as what I told you about Floretta." He spoke slowly, as if he could not believe what he was saying. "How could I not have seen that?"

We both were silent a few minutes, then I said, "Could the answer lie in what you've already suggested when you said, 'But I don't let myself think much about what happened anymore, because after we stopped I was so sad I didn't want to think about all the good feelings I had about it because I'd just get sad again'? Your feelings seemed to be telling you that they couldn't bear again the pain of Sandra's rejection when she pulled the floor from under your heady moments with her, that you felt desperate to get her back, and that you had to push those feelings underground and not allow them to come back until they would be safe, which they were for a while with Floretta."

He thought a few seconds, then said, "I know that's right,

because long before we began this work, when I'd have fleeting memories of what Sandra did to me, I'd immediately push them out of my mind. But I don't understand why I didn't just swear off, and say to myself, 'I'll never let this happen again.' Why did I do it all over again with Floretta?"

I said, "I'm sure you did say something like that to yourself, but our subconscious feelings have an agenda of their own and can override even our best judgment and most firm resolve. What I've heard your feelings say is, 'I loved Sandra so much, and I wanted her to love me like I loved her, that somehow I've got to get her back and make it come out right.' So when the right person came along at the right time, your feelings were compelled to make come out right with Floretta what didn't come out right with Sandra."

After reflecting on my interpretation, he responded, "That last thing you said, 'your feelings were compelled to make come out right with Floretta what didn't come out right with Sandra,' really resonates right. I told myself a thousand times, things like, 'Stop this, this is crazy, you're throwing good money after bad, this cannot possibly work,' but I felt driven to try to make it come out right anyway. I wonder if things ever do come out right if they're done for the wrong reason, like my love affair with Floretta was."

He mulled over what he had just said, then looked into space. "The other thing I'm still puzzled about is why I couldn't see the connection between what I just told you about Sandra and what had happened with Floretta, even when I kept saying to myself, 'this sounds familiar.'"

I responded, "Since you are inside yourself, perhaps your feelings can tell us more than we said earlier about the fear of remembering your hurt from Sandra's rejection. What comes to mind about it?"

"I don't really know why I asked you, as if I didn't already know the answer. I thought Floretta's and my love was so special that I just knew there couldn't possibly be any connection between it and any other love, that our love was so pure, and precious, and wonderful, and unique, there never had been, and never could be, anything like it, for anyone, anywhere, ever."

We both were silent, as he digested what he had said.

He continued. "After Sandra stopped letting me feel her breasts, seeing Ruth smile and playing games with Janice were, at first, a kind of let down, but pretty soon they felt a lot better than the roller coaster I had been on with Sandra, and that's also been true since Floretta."

"Ruth's smile didn't make you soar to the heavens like feeling Sandra's breasts did, but it did give you the warm confidence that made you not feel so helpless. Has anything like that happened since Floretta withdrew from you?" I asked.

He responded, "It's more complicated this time because of what you and I are doing. I remember telling you soon after we began that I knew I could actually do most of the things I was afraid I couldn't do without Ruth's smile. Of course that was obvious, since I did them, because all her smile did was give me the confidence to use the abilities I already had, like the ones that got me into graduate school or a new job. Her smile hadn't, nor could it have, created in me any new actual abilities, but I got so dependent on the confidence and energy I got from Ruth's, or Evelyn's, or Floretta's, smile, that I got to believing I'd be a failure if their smiles weren't there.

"That's where this work comes in and why this time is different from when I was little. You and I started working together shortly after Floretta stopped smiling at me. Before, that would've made me desperate for some other woman's smile. But, as you and I have worked out those inferiority feelings of having had my nose rubbed in being the smallest, especially the ones I felt from Sandra, I don't seem to need those smiles any longer. These days I can pretty much do whatever I'm called on for, whether it's for me or something I have to do for someone else—and I don't need a woman's smile to do them."

Shortly before completing his self-knowledge therapy, Mr. Stetson reflected, "It was as if I didn't know what I knew, that there aren't any magical solutions to real problems. If there's one thing I learned from my computer work, it's that you can't just kick, slap, or bless a computer and expect that all of a sudden its bugs will go away. There's no substitute for facing and working out the problems in computers or relationships, especially the unavoidable differences that come up when two people try to work out their lives together. Of all the things you've said, I remember the story of your three marriages the most."

Mr. Stetson was referring to my response to something he had said much earlier in our work. When he once said, "You talk about marriage with a view I don't have yet," I had responded, "Well, maybe that's because of my wife's and my three marriages." When his face showed puzzlement bordering on alarm, I continued, "Our first marriage lasted, oh, probably fifteen to twenty years, when we not only loved but also resented each other at times for not satisfying each of our infantile expectations we had convinced ourselves would be fulfilled by our partner when we got married." His puzzled look continued, but a slight knowing smile suggested that he was already getting the point. "And in our second marriage, which lasted, oh, ten to fifteen years, we each learned to accept, and respect, and love each other as separate persons, each with our own individual identities and needs." By then his broader smile and nod indicated he understood, so I continued, "And in our third marriage, by now ten to fifteen years, we're enjoying living out our lives with the happiness, and contentment, and rewards that go with two people who have ironed out the wrinkles of their lives together."

Every married person or couple, young or old, to whom I have told this abridged version of a marriage that has lasted, has indicated that of all the insights they have gained about the qualities necessary for an enduring intimate relationship, the observations embedded in this story were the most meaningful and memorable.

Society's values today are different from earlier generations; people now are more apt to avoid the rough spots of marriage by divorcing their spouse, rather than hold fast to their union and solve its problems.

The unspoken expectation in the beginning of all marriages is that one will recapture through one's partner the ecstasy of wish fulfillment and happy bliss one had in infancy and early childhood, as Mr. Stetson tried to do. If one intends to succeed in marriage, and sticks with that goal, though, one will be forced by nature, sooner or later, to respect and fulfill his partner's unreasonable, as well as reasonable, wishes, and to compromise and, at times, relinquish, rather than expect full gratification of, one's own desires. People who want to grow and mature learn there is no way to avoid facing, accepting, and solving the normal conflicts of any intimate relationship.

Enduring marriages have certain notable advantages: the core family remains intact, memories can be relived and shared, the security of accumulated assets is preserved, and both partners mature more solidly by working through their differences. These advantages, however, are not usually given much weight when one feels desperate to relieve his disappointment, and believes that his fantasy of regaining the heavenly bliss that life seemed to have promised could be found with another partner.

Several months after Mr. Stetson concluded his self-knowledge therapy, he called to discuss the referral of a friend to me. While we talked, he said, "Sarah and I have remarried and our life together is going extremely well. I've grown, and she's grown, too. She works hard at being more sexually interested and involved, and that feels like the kind of real smile healthy marriage partners normally give each other. But it's not just what she does, it's also that since I no longer have to have a woman's smile to reassure me, or for her to be sexually responsive every time I want to make love, I can respect and love her for who she is, and that makes it so much easier for both of us to do what we need to, to make our 'second marriage' work. Sarah was as genuine before as she is now, but I was so desperate for that special smile I couldn't see anything else. You said once that 'infantile expectations' are the cardinal enemy of marriage. I didn't know what you meant then, but I know now that mine was needing that great feeling I got when I saw Ruth's smile. Since I'm beyond that now, I can see that someday Sarah and I will have that "third marriage" you talked about.

7

The More He Mistreats Me, The More I Love Him

Marcia Green, a well-dressed, naturally attractive, thin woman in her early thirties, avoided my eyes when I greeted her in the waiting area. She nodded when I introduced myself, and remained expressionless as she entered the consultation room, sat, and adjusted herself in the chair. In response to my invitation, "Perhaps you can begin where you feel comfortable, and we can take it from there?" she looked at the floor and said nothing.

After two or three minutes of silence, still looking at the floor, she said, "Mr. Bernard [her attorney] sent me to see you because he says I can't cooperate in my own defense. He said my husband, Fred, is making outrageous demands on me in our divorce settlement, and I'm acting crazy because I won't do anything to stop him."

Another long silence passed.

"I wasn't sure about seeing you," she said, frowning. "I don't really want to hear what you think. Mr. Bernard says I need to fight my husband, but I can't bring myself to do it. I assume you and Mr. Bernard are realistic about these things, but he's so hard-hearted, and I don't want to hurt my husband."

Several moments later, she lifted her head enough to look at me and ask, "Has Mr. Bernard already told you all this?"

"He did call to pave the way and give me an overview, but he didn't go into detail. Can you tell me more about what brought you here?" I asked.

"What did he tell you?" she asked.

"Actually, even less than you just did, so I know very little."

While she paused again, I pondered whether I could ease her way best by offering a lead, or by remaining silent so she could respond when she felt ready. Before I could decide, she took a deep breath, exhaled in a big sigh and said, "Well, here goes.

"Fred and I have been married five years, and we lived together for two years before that. We dated in college six years before that, but he left me for someone else."

Another long silence followed, but her expression told me she was concentrating on her thoughts, and I did not want to intrude.

Frowning slightly, she resumed her story. "A few months after I finished college I married Mitchell. Then instead of going to work I took care of his two kids while he drank with his friends and played around with other women. We stayed married two years, until he found someone else and divorced me."

She stared into empty space; her frown faded, then reappeared. After a few minutes I thought some troubling idea with mixed feelings must have occurred to her and she didn't know where to start, so I asked, "Can you say what you're thinking?"

Looking directly at me, she sighed, glanced out the window, then turned back.

"Fred and I saw each other at a party a year after my divorce from Mitchell, and we immediately picked up where we had left off before."

Her hands flew to her mouth as she tried to swallow her tears, but could not, and she cried for several moments.

"I still loved Fred," she choked out, "and wanted to get married, but he said he'd leave me before he'd marry, and that would've torn me apart, so we just moved in together." Tears flowed down her cheeks. "He never would have married me if his mother hadn't pushed him. I was surprised when he finally did, but she has more of a hold on him than anyone, least of all me."

Burying her face in her arms, she cried for several minutes before she could sit up and continue.

"The truth is, we've never gotten along. He's impossible to please. I wanted children—I still do—and begged him to agree, but he said he would leave me first. I could've gotten pregnant anyway, but I knew he'd leave if I did, and that scared me to death."

I waited while she cried silently and stared out the window, then I asked, "Can you say more about being scared to death if he left?"

Her face tightened as she looked at me, wary and undecided.

"I've lived in constant fear our whole marriage that he would leave," she said, at last. "But he's always been a good provider—he works for a developer finding land for building resorts and housing developments. But he travels a lot and leaves me alone most of the time—just like my father did—and when he is home, he's always critical. He never agrees with me and always demands that I go along with whatever he wants. We never take vacations I want or go to movies I like, and I think he insists on getting his way just to say no to me. But whatever reason he gives, we always do what he says."

Returning her gaze to the floor, she said, "I sound like a crybaby, and you probably think I'm making all this up. But if you don't believe me, talk with Mr. Bernard. He said even Fred's lawyer rolls his eyes when they talk about Fred's demands."

Her having given only a one sentence response to my question about "being scared to death" if Fred left, before she avoided the question by quickly assuring me "he's always been a good provider," then going on to express her hurt about his self-centeredness, suggested to me the power and depth of her fear of losing him. Her worry that I might think she was a "crybaby" was equally striking since her grievances had already been validated by two professionals—Mr. Bernard and, implicitly, Fred's own attorney. Experience had taught me, though, that this early in our work she would not feel ready to talk directly about either her fear of losing Fred or her resentment about his selfishness, and any attempt to explore it at this time would be counterproductive.

"Fred was an only child and never had to share anything with anyone," she continued, with a hint of scorn. "Even his mother told me, 'I love Fred because he's my son, but I know he's a spoiled and selfish child who mistreats others to get what he wants.'" She pursed her lips. "I don't know why, but I love Fred no matter how badly he treats me, and sometimes I think the more he mistreats me, the more I love him and am afraid I'll lose him," she said, as tears formed.

As she began crying again, she said, "I'm so mixed up I don't know how to feel. Fred wants a divorce, but I'm so afraid of losing him I can't say no to anything he wants, and Mr. Bernard says he can't protect me if I don't agree to his fighting Fred, but I can't fight back because I'll hurt Fred and make him mad at me and I'll lose him for sure, and it's all so crazy because I've already lost him anyway."

She held her hand to her mouth until she stopped crying enough to say, "Mr. Bernard is right, Fred's demands are outrageous and I should fight him, but I just can't."

I waited for her feelings to settle, then asked, "What all is he demanding?"

Looking at the floor, she sighed quietly. "He wants everything but the house and family car, and Mr. Bernard says that's unfair."

"What makes it unfair?" I asked.

She shifted, as though in pain, and glared at me, as if I, too, were being unfair.

"We bought our house a year ago with a minimum down payment that left us with $3,000 monthly mortgage payments," she said, looking back at the floor. "I'm a wholesale buyer of women's clothes, and I don't have the income to pay bills like that. I'd have to sell the house, and, with very little equity in it and the housing market down like it is, I'd have to take a big loss and wind up in debt. Our Chevy is paid off, but it's eight years old and every month it needs repairs I can't afford. Mr. Bernard says this is unfair because it leaves me with nothing and puts me deep in debt."

She stared at the floor.

"You haven't yet told me what your husband gets according to his plan."

Again she glared at me. "Well, he gets our beach house."

Silence.

"How much do you owe on it?"

"Nothing, it's paid off."

Silence.

"What else does he want?"

"The Porsche."

Silence.

"How much does he owe on it?"

"Nothing."

Silence.

"What else does his plan give him?"

"His retirement."

Silence.

"What other savings do you have?"

"None."

Silence.

"How much alimony would he give you?"

"None."

Silence.

"Who wants this divorce?"

"He does."

Silence.

"Can you sense how come I'm having to practice dental psychiatry and extract all this from you?"

With a hint of a forced, knowing smile and nod of her head, she responded, "Yes, because you're trying to make my husband look bad. You're just like Mr. Bernard. Fred is a good man, and I love him, and all these questions make him look bad. He's not all bad. He takes good care of his mother, and the people at his work like him. And he can be very sweet at times. You should have seen how tender he was with a little sparrow the other day when it flew into our picture window and was knocked unconscious. It brought me to tears when I saw him pick it up and hold it so gently until it could fly away."

She looked relieved, as though she had acquitted her husband of appearing selfish and greedy.

I asked, "Earlier you put together Fred's mistreatment of you with loving him and being afraid to lose him. Has this ever happened before with anyone else?"

Looking out the window, she frowned before continuing.

"I've never thought about it like that," she said slowly, returning her gaze to the floor.

"Now that you are thinking about it that way, what occurs to you?" I asked.

A minute of silence passed.

"Well, I really don't want to think about them now, but before I married Mitchell and Fred, I had several boyfriends who didn't last long. Nothing really bad happened, but all of them, including Fred, took me for granted. They stood me up on dates while they went out with other girls, or came by out of the blue just to have sex. Whenever I was committed to someone, I never had sex, or even went out, with anyone else. In college, and when we got back together later, Fred treated me well in the beginning, and I thought he was the man of my dreams, but it didn't last long either time."

Brushing away the tears that had crept into her eyes, she went on.

"I hadn't thought about them being the same, but Fred does act like my father did when I was growing up. Well, maybe I have thought they were a lot alike, but I never thought it meant anything. I've always just assumed that was the way life was."

Her voice sounded mournful, yet with this insight she began to have an awareness of her despair from a lifetime of accepting others' abuses.

"I started getting depressed a few months ago. I had been trying so hard to make our marriage work, then Fred started hinting he wanted a divorce and what he would expect in the settlement." She held her hands to her mouth until she could suppress her tears. "When I talked to Dr. Russell, my family doctor, he referred me to a psychiatrist who gave me some antidepressant drug that didn't help. I did feel a kind of lift, but it didn't fix my marriage problems or help me think about how to fix them," she said, drying her eyes with a tissue.

"When I told Mr. Bernard about the drug treatment and that I didn't want to fight Fred, he said, 'Of course drugs didn't help, even a lawyer can tell you that. You have good reason to be depressed when your husband wants to force a preposterous settlement on you, and you can't bring yourself to fight it. Drugs can't fix that any more than lawyers can without your cooperation. If you weren't depressed about all this you'd have a bigger problem than depression.'"

As she quoted Mr. Bernard, she leaned back in her chair and spoke with a focus and ease not present before.

"At first I thought Mr. Bernard was just against people taking those kinds of drugs, but then he said, 'Medication can help some problems but yours is not one of them. Your problem is you can't stop yourself from giving in to a selfish, mean, undeserving husband, and if you don't do something about whatever inside is making you behave this way, it will not only ruin your fair rights in this settlement and wreck your future finances, it will continue to destroy any hope you have for a meaningful relationship with anyone.'"

I asked, "What did you think about what he said?"

She hesitated for a moment. "Before answering that, I want to say that when I just told you what Mr. Bernard said, that was the first time I had ever said it out loud, even to myself, and, as soon as I said it, I realized I had taken his opinion seriously. What he said actually didn't come as a real surprise. A lot of people have told me I'm my own worst enemy, so when he said the same thing, it rang enough bells for me to do something about it, so I called you."

Ms. Green's voice had become stronger and more confident as she described her new perspective.

"When the psychiatrist gave me the medicine, he said a 'chemical imbalance' caused my problem. But when I asked him what caused the imbalance, he said he didn't know, and when I asked, 'Why can't I stand up against Fred,' he said, 'It's because you've been depressed your whole life.' But that didn't make sense either, because I haven't had trouble standing up for myself with people who aren't important to me."

She glanced at her watch, looked startled, then asked, "Is our time up already? When do we meet next?"

I asked if the same time two days later would work out for her, and she said it would. We stood, shook hands, and, on leaving, she smiled, and said, "This time went faster than I'd expected, and I've got a lot more to say."

We had actually met for a double session, which I customarily arrange for a first visit.

The next session, she grimaced as she began.

"When Mr. Bernard said that my behavior would continue to destroy any hope I have for a meaningful relationship with anyone, it really bothered me, but I think he's right because of the men I choose." She glanced out the window, then at the floor.

After several seconds, I said, "I can sense this is painful. You said Mr. Bernard told you Fred's demands were unfair. Does it hurt to recognize that you, too, think Fred is unfair?"

"Yes, I feel hurt, and I'm afraid."

"Can you sense afraid of what?" I asked.

She closed her eyes, her whole face tightening in pain.

"I think I'm afraid that if I really let myself see how selfish and unfair he is to me, I'll lose him. But that's stupid, because you can't actually have somebody who thinks only of himself the way Fred does, and the truth is I've never really had him anyway."

In what by now had become her manner when mulling over thoughts, she looked out the window for several moments.

"I said earlier," she began slowly, "'the more he mistreats me, the more I love him and am afraid I'll lose him,' but now I think it's the other way around—the more I'm afraid I'll lose him, the more I love him and have to have him and am willing to let him mistreat me.

"He's never physically hurt me, but he does hurt me in every other way, and I don't do anything about it, and I know it's because I'm afraid I'll lose him." She began fiddling with her earring. "I've been so down about this I don't have as much energy as usual. Most mornings I don't even want to get up. I don't sleep well anymore, and my appetite isn't what it used to be, although I haven't lost any weight."

Putting her hand to her eye, she said, "Excuse me for a moment, my contact is blurry," then removed and reinserted the lens.

"My life with men has always been this way, but I've never been down like this before. I usually get along well with my clients and friends, and most people don't take advantage of me. Even if they try to, I don't have any trouble stopping them, but with Fred it's like it's been with almost every man I've ever known." With a rueful smile, she added, "I said 'almost' because I've known a couple of men who were interested in me and treated me well, but for some reason I was never interested in them."

Raising her eyebrows, she looked at me. "I said I'd let a man mistreat me rather than lose him, but why would I choose someone like that in the first place? I know I'd be far less likely to lose a man who treated me well than someone who treated me like Fred and Mitchell did."

As her emotional curiosity took hold over the following months, she became able to work through her resistance to recognizing how her fear of loss made her afraid to feel anger toward her abusers. Each session she had fewer long silences and less need for me to drag thoughts out of her.

In one session, when reflecting on why she had needed to choose men who mistreated her, she said, "Sooner or later men seem to know I'm afraid of losing them, and

Fred has known this all along. He's never concerned about me or what I want, or I how I feel about what he wants. He got his new Porsche even though we couldn't actually afford it. I can live without having my way, but why should I always be the one who has to give in? He and I have never talked about it, but he's known from the beginning that I'm so afraid of losing him, or even his being unhappy with me, that I can't even disagree with him. Sometimes he's outright mean," she said clenching her fist, "like when he's willing to leave me in debt in this divorce settlement."

I said, "This is first time you've allowed yourself to know how angry you feel about the way he treats you. Can you sense what freed you?"

Raising her clenched fist, as if ready to strike, she responded, "It came when I said 'he's outright mean.' I've always known this has been inside, but I've never really felt it before. I just wish I could put him through the wringer like he does me, and maybe I can before this is over, although I don't have anything to threaten him with since he's not afraid of losing me."

Looking determined, she sat up straighter.

"After I said earlier that I get along well with clients and friends, I realized that sometimes it's because in small ways I give in to them the same way I do with Fred. Not as bad as with Fred because they don't demand as much as he does, but I almost always do the accommodating and don't insist that they do what I want. My clients like it and want to do business with me, and that's okay because it's part of 'the customer is always right,' but when my friends make me give in to them, I feel like I don't really count," she said, lifting her open palms in a gesture of confused helplessness, then dropping them into her lap as she drooped into her chair.

"Now that I'm thinking about it, I see I've done this my whole life. I choose men who take advantage of me and then, when we have trouble or disagree, I give in to them and hate myself for it. I did it with Mitchell in my first marriage, and if he hadn't walked out on me I'd have stayed with him and let him use me as a baby-sitter for his kids, and I'd never have had a life of my own. And before that, I'm sure I would've stayed with my father, too, if I hadn't run away and married Mitchell. And I suppose I'd have clung to Fred and let him keep abusing me if Mr. Bernard hadn't talked to me the way he did and sent me to you."

Her inclusion of her father with the men who had abused her and to whom she would have continued to cling, had external events not supervened, opened the door to our understanding how her lifelong self-defeating behaviors had become ingrained during her developmental years. Although she had mentioned certain elements of this history earlier, it had been before she had become ready to make use of them with her new take-charge-of-my-own-life attitude.

I asked, "You said you would have kept doing it with your father, too, if you hadn't run away and married Mitchell. What did 'doing it with my father' mean?"

The room was warm, but she wrapped her arms around herself as though she were cold.

"I only had my father at home, not even a brother or sister. I was close to Dad, but he was a salesman and out of town most of the time, and my mother was so far away. They divorced when I was six."

As she held herself, her eyes drifted and she seemed to disappear into the past right in front of me. After a few minutes, she sighed and continued. "I didn't see her much after that," she said wistfully. "She moved to Sweden, where she was from, and I went to visit her every two or three years, but I hated going because she was so distant— she pretended to love me, but I always knew she didn't, really. After I'd travelled all the way to Sweden just to be with her, she'd go out on dates and leave me with some Swedish sitter who couldn't speak English, and then when I had to leave to come back home, that was terrible too. I didn't really want to stay with her, but leaving her was much worse." Her voice had sunk so low I could barely hear her.

"Mother was Swedish, and she and Dad married while he was on furlough from his army post in Germany. She had won a beauty contest, and she always acted like being a beauty queen was the most important thing in her life. She always seemed more interested in who made her feel pretty than in wanting to be with me."

Then her face showed a ghost of a smile. "People have told me that she and I were very close when I was little, before they divorced. I don't remember it well, but I have good feelings about it."

Still slumped in her chair, she gazed out the window. When she turned back to speak, her face had become mournful again. "The last time I saw Mother was when I was sixteen; she died of cancer two months after I came back from that trip. I didn't find out until much later that she had died, and I never got over the shock," she said, as her eyes filled. "I still don't understand why Dad waited so long to tell me. I've always wished I could have had time to know her better," she said, and started to sob.

She cried for several minutes. As her tears lessened, she wiped her eyes, and continued.

"After Mother left, Dad was all I had. He remarried when I was eight, but his second wife, Nancy, was mean and cold. I think she hated me. She was always busy, and I was glad because I was afraid to be around her. There were sitters who came and went, but none of them stayed long. Whenever I got to know one well, something would happen and she'd disappear. My father never told me why the sitters didn't stay, and when I asked him, he'd get irritated so I didn't ask any more. Aunt Eva, Mother's sister, who didn't like Dad, told me after I grew up that they left because Dad came onto them sexually, but I never saw any of that, and I don't even know if it was true."

I said, "When I asked you to talk about accepting abuse from your father, like you did from Mitchell and Fred, you talked about your mother's abandonment and your stepmother's coldness. Say more about how they belong together?" I asked.

Her eyes widened and she stared at me.

"I don't know," she said, "let me think about it a minute."

"Dad was the only one I had," she resumed. "He was inconsiderate and insensitive, but I knew he loved me. No one else did. He didn't really treat me so bad, it was just that I would've done anything not to lose him. He divorced Nancy when I was twelve, and I was his housekeeper after that. He usually criticized how I did things, and he came and went as if I didn't count. But at least I had him. I would have done anything for him, because nothing was as bad as when Mother left, and I never," she shook her head, "wanted to feel that way again."

She glanced at her watch, then said, "I guess I'll have to stop. I know we're already overtime, and I heard your next appointment come in, but I'll start next time with where I left off today." She stood, smiled, and said, "See you Tuesday."

The next session, she began as though no time had passed since we had last met.

"Before I married Mitchell, I always wanted to be at home with Dad and be sure he was all right, so I didn't go out or date much in high school. About all I did outside home was go to church with Dad, which I loved because it brought back good memories of when Mother and he and I all went to church together. I don't know why, but I always felt so comforted when I sat with Dad and saw Christ on the cross. I don't remember feeling that way when I went with Mother, I just know I did. When I was a teenager, most of my friends were in the church youth groups.

"After high school I went to the community college instead of the state university just so I could live with Dad. The only way I ever could have left home was to elope with Mitchell the way I did. Dad really got upset when I ran away, and I was so afraid of facing him I didn't go to see him for two months, but since I had Mitchell, I wasn't afraid of having the bad feeling."

"Can you talk about the bad feeling?" I asked.

Her eyes darted away from me, first at the woods outside, then at her wedding ring she was rolling between her fingers.

"I can't even think about it. It's too upsetting."

"Say more about upsetting?" I asked.

Shooting me a hostile look, as if I were an enemy, she said, "I said I can't talk about it."

"Actually you said, 'I can't even think about it'. Are you saying you're afraid to think about it because just thinking about the bad feeling brings it on?"

The question hung in the air. At last she responded, "It isn't the thinking or talking about the bad feeling that's upsetting, it's having the feeling, but the problem is that the bad feeling comes even if I just think about it." Then she became quiet for several moments.

"I've told some people what happened with Dad and Mother, but I've never talked about it in a way that made me have the bad feeling before," she said.

"Did you notice the feeling creep in when you were talking just then?" I asked.

"Yes, but only for a second."

"Can you say what made it too upsetting?"

"No, it didn't stay long enough," she answered, testily.

"Can you sense what made it go away so quickly?"

"I don't know," she exclaimed, "it's just too upsetting."

After a short pause, she smiled faintly. "I'm learning I don't really want to find out." Then, she relaxed and settled into her chair. "I guess I push the feeling out of my mind because I know it will be too upsetting."

I asked, "How long have you known the bad feeling?"

"As long as I can remember," she answered, and her pained tone suggested to me she felt stymied and needed help.

While she paused, I thought about her fear that the bad feeling would make her too upset, and wondered to myself how I could help her feel safe enough to expose the feeling so we could work on it together and help her understand what made it dreadful.

I said, "When you said you pushed the thought out of your mind because it would be too upsetting, and later added that it had been there as long as you could remember, I wondered if when we put the two together, did they become something like many people feel about green vegetables. As children, we often think spinach and broccoli are so yucky we refuse to eat any green vegetable, and, never knowing anything different, many of us continue to feel that way when we grow up. Only after we discover as adults that vegetables can be made tasty are we willing to eat vegetables we would never have even considered as children."

Her frown of concentration told me she was following my analogy, so I continued.

"In the same way, when we are little and feel alone and hurt, the feelings seem unbearable and as though they will last forever because at that time our undeveloped mind is too helpless to know we can understand our feelings from a position of strength. But then, as adults, we find we can master our feeling problems in ways we couldn't as children, like you did when you eloped with Mitchell. The marriage to Mitchell may not have been a good one, and it didn't erase your bad feelings forever, but it did show you that you did not have to accept being held hostage to your feelings and remain your Dad's slave."

Nodding her head subtly, she responded, "What you said makes sense to me. I've lived long enough to know I'm not really dependent on Fred, and some part of me wants him out of my life. The problem is the bad feeling I get when I think about him not being with me."

In the previous weeks and months, step by painful step, Ms. Green had become aware of the price she was paying for her "bad feeling" and had begun the process of overcoming her self-defeating behaviors by confronting the feeling. Now, rather than avoid the feeling, her response showed she was no longer as intimidated by it.

I said, "Your thoughts about the bad feeling keep coming back. Perhaps that's the bad feeling's way of saying, 'Maybe it's time for you to be free of me, that you don't have to fear me any more, and that if you will bear me a little bit at a time, you will gradually understand I'm not as fearsome now as you felt I was when you were still a little girl'."

In the silence that followed, her eyes filled with tears. "I've never done this before," she said. "This feeling is so awful because it makes me feel empty, like there's nothing inside me, just big holes in my stomach and chest." She clasped her hands to her chest. "When I think of never seeing Fred again I feel so alone in the world, and that I would do anything to get him back. I feel alone even though I have friends, and sad even if I lose someone who treats me badly. I don't want to eat, or work, or even go on living." Her clasped hands gripped each other tightly, and her face had gone white.

"It's these holes in my chest and stomach that keep me from thinking and talking about the bad feeling. They're the worst feelings in the world because they make me feel like I'm nothing," she said, in a flat, barely audible voice.

"It was horrible when Mitchell left me. I felt like dying, like I had no reason to live. I didn't like his kids, but taking care of them made me feel connected to Mitchell. And now I don't have anybody. I just want to cry forever."

"If the crying could talk, can you sense what it would say?" I asked.

Fighting to hold back her tears, she said, "I hate looking like a blubbering idiot, it makes me feel so weak. I think the reason I want to cry is because I started to talk about running off and leaving Dad, and I felt so guilty about deceiving and hurting him." She began to cry. "I just ran off. I'm an honest person, and I wasn't honest with him. He was worried sick about me for three days before I called to let him know I was all right. It was like I was telling him he wasn't important to me, and I know how that hurts," she said, and broke down, sobbing uncontrollably.

"I told him how sorry I was so many times," she looked away and cried, "and he understood, but I feel guilty anyway." She held her hands to her face and cried more. "I knew that eloping with Mitchell was the only way I could leave home," she broke down and sobbed, "but I never understood that I did it so I wouldn't have to face how I felt about leaving Dad."

She cried uninterrupted for several minutes before she

could continue speaking.

"It's harder to remember how I felt when Mother left, I was so little, but I do remember some things." She paused to dry her face with a tissue. "I was six and I remember liking my first grade teacher and playing with my friends at school. But I'm so mixed up about it all. I really loved my mother, and I remember when I was really little how she'd read to me, and we'd go to Sunday school and church together."

Though her crying had eased momentarily as she recalled pleasant memories, she suddenly burst into tears, saying, "Then she left without ever saying goodbye to me. Someone said she had a nervous breakdown, but I didn't know what that meant so I never understood why she left."

"Did you ever find out?" I asked.

Still crying, she shook her head. "I remember Aunt Eva explaining to me what happened, but it was so soon after Mother left that nothing made any sense, and I never wanted to ask her or anyone else after that."

"How did you explain it to yourself?" I asked.

She burst into profuse, uncontrollable sobbing, unable to talk for several minutes, then, trying to make herself talk over her tears, she cried out, "I never understood, I never understood. Mother just disappeared, and I never understood why. She was there, and then she was gone. I loved her and needed her so much I didn't understand how she could have left me, and I've never understood," she wailed, as her tears overwhelmed her. "I always blamed myself for it, but I never knew what I did wrong. I was so sad after she left. I was all alone. I didn't know where she was, or what had happened to her, or what was wrong with her."

She cried for several minutes, until she was able to talk.

"Dad was gone so much, and when he was there he didn't talk to me, and he never told me about Mother, and I was afraid to ask because I just knew something bad had happened, and that I'd caused it, and I didn't want him or anyone to say she was really gone and would never come back and that I had caused it." She took a tissue from the box on the lamp table and wiped her eyes. "It was so terrible knowing I could never have her back; I would have done *anything*, and would still do anything, to have her back and make up for what I did wrong."

Overwhelmed by her feelings and tears, she sat quietly for several minutes.

By having faced and survived her most dreaded feelings—her helpless loss of her mother and guilt for thinking she had caused it—she had reached a turning point in her self-knowledge therapy and her life.

After several weeks of digesting and integrating into her emotions what she had come to know about herself, she said, during one session, "I think I haven't really told you how far I've gone sometimes to make the bad feeling go away." She shook her head and looked disapproving. "I was too ashamed to tell you before, but I've clung to men any way I could. I didn't just give in to Fred and take care of Dad and Mitchell, I let some men use me for sex just so I wouldn't lose them."

Her eyes filled with tears, as she began to speak. "I once read a book called *The Fifty Minute Hour*, about a psychotherapy patient who said, as best I remember, 'I miss my father so much I would scrub Charles Street [Baltimore] from one end to the other with a toothbrush if I could just have him back.' That feeling has been with me as long as I can remember."

Glancing out the window, she said, "This seems farfetched now, but I was willing to fail if that was what it took to keep someone I loved from leaving me. The reason I went to community college wasn't just to be near Dad and take care of him, but because he didn't approve of the highly educated, successful women he thought came out of the university. I intentionally made bad grades until I realized," she smiled slightly, "that I didn't have to tell him. Once, after I was working and no longer living at home, I turned down a promotion at my company because I knew he would disapprove. I did accept it when they offered it again a year later, though, but I didn't tell him."

As she sometimes did when she began to feel angry, she starting swinging her right leg.

"I really hate stories about women playing dumb to 'get a man,' but that's what I did. Actually, I didn't do it to get a man, I did it to keep him so I wouldn't feel desperate about losing him."

I said, "You talked about men who abused you when you were an easy mark, and then you said—in your tone even more than your words—how much you hated stories about women doing anything to 'get a man,' or, for you, keep a man. What are you saying about your feelings toward men who made you do anything they wanted, knowing that you would do anything not to lose them?"

She did not respond at once, but her face became grim. Then she said, "I'm bitter beyond words. I've always known I hate anybody who abuses other people, but I especially hate the men who've exploited and taken advantage of me, which is what Fred is trying to do to me right now."

With her leg swinging rapidly up and down, she folded her arms tightly across her chest. "These feelings are so strong, it's hard to believe I wasn't aware of them before we started working, but I've been so afraid this bitterness would show and I'd lose Fred or any man I hated." She paused and clenched her teeth, and I could almost see steam shooting from her nostrils and ears. "I feel sorry for women who let themselves be abused like I have, but even more I hate the fucking bastards who do it to them. I hate Fred and I hate Mitchell for what they did, and I hate my father for taking me for granted." Again, she clenched her fist. "I feel this so deeply, it's in my soul, and it's been there as long as I've needed someone so much I'd do anything to keep them."

She abruptly stopped swinging her leg, dropped her fist into her lap, and heaved a big sigh.

"It's not the same with Mother. I know I felt she abandoned me when she went away and then died, but she was sick and couldn't help it, and anyway she didn't hurt me and exploit me like men have.

"I know the fact that I've kept all this bottled up inside has made my depression worse, and I feel some relief just talking about it." She almost smiled. "Since you didn't get mad and walk out when I talked that way about men—and I'm very much aware you are one, too—I think I won't be as paralyzed as I have been."

This was the second major turning point in Ms. Green's self-knowledge therapy. The first—rooting out the causes of her unbearable pain left over from the loss of her mother —had allowed her to work more freely within the therapeutic sessions, and now—facing her fear of losing the men who had abused her, and her rage at them—would give her more freedom in her regular life, including becoming able to work effectively with her attorney in challenging Fred.

Ms. Green solidified her progress still further by actively recalling the mechanisms she had used in earlier years to manage her fears. "The hardest part when I was growing up was feeling so helpless. Until we put my being Dad's slave girl and taking shit from Mitchell and Fred together with Mother's going away, which I'd barely remembered, I didn't know what was wrong or what I could do about it.

"When I was young, what helped me most was going to church, and I'm sure that's why I still go." She smiled at the warm memory. "I got especially involved when I was a teenager because I needed something to help me through the emptiness at home. By then Dad had divorced Nancy so she wasn't even there, and even though she'd been distant and I didn't like her, at least she'd been there until then. We'd had good conversations sometimes, and she went to church with Dad and me."

The depth of Ms. Green's absorption in recalling how she dealt with the emptiness and bad feelings of her teen years made unnecessary and out-of-place any remarks I could have offered.

"I always felt comforted when I saw Christ on the cross and when I heard people say that someone was a good person because 'she carries her cross well.' When I was married to Mitchell, and, until recently, with Fred, I lifted my spirits by thinking that I carried my cross well," she said, with a smile that reflected her inner calm.

"I also used to console myself by remembering that Jesus said to 'turn the other cheek.' For a while that made good sense if it happened only once, but I never understood why I had to keep turning my cheek when people would slap me, first on one side, and then on the other as long I was willing. But that's what I did; I felt stronger and it seemed so right since God approved of it.

"Mr. Bernard was right about most things but not about why I was depressed," she said with a knowing smile. "He thought I was depressed because Fred mistreated me, but that wasn't really it. Actually, I felt good knowing I could bear my cross like Jesus. I was depressed because I was afraid of losing Fred and was helpless to do anything about it."

Ms. Green's awareness that her depression was due not to Fred's abuse of her but to her helpless fear of losing him, shows how assuming a seemingly obvious reason for a person's depression, or any other emotional condition, can be misleading, and how the actual cause usually lies in the mind's deeper layers that are accessible only through self-understanding.

The critical elements of clinical depression are feelings of loss, helplessness, and, frequently, suppressed rage, and Ms. Green faced all three. A sense of utter, hopeless futility also occurs in severe instances, and is the primary factor that disposes a depressed person to suicide. Ms. Green's feelings of strength and worthiness, through her identification with Jesus in enduring abuse, protected her from this additional symptom.

These elements of depression are especially powerful when a child experiences in early life the loss of her primary love-giver and source of self-identity and self-worth. Ordinarily, the earlier the loss, the more powerful its impact, the deeper the scars, and the greater one's later susceptibility to depression. When such a loss occurs, the extreme helplessness of infancy results in a child's inability to protect herself from the overwhelming pain of loss, express her rage in protest, or supply her own sense of self-identify, self-worth, or being lovable.

Though the availability of a loving caretaker to replace the lost loved one is invaluable in lessening this trauma, the pain of internal loss, due to both the wrenching away of the child's deeply bonded loved one and the living in lonely emptiness that follows, can cause the child to feel these states even when the loss is softened by the nurture of a fully devoted surrogate caretaker.

Marcia had not lost her mother until she was six, and, as a result, her trauma was not as great as it would have been had the loss occurred much earlier. By six her development had enabled her to weather the two years between her mother's going away and her father's marriage to Nancy, the relative emptiness during the Nancy years that followed, and the teenage years after Nancy left. Her early church experience, where she felt especially close to her mother and father, laid the groundwork for her identification with Christ—who also endured great suffering—that would reinforce her internal strength and sustain her through her worst times.

When the scars of such losses, and the child's inevitable reaction of rage to those losses, are etched into her emotional foundation, where they simmer through childhood into adulthood, later losses, as from death, divorce, broken relationships, geographical moves, job or career failures, and even normal retirement, can, and usually do, arouse the original emotions. When this happens, the later losses are not experienced solely as specific adult events, but include reexperiencing the original loss as one felt it as a child, now made more potent by the added experiences and intellect of adulthood. This pattern is commonly seen in those who fall into clinical depression following the death of a loved one, or other powerful losses, including retirement from a fulfilling lifetime career.

Some Nobel Prize winners and other high achievers have become depressed after receiving their honors when they discovered that their "business as usual" life meant they had lost the fantasy and grand feeling they had anticipated would continue after receiving their award.

In severe psychoses, these emotional dynamics are often responsible for the puzzling events we hear of when a person who had been orphaned at three and then cared for by a loving caretaker suddenly goes berserk and kills at random or murders the very ones who saved and nurtured him through his most vulnerable years.

Though the fear of loss can lead to clinical depression, it can also create severe anxiety in addition, or instead. Following are illustrations of two individuals, both highly personable with intact families and successful careers, and their particular sensitivity to triggers of feelings of loss and separation.

One had emotional inhibitions that crippled many of his career requirements, such as traveling away from home overnight. His inhibitions also prevented him from flying kites with his children because he feared the kite string would break and he would have to watch helplessly, while feeling unbearable desolation, as the kite drifted away, forever. The inhibition resulted from his dread of reliving the feeling he had had at twelve when he saw his mother leave home on a stretcher, for the final time, to go to the hospital where he knew she would die of cancer.

The second person had emotional restrictions that kept her from playing tennis—one of several crippled activities. Each time she swung the racket, anxiety seized her at the sight of the tennis ball going away and her having to wait three seconds—an eternity in one's subconscious mind — until it returned. She had lived in an orphan's home from when she was ages three to eight, and had had to watch helplessly each time her alcoholic mother or deadbeat father left after their cherished—by her—but short, infrequent visits.

The man overcame his anxiety and went on to enjoy flying kites with his children and traveling on vacations with his family. I saw the woman only once, when I was teaching psychiatric residents in a hospital, and never learned her outcome.

Because the infant or small child's mind cannot understand or express its emotions rationally, when unbearable loss and impotent helpless rage are overwhelming, the child must shut down her mind and push these emotions into her mental underground.

After her mother died, little Marcia had to turn to her frequently absent father for emotional support, yet her only way of feeling connected to him was to sacrifice her own wishes and comply with his needs. While originally intended to ensure her father's love, this pattern evolved into self-defeating behaviors with other men, behaviors that finally became unacceptable to her after her attorney confronted her with, and her self-knowledge therapy helped her realize, the enormous emotional, as well as financial, price she was paying for being unable to "cooperate in her own defense" against someone who was completely indifferent to her needs.

Frequently, a loss not evident to an outside observer is devastating to a traumatized person's exquisite sensitivity, and each of us is predisposed to experience the fear that results in a unique way—the man by fearing his child's kite drifting away forever, the woman her tennis ball zooming away over the net, and, much more often, as with Ms. Green, fearing the loss of our secure loved ones.

We also cope with our fear of loss in our own special way. The two people mentioned earlier handled their fears of loss by avoiding flying kites and playing tennis. Ms. Green tried to handle her fears more actively by adapting to the demands of her abusers, until she discovered her pain was unbearable, and the cost to her well-being and goals was too high.

Toward the end of Ms. Green's self-knowledge work, she said, "The most important part of this therapy, and what has changed my life, has been knowing in my deepest mind that I no longer have to fear the bad feelings I had when Mother left, and when I didn't have Dad or Fred. I can understand why I felt the way I did when Mother left, but I'm strong and independent today and there's no reason for me to be afraid of those feelings now."

As she talked, I was struck by the contrast between the insecure, compliant, yet obstinate, woman who had begun self-knowledge therapy two years before, and the even tempered, emotionally free, straightforward person she had become. Relaxed and confident, she spoke with ease of the perspective she had gained from her self-knowledge therapy.

"When I talk about this to other people, it sometimes sounds easy, that all I had to do was say, 'Well, that happened a long time ago, but I'm an adult now, so what's the big deal.' But when I started this, I didn't even know what the problem was, much less the feelings causing it—my feeling hurt and abandoned about Mother leaving without anyone telling me, not understanding why she left, blaming myself for it, and then being alone and eventually realizing I could never get her back. Even when I began to know the feelings, they felt so bad I couldn't make myself think about them." She smiled. "Except for needing Dad and others so I wouldn't feel so alone, I've always taken pride in being able to do things by myself, but there was so much about myself that I had no way of knowing until we uncovered it here, that it would have been like doing my own cancer surgery without knowing anything about cancer or ever having done any surgery."

Her smile faded and she became thoughtful.

"I realize that while understanding childhood feelings that made me so vulnerable to abusive men has changed my life, I also know it can never bring Mother back, and, as painful as losing her was, I've had to accept that she's gone forever. I still don't know which was worse, her leaving or her being gone. They both were terrible because I was so helpless. And as bad as my solutions have been in making up for her not being there, there was nothing I could have done to have kept her from going away. I couldn't have felt any different about it as a child, but I can change how I feel about it now, and how I handle those feelings, and that's really what this work has been about.

"One way I know I've changed is that for the first time in my life I want to have a meaningful relationship with a man who treats me well. I've always wondered why I've chosen men who've used me and then rejected me, but now I know that with each one, just like with Mitchell and Fred, I was trying to make this thing with Mother come out right."

Mr. Bernard had stalled the divorce proceedings until Ms. Green could overcome her depression and self-sabotaging behaviors and marshal the strengths necessary to combat her infantile, heavy-handed, mean-spirited husband. Now, able to cooperate with her attorney in securing her best interests, she turned the tables on Fred and left him with little more than the shirt on his back. At one point in the proceedings he even asked her, "Why do you have to be so hard-hearted?"

Several months after she completed her self-knowledge therapy, Ms. Green began a relationship with a former colleague, Bennett, who for several years had shown his respect and care for her, attentions she previously had been unable to accept. A year later they married and went on to have two children.

Ms. Green and I last spoke by telephone two years ago when she called to refer a friend. When I asked her, "How are things?" she cheerfully responded, "They're going extremely well. Bennett and I and our children are happy and devoted to each other. He's an entirely different man than any I've ever known before. He treats me with love and respect, and he would never abuse me the way I used to take for granted."

Then she chuckled, and said, "Well, I'm not entirely free of slaving and sacrificing myself. I do it all the time for my children because that's what being a parent is all about, but I do it with them because I love them, not because I'm afraid they'll leave me if I don't."

8

I Can't Do It All By Myself

The voice on the telephone sounded hesitant and un-sure.

"This is Michael Morris, uh, Susan Morris is my wife. She, uh, uh, told me you would, uh, be expecting my call, excuse me," he coughed a couple of times. "I'd like an appointment, and, uh, if you could, as soon as possible."

I answered, "What about tomorrow morning at six?"

I could hear alarm in his silence. After a few moments, he said, "Uh, uh, uh, do you have anything later in the morning?"

He had called on a Wednesday, and I replied, "Not tomorrow, but we could meet at the same time on Friday of next week."

He cleared his throat, and said, "Uh, tomorrow'll be all right. I have your address, and Susan will, uh, give me directions. I'll be there at six."

Susan Morris had consulted me originally after being referred by her attorney for help in sorting out her mixed feelings about separating from Michael. Although she had already made the decision to divorce Michael, she felt guilty about leaving since she knew that Michael's problems that had contributed to their separating were also destroying his career. She wanted not to hurt him more than neces-sary, or to make his problems worse than they were already, so she encouraged him to see me for his own reasons.

Michael, who had been even less concerned about organizing his mind than managing his office, had not thought of obtaining professional help, but when Susan had outlined for him what he should do to straighten out his life, and then gave him my name and phone number, he called me immediately.

The next morning, a bitterly cold winter day, Mr. Morris arrived ten minutes early, dressed in a black astrakhan hat, bright red scarf, and plaid mackinaw jacket. He smiled as we introduced ourselves and, on his way to the chair, said, "Well, this early time wasn't as bad as I'd thought, but I sure hope it won't be regular."

I, too, smiled and said, "We're all different. Some of us are early morning sorts and some aren't. We'll find what works best for us."

Before I could segue into asking what prompted him to call me, he quickly added, "I don't really know if I'm a morning person. Twenty or thirty years ago, or even ten—I'm fifty now—I got up every day at five, but recently I don't even get started til nine-thirty, or even later. I don't know if it's my age or what, maybe it's because I'm in such a mess I just don't want to start the day, but I do know that getting up and going felt good this morning, like there was some hope," he said, sitting comfortably in his chair.

He had begun his last thought with a solemn expression, but his face and tone brightened when he spoke of the hope he felt today.

"When you said 'hope,'" I responded, "you implied it was for getting out of what you called the 'mess' you're in. Is the 'mess' a good place to begin?"

"No place is a good place to begin," he said, with a twisted smile. "I don't know what Susan told you, so I'll start with what I think is the problem."

His smile disappeared, and his face went blank.

"I'm an engineering consultant, and my business is going to pot. I've always had a good reputation, but now I'm losing clients. My office is disorganized, I'm in trouble with the federal and state tax people, the banks won't give me a loan, and I can't even get a credit card. My personal life is in shambles too. Susan is leaving me for the same reason Ella did twenty-five years ago. Both of them said they couldn't live with the chaos I create." He recited these facts in a flat voice, as if reading from an engineering manual. "Ella and I were in our early twenties when we got married, and she was as devoted and patient a woman as any man could ask for, but she said she just couldn't continue to live in the misery I caused her."

When he finished speaking, he looked out the window, then abruptly exclaimed, "Look, there's a pileated woodpecker, they're so majestic, and so rare around here you almost never see one."

"Yes," I said, "I know they're very impressive, but did you just tell us an important reason why you haven't been able to get out of the 'mess' you described?"

His gaze shifted back to me, surprised and curious, but with a hint of wariness, perhaps about what I might say.

"What do you mean?" he asked.

I continued, "Does it strike you, as it did me, that right in the middle of telling me about the downhill course of your career and the loss of two marriages, you allowed a little bird—and I agree that pileated woodpeckers are more impressive and unusual than most birds—to distract you from thinking about and dealing with your most serious problem?"

Startled, he straightened himself in the chair, looked at me cautiously as if he had been "found out," then responded, "Susan says the same thing in different words. You wouldn't have any way of knowing it because my field is so specialized, but I've had an extremely successful career," he said, as he smiled and knocked on the wooden bookshelves. "I'm retained, or at least I have been, by firms all over the world who need my help, and the media still regularly ask me to appear on television as an expert and also to write articles for the lay press. But Susan says my disordered life has almost destroyed my standing."

"Can you say more about what Susan means?" I asked.

Looking straight at me with a thoughtful expression, he answered, "As an engineer I can diagnose and fix, or tell someone how to fix, almost any problem, which is how I've gained prominence in the field. But I've never been able to make my business run right." He frowned and shook his head. "Right now my office manager, Laurie, is the problem. She's had no experience as a manager, and she gets upset if I try to tell her what to do, and then I feel stonewalled, and don't know what else to do."

"Did she seem capable when you interviewed her originally?" I asked.

"Well," he hesitated, "I didn't really interview her. She was one of the 'Temp Girls,' and when she learned I didn't have an office manager, she said she'd like to have the job, and she seemed like a good secretary, and nice enough, so I said okay, but she doesn't know anything about managing an office. And I don't know what to do about her," he finished, in his monotone.

Mr. Morris' helplessness, and resignation to it, helped me understand why he had said earlier, "My office is disorganized." This problem, however, was too great to pursue before we understood more about it, or had established a sufficient rapport, so I continued to ask about the problems threatening his career and personal life.

"You also said, 'I'm in trouble with the federal and state tax people.' Can you say more?"

He shifted uncomfortably.

"I owe several years' taxes to the Internal Revenue Service and state tax bureau, and the only reason they haven't seized my assets is that I don't have any."

"How much do you owe?" I asked.

He hesitated, then said, "About $250,000 for the last three years. The taxes alone weren't that much, but that figure includes penalties and interest which have more than doubled the original amount," he added, looking stoic.

"You also said the banks won't give you a loan, and credit card companies won't extend you privileges," I commented as an invitation for him to say more.

With no change in expression, he continued, "Yes, but that's like my tax problem. I don't have anyone to pay my bills and take care of things for me. I had a full time secretary the employment agency sent—I've forgotten her name now—when I started my business three years ago, but she quit after two or three months, and since then I've gone for two years with only part time 'temps', and they don't know enough about my ways to be of any help. Laurie's been with me only a couple of months, and she doesn't know yet what's going on either."

Since his complaint was about not having someone to run his office, I wondered what steps he had taken to rectify the problem. "Have you spoken with the employment agency about finding someone to replace Laurie?"

He looked away from me, first as if he were studying the titles of the books on my shelves, and then at the snow beginning to accumulate on the trees.

"I don't really know how to talk to those people, I've never done that kind of thing," he said impassively.

"You said the agency sent you the first secretary," I said. "Has something happened since then to keep you from asking them to find you someone now?"

"Well, I never actually talked with the agency," Mr. Morris said. He paused, and added, "Bernie did."

"Bernie?" I asked.

"He's a friend who knows how to do those things, so he talked to the agency and made all the arrangements for me to hire her."

He looked away again, and, when he turned back, he did not look directly at me.

I noticed I had begun to shift from one side to the other in my chair, and experience has taught me that when I feel restless it is most likely due to my feeling stymied in trying to understand the emotional meaning of what the person is saying, but that I haven't yet crystallized how best to therapeutically approach the issue with him, and that this reaction is even more pronounced when I'm working with someone who appears resigned to his helplessness. Since my nature is to solve problems, when a person appears as totally helpless as Mr. Morris did, I usually have to make an effort of will to remind myself that practical, fix-it interventions are worse than useless, and that I can benefit a person most by helping him understand the cause of his problem, so he can learn the tools to solve it himself.

I asked, "How have you explained to yourself the problem of your wives and office managers and secretaries leaving you?"

Raising his eyebrows, he began, "It's hard to remember about Ella because she was so long ago, but Susan says that my dependency on her to take care of me upsets her peace of mind too much, and that my financial incompetence is ruining her credit rating and career. She's a business consultant, and when I don't file or pay taxes on our joint returns, the tax people go after her as well as me. She says those things are impossible to explain to people, especially by someone who provides consultation on business efficiency like she does, and that her reputation is being damaged because of me."

His monotone continued, but a barely perceptible self-conscious smile had begun to form.

"Losing my office managers is the same thing. Susan said, 'Many people can manage a normal office, but they can't run one whose employer is so disorganized and helpless he can't keep a schedule or make enough money to pay his office manager's salary,'" he said, opening his hands and giving me a what-can-a-guy-do smile.

Having heard the waiting room door open and close, he looked at the clock, then asked, "Do I have to leave now? When can we meet next?"

"Our time is up, but we can meet at this same time tomorrow, if you'd like."

"Good, that'll work out fine with me, too. See you at six tomorrow." He gave a big smile, and looked back at me as he left.

The next day he began as soon as he sat down. "I've grown up some since Ella left me, at least enough to realize that if Susan is moving out, and my career is almost on the rocks, then I must be doing something wrong, even if I don't know what it is or why I'm doing it. I've got sense enough to know that when someone as smart as I am is in the kind of trouble I'm in, and doesn't get out of it, then he needs to make some kind of change. My friends and colleagues, like Bernie, who used to respect me, are starting to make snide remarks about me, and if I don't fix my problem I know my career will go under. And now, with two failed marriages, I doubt that many women will want me in the future."

"When you said 'change,' and 'fix my problem,' what were you thinking?" I asked.

He focused his eyes on me. "Until we started talking, I hadn't thought that my problems had anything to do with me. I guess I've had the feeling that either 'things just happen,' or that 'people aren't doing what they are supposed to.' But listening to myself answer your questions about my wife and office manager has made me start to think."

"Can you say more about what you heard yourself say?" I asked.

"Well," he narrowed his eyes in concentration, "one of your questions implied I should have interviewed the first office manager myself, but that never occurred to me, since the people at the agency said she was good, and Bernie had recommended her. And I also had never thought about what affect my not paying taxes might have on Susan. I don't know of anything I can do to change this, but maybe now you'll tell me," he smiled. "Usually I just hope that somehow things will get better."

After a moment, his smile faded and was replaced by a look of incredulity.

Shaking his head, he said, "This sounds crazy, doesn't it?"

Mr. Morris's assumption that "things just happened" to him, while he sat by as a dumbfounded bystander, and his apparent helplessness to do anything about them, were the primary topics of his first several weeks of work in gaining self-knowledge.

During one session, he said, "What I really need is my own 'manager,' a 'personal manager.'"

"A 'personal 'manager'?" I inquired.

He smiled and looked sheepish.

"I know what I'm going to say could sound like I'm lazy, but I'm really not, you can check my record on that. But if I don't have a manager to run my office or home, actually every part of my life, then I don't know what to do. Anytime I'm supposed to do something alone, no matter what, I always feel I can't do it all by myself. It sounds nutty for an engineer to talk like this, because I fix problems all the time, but I need someone, like an employee, or wife, or friend, to help me plan my activities, and then be around while I do them. Bernie did this for me until he got tired of me using him that way."

I replied, "Who did this for you in earlier-"

Interrupting me, he exclaimed "Booba!" in an eager voice.

I knew immediately an important moment had arrived.

"Booba?" I asked.

He smiled warmly. "Booba was my aunt, and the only one who really loved me. I always felt special when she was near me. I hardly knew anyone else until I was six. I was born in 1939, just before World War II, and when I was two-and-a-half, my father went off to the army, and my mother went away to work as an electrician in the shipyards, so Booba took care of me until the war was over in '45. Booba told me my parents weren't around much, even before they went away because of the war, and that mostly baby sitters took care of me." He had become pensive. "I have a vague memory of my mother coming home sometimes, but she always seemed like a stranger, and I never saw my father until he came back after the war, and I didn't like him from then on, because he seemed like he didn't belong with us.

"Until I went to college, Booba was the only one who was always with me. Even when my parents returned after the war, both of them worked long hours. I couldn't do anything without Booba. She was so good to me," his smile returned, "and always made me happy. She'd tell me what to do and how to do it, what games to play so I wouldn't get hurt, and what decisions to make, and then later she helped me organize my schedule for hours and days ahead. I always obeyed her, not out of fear that she would punish me, but because I felt so good when she approved of what I did and admired me when I did it well."

He raised his eyebrows. "I just realized that while it's true I wasn't afraid that Booba would punish me, I did get anxious when I thought she might disapprove of me, or something I had done, or if I felt we weren't connected. My whole life was centered around her." He smiled again at the memory.

"When I was in high school I did a lot of things that made me popular—my grades averaged nearly 4.0, I played wide receiver on the football team, and I ran the fastest mile in track. Everyone thought I did all this on my own, but the truth was I always knew Booba was not far away, and I couldn't have done it without her. She was always by my side, literally and figuratively. We talked together every day about my studies, and she went to all my football games and track events," he said with great warmth.

The seeds of Mr. Morris' helplessness were beginning to emerge.

I asked, "A few moments ago, when you said, 'Until I went to college, Booba was the only one who was always with me,' what were you suggesting about needing her after that?"

He look puzzled, and hesitated before answering.

"I've never thought about this before, but in college and graduate school, I guess it was Donald I turned to. He was a junior when I was a freshman. We took to each other right away, and he became a sort of mentor to me."

Michael had become more focused than at any time since he had begun our work.

"Donald and I often slipped into the college auditorium at night so that, with him as my critiquing audience, I could develop my public speaking abilities," he said, as a nostalgic tone crept into his voice. "I gained a self-assurance from those experiences that's been with me ever since and is invaluable now when I speak to large audiences and give television interviews," he added with confident vigor.

Then he looked at me, "In case you're wondering, there was never anything sexual in our relationship.

"Our mentor-protégé friendship lasted a long time," he continued, "long after college, about twenty years altogether, and well into my marriage with Susan. He and I met as often as we could because his advice was always so helpful, even on holidays and vacations when my wives, first Ella, and then Susan, expected me to be with them. Ella adapted to my being away, but Susan was flabbergasted about Donald and me, and she eventually laid down an ultimatum. By then I was much older, and I also didn't want to lose Susan like I had Ella, so I stopped meeting with him." He sighed, his lips pressed into a flat line.

"But by then, Susan was so hurt she stopped trying to make our marriage work, and she began having what turned out to be several affairs. She denied what she was doing, but she didn't try to hide it from me. She came and went with men she introduced as 'office colleagues.' Once I came home and found her in our living room with some guy without his shirt and shoes on and still buckling his belt. Our marriage went downhill after that, and our separation from then on was inevitable," he said, as his face drooped.

"Susan doesn't see it the way I just said, though. She says she told me she'd leave me if I didn't stop spending so much time with Donald, but that she didn't give up on me until after I stopped talking with him and then started expecting her to tell me what to do, and take care of me, every minute of my, and her, life like I had done with Donald and others before. I don't know what truth actually is," his voice sounded strained, "but there is something to what she said. When I no longer had Donald to help me, I usually felt totally helpless, and needed Susan more and more.

"When I don't have someone to manage me, my mind goes blank, and I don't remember to do even ordinary things, and, more often than not, it can be really expensive," he said, shaking his head. "One time I left some irreplaceable, and invaluable, professional notes on an airplane, and, another time, I left my appointment book in a taxi. Once, I caught a plane home from Russia and half way over the Atlantic I discovered I'd left the only set of keys to my car, and office, and home, in my Moscow hotel room.

"But the real doozy, and I feel awfully stupid telling you this, happened when I'd taken a few days off to get caught up on things at the office and around the house. FedEx delivered a five thousand dollar specially ordered computer part for an engineering instrument, and I put it in the pocket of some short pants I wear when I'm off work. Then, on my way to the office to install it, I dropped by my sister's house where my niece and nephew were in the backyard swimming pool, and when they saw me, they yelled, 'Hi Uncle Mike, come on in,' and so I just jumped right in the pool with them.

"I had completely forgotten that the computer part was in my pocket, and, of course, it was ruined. Not only did I have to buy a new one, but I had to wait two months to get a replacement, and by then I'd lost the client because his work needed the computer part then, not two months later, so he had to get someone else who could do the job sooner." He threw up his hands, shook his head, and frowned in bewilderment.

Looking at his watch, he stood, and as he turned to leave, said, "I'm sure we'll talk about this again, because this kind of thing has happened too many times to be accidental, and, as you see, it sets me back every time." He smiled and nodded as he left.

A week after this session, Mr. Morris appeared for our appointment with a red and swollen left eye. After he spoke for a few minutes with pride about his son's recent eighty yard touchdown run playing football for his college—Mr. Morris' alma mater—all the while frowning with a pained expression that favored the eye, and had made no mention of his obvious medical problem, I asked, "What's going on with your eye?"

He replied, "I guess I should say something about it. It's been hurting and I've had trouble seeing the last couple of hours."

The medical alarms in my mind went on high alert. I asked, "What else?"

"Well, my vision is blurry, and I see halos like I did when this happened two years ago. I also have a headache, and feel nauseous, like I want to vomit. When this happened before, my eye doctor told me it could happen again." He paused and looked at me as if he were waiting for me to tell him what to do.

Incredulous at what he was saying, I asked, "What else did the eye doctor tell you?"

"He said that when this happened it was what he called 'an acute glaucoma emergency.'" Again, he waited for me.

Containing my disbelief that even Mr. Morris could dissociate himself so outrageously from his body's screams for help, I asked, "What else did he say?"

"He said that if I didn't do something about it immediately, I might lose my vision." Once again he waited for me.

Increasingly astounded at Mr. Morris' passivity, I persisted, "Did you call him as soon as you began to notice the symptoms this morning?"

Mr. Morris began to look sheepish. "Well, no. If I called him, he would have just wanted to see me right away or tell me to go to the emergency room, and I thought that would interfere with my coming here, so I figured I'd wait and see if it got better as the day went on, or if you'd tell me what I ought to do about it."

As I witnessed Mr. Morris's alarming capacity to deny the gravity of his symptoms and signs, I was afraid for him to leave my office without specific directions, so I immediately, in his presence, called his eye doctor and made arrangements for Mr. Morris to see the specialist within thirty minutes. The ophthalmologist later said that had Mr. Morris delayed even an hour longer, he would have lost significant eyesight.

Several months after the eye crisis, Mr. Morris' pattern of denial created a nearly mortal crisis. One day Mr. Morris let slip something about having seen a GI (gas-

trointestinal) doctor, and when I inquired about it, Mr.
Morris allowed as how several months earlier his internist
had found blood in Mr. Morris' stool, and had referred him
to a gastroenterologist who did a colonoscopy and discovered a cancerous polyp. Not only had Mr. Morris failed to
tell me about his condition, either before or after the procedure, he had also promptly denied the findings and ignored follow-up notices from both the GI specialist and
his internist. Not until I insisted that he tell me what was
going on and then oversaw his every step did he see a surgeon and have life-saving abdominal surgery.

The success of self-knowledge therapy depends on the
willingness of the person seeking it to overcome his infantile expectations, and for Mr. Morris this meant overcoming his pathological need to be "managed." Ordinarily,
therapeutic prudence leads a self-knowledge therapist to
frustrate such wishes, since satisfying infantile yearnings
removes the motive to overcome them. In acting as Mr.
Morris' emergency physician, I was aware I had collabo-
rated with him in living out his lifelong quest for a "Booba"
stand-in, rather than taking the more effective action of
frustrating the patterned behavior so we could understand
its underlying wish and he could overcome his self-destructive behavior. But there are certain instances when a
self-knowledge therapist must act as one would in everyday life, and these were two such times. When a deadly
time bomb is involved, common sense dictates that, at that
moment, one does not have the option of conducting "ideal"
therapy. Surgeons have a gallows humor expression for
such a misapplication of medical priorities: "The patient
died, but the surgery was a success." Obviously it is far
better to struggle with a temporarily complicated therapeutic procedure than with permanent blindness, or death.

A few weeks after the surgery, and still shaken from
having recognized his close calls, Mr. Morris could observe his behavior more rationally.

He looked out the window, smiled pleasantly as he
saw a lone titmouse on the snow covered brick ledge and
squinted his eyes in thought for two or three minutes. "I

haven't talked about this before, but I think my not attending to my eye problem and cancer surgery, as well as leaving my keys in Moscow and jumping into a swimming pool with a high-priced computer part in my pocket, is all part of what I call my 'pile of junk.'"

"Pile of junk?" I asked.

"Yes, it means I always have to have something hanging over my head," he said, with exasperation, "something I've forgotten, or done wrong, or simply failed to do.

"Right now it's my publisher who's hounding me to write a second edition of a book that came out about five years ago. It has sold reasonably well, and by now there've been enough advancements in my field to make a second edition timely. My editor for the first edition was a take-charge woman who helped me organize my writing and revising schedules, but she semi retired last year, and the publisher doesn't have anyone to help me like she did. I think I'm waiting for her to call me so I can get started again."

"Does she know you want to revise the original edition?" I asked.

"No," he responded, shaking his head in bewilderment.

I was encouraged by the tone of Mr. Morris's observations, because it reflected his increasing ability to look inside himself.

I asked, "Are you putting the need for a 'pile of junk' together with waiting for someone like Booba to show up and pay your bills, or make sure you get your cancer surgery, or write your book, even if the person would have no way of knowing you need them?"

"I guess I am, but I'd never really thought about the consequences of it until my waiting for you, or someone, nearly caused me to go blind from that glaucoma attack, and then the cancer that could've killed me. I'm sure you've seen this all along, but I hadn't realized my life was falling apart even when Susan left me and insisted I call you. This must be what they call denial, since I've been willing to ruin my marriages and now my career, or go blind or die from cancer, rather than recognize the price I pay for depending on others the way I do."

I was struck with his increasing willingness, even active interest, in looking within to understand the role that he, himself, was playing in creating his predicament.

I asked, "You said, 'I'd never really thought about the consequences of it.' Does that mean you had thought some about it?"

He stared at the floor a few minutes, then lifted his head and responded, "What I meant was that in the back of my mind I had a vague feeling, it wasn't really a thought, that went something like, 'Soon, Susan will see how much she loves me, and will quit her business so she can take charge of my office, or the surgeon will learn of my importance and call me to make sure I have the operation, or my editor will come out of her retirement so she can work with me.' Also, and this is even more vague, I feel kind of stubborn, like if I wait long enough, they'll come."

I replied, "Are you saying that the denial is not all passive, it's active, too, and that it's driven by the determination that waiting will eventually make the person come and take care of you?"

"I guess I am. Feeling this way has always seemed so natural, and that must be why I never questioned it until now. If I needed Booba, and she wasn't there, I knew she'd come eventually, and if she didn't, then she'd really know I was angry when she finally did come." His jaw was set and his eyes were stony. "I'd dig in my heels and wait, not just with Booba, but with Ella and Susan, and now that I look at it, with anyone I need but don't have, and sometimes for someone who doesn't even know I exist. And while I waited, I'd refuse to do what I could, without realizing the harm I was doing to myself."

His face had released some of its stubborn grip.

Denial mechanisms, and the patterns they create, like the one afflicting Mr. Morris, begin in the earliest months, or even weeks, of our lives to protect us from our fear of helplessness to loss and other emotional trauma. The more forces converge to threaten us, whether from our outer world or inner mind, the greater will be our need for denial mechanisms. Since helplessness is ever present in infancy, a small child is constantly in its peril, and while parents usually do their best to spare their little one pain, such as changing the infant's diaper when it cools and becomes uncomfortable, even the most sensitive and responsive parent cannot completely spare a child awareness of his helplessness. When the child is older, and ready to integrate the experience, however, learning to cope with the reality of helplessness is a vital step of emotional growth. At that point, a prudent parent will allow the child to make his own mistakes and discover his ability, or inability, to meet the challenges of everyday life, so he can gain the ". . . serenity to accept the things I cannot change, the courage to change the things I can, and the wisdom to know the difference," as expressed in the Alcoholic's Anonymous' adaptation of Reinhold Niebuhr's, The Serenity Prayer [1934].

One illustration of a small child's use of denial occurs frequently when Mommy and Daddy leave their three-year old with a sitter to go away for a weekend holiday, and then eagerly return expecting to see their smiling cherub happy to see them, only to find him stone faced, looking away, and refusing even to acknowledge their existence. The little one must deny his beloved parents' presence, and his own feelings of joy for their return, for fear that reinvesting his love and trust will only bring more abandonment and hurt.

A small child may not suffer grave consequences immediately from this form of denial, since, when his parents smile with love and understanding, he usually will soon feel reassured enough to thaw and resume his former trust. And, normally, as he gains strength and confidence, his need for the unhealthy use of the denial mechanism will fade. But if faced constantly with such trauma, his persistent denial may create a reflexive pattern that can, in later life, disrupt the development of his basic trust in the reliability of others, even loved ones. This same pattern may also cause him to suffer the consequences of denying a destructive reality until it is too late, like someone with anorexia nervosa who starves herself to death.

I Can't Do It All By Myself

245

A person with such a pattern may react to even minor stresses or challenges as though he would be as overwhelmed as he had been by the original threat, when he was small and desperately needed to be protected from it. This pattern can continue long after the child has acquired the strengths to handle threats and has no need for the denial mechanism to provide him with illusory protection.

When this happens, as it did to Mr. Morris, the child is deprived of knowing he can fare well by using his own independent strengths. Little Michael learned he could blackmail Booba into always being by his side; only later did he find that in the adult world such a person is almost never available.

This outcome is similar to the fate of Ms. Tillman (Chapter Two, "You Can't Mollycoddle Them) who, as a child, used the mechanism of "fierce independence" to protect herself from her helplessness and humiliation in the hands of hospital authorities who barred her from seeing her mother and with her older sexually abusive brother. But when she applied this pattern in adulthood, it created problems rather than solutions for her. Because her "fierce independence" had worked so well when she was as a child, she had failed to learn that she had developed other strengths and no longer needed the childhood mechanism.

As a young, wide-eyed psychiatric resident, I had a shocking wake-up call to the tragedy of adult denial when I learned, several months after his death from colon cancer, that my idealized teacher, a professor of psychiatry and certified expert on the mind and emotions, had had blood in his stools for ten months before seeking medical help.

I have also worked with other people whose quiet denial has led them down a fatal path. A patient, whom I saw weekly, died of metastatic cervical cancer. She told me that her gynecological surgeon had excised a lesion on her uterus and that the surgeon was "watching it." When, several months later, my patient's weight plummeted almost overnight and I insisted she account for it, she, unable to maintain her denial, met with her surgeon. But it was too late and she was dead within six weeks. After her death, I found that her reassurances to me had been outright falsehoods; at the same time she was guaranteeing me that she was having regular office visits with her surgeon, she had been consistently avoiding the appointments.

Such experiences humble anyone directly responsible for helping others. Self-knowledge therapy is founded, at least in the mind of the therapist, on a presumption of mutual trust. Patients ordinarily divulge the most sensitive and critical matters in the interest of overcoming their problems, and we therapists are always taken aback when confronted with our helplessness in the face of a patient's denial.

Arnold Palmer, the great golfer, in a television interview, addressed indirectly the potential deadliness of denial when a television reporter asked Palmer, a survivor of prostate cancer, "What advice do you have for the viewers?" Palmer responded, "Men, get your PSA," referring to the prostate-specific antigen laboratory test for prostate cancer. Implicit in Palmer's comment was his awareness of the common, everyday version of human denial imbedded in, "It can't happen to me."

The self-destructive effects of defensive denial can pervade virtually any aspect of one's life. Denial inevitably creates an assumption of dependency on others' conscience or sense of responsibility that is usually incompatible with real life. Some people may find partners who are willing to narrow their lives to the simple function of gratifying a loved one's excessive expectations, but, as Mr. Morris found, counting on such a highly precise fit is not realistic.

Any "manager," as defined by Mr. Morris, inevitably has her or his own agenda that is different from the expectant one's wishes. Donald, for example, had eagerly interpreted Michael's wish for a manager as a license to dominate and control Michael. As Michael said, "I guess he saw in me an appreciative, eager-to-learn protégé who needed him, and whom he could tutor in his studies, tell how to handle his problems, and help develop his talents." Michael's wives also had their own normal human needs.

Susan once said to him, "Why do you think I would want to stay married to you? I thought I was marrying an adult man, not a child who wants a full-time manager and admirer."

Likewise, government and other institutions that provide welfare, on which many people rely as the ultimate caretakers, are also composed of people who, in the end, are concerned primarily with their own goals and personal wishes and are usually helpful only as long as their work serves their own needs, even if those needs are subconscious. One of the most frequent versions of this attitude occurs when institutional personnel avoid the bother and stress of work by responding to a caller's request with unassailable reasons for bogging down the caller in "red tape" or endless referrals to "another department."

Too, when anyone depends on others to provide for his needs, as did Michael, one is at the mercy of the other person's availability. In a class I taught for student psychoanalysts on "Internal Repair vs External Repair," referring to the advantages of relying on oneself, rather than others, for one's sense of well-being, we discussed the hazards of depending on "external repair." In posing a hypothetical question, I said, "The other day I was feeling down, but when I remembered how much I enjoy talking with Cohn [a class member], I said to myself, 'I think I'll call Cohn so I'll feel better.'" When I then asked the class, "What's wrong with that solution?" one student immediately responded, "You may get Cohn's answering device."

In one form or another, my illustration of momentary frustration with not reaching Cohn happens to each of us daily, and ordinarily does not cause us a second thought. But until Mr. Morris understood and mastered his profound dependency on Booba, and her illusory successors, when he felt he needed a Booba-type manager and she, or he, was unavailable, Mr. Morris became immobilized with stubborn passivity, at times inviting disaster.

The trait of strong-mindedness, like Mr. Morris's stubbornness in waiting for Booba to rescue him, takes a course similar to denial. Aggressive urges begin to develop in a child's first year, and, during his second year, when his nerves and muscles mature, the urges become more focused and make him less willing to accept being helpless. This normal, healthy phase sets the two year old on an active course of using his aggression to gain independence, by excessively demanding to have his way, a period that harassed mothers call "The Terrible Twos."

Ordinarily this distortion and overuse of aggression in the second year will run its course and become the foundation of such adult strengths as independence and determination. But if his early years are marked by excessive trauma—as they were with little Michael when, at two-and-a-half, his mother and father summarily disappeared—the child can become stuck at that level of emotional development, both in his perceived trauma and method of dealing with it.

For Michael, this meant that before his normal two-year-old stubbornness could be refined as healthy independence and perseverance, it became engraved in his emotions as unyielding dependency and bullheadedness. When this bullheadedness then merged with his defense of denial, the combination created, and endured as, a powerful mechanism that caused him to react with self-defeating, dogged denial to even minor losses, real or imagined.

Overcoming these self-saboteurs began with identifying the helplessness he felt when alone in the face of demands and expectations. While he could perform some routine chores independently, he was paralyzed when faced with requirements that focused solely on him, with no manager nearby.

Over several months, Mr. Morris learned to look inside himself to understand and master his role in bringing about his business and marital failures.

As he began one session, he said, almost in passing, "I really miss Susan. Everything hit me all at once yesterday. The telephone company cut off my service, my landlord said he would evict me if my rent wasn't up to date by the end of the month, and the IRS garnisheed my office bank account, all because I hadn't paid my bills. Susan used to take care of things like that, but with her gone, nothing seems to get done."

I responded, "What you just said about, 'with her gone, nothing seems to get done,' sounded like a euphemism that you substituted for something more unpleasant. Can you sense what I might be picking up?" I asked.

"I don't know what you mean," he said, sounding puzzled, then waited for me to reply.

"The idea, 'with her gone, nothing seems to get done,'" I replied, "implies that there is someone, or something, somewhere out there that's just not doing their job, and I was wondering if that idea might be a less disturbing way of putting some kind of feeling you recognize about yourself."

"I still don't know what you're saying," he replied, and again waited for me to answer.

I said, "I was thinking about the telephone company, and the bank, and the IRS, who have the idea that you're the one who's not paying his bills, and I was wondering if something about their messages was too unpleasant to face, and that it might be less disturbing to think, in some global kind of way, that your bills, somehow, just aren't getting paid?"

"Oh, I see what you mean," he responded. "Well, I don't know. Susan, or my secretary, or someone, has always done things like that, so I just don't know how to do them."

"Say more about what, 'I just don't know how to do them,' means?" I asked.

"It's just that I've never done them before. Maybe I could if I absolutely had to." He thought several moments, then added, "But I don't think so."

He became silent and appeared to be mulling over what he had said.

"What were you thinking during the pause?" I asked.

"I was thinking about what we just said, and why I don't write checks myself, and then I wondered how I would feel if I sat down and tried, but then my mind just went blank, like something was missing."

"Something was missing?" I asked.

"I can't say, I don't know, my mind just went blank, like, as I said, something was missing. And that's peculiar, because usually I don't have trouble putting words to things —like when I'm angry or embarrassed—but this is different somehow. There aren't any words for the feeling. How do you describe something that's not there?" he asked rhetorically.

"Is the feeling that has no words familiar to you?" I asked.

"What do you mean, 'familiar'?" he replied.

"Like some feeling you've known before?"

"I don't know," he said, sounding puzzled.

"Did your mind go blank just then when I asked you that question?" I continued.

"No, no, that's not what happened just then, this was different, my mind wasn't blank. I wanted to answer you, but I couldn't because I really didn't know the answer. This is the first time, at least that I can remember, that I've ever tried to think about this. Usually someone, like Susan, or my secretary, does these things for me, so I've never thought about how I would feel if they didn't."

He was silent two or three minutes.

"Can you think out loud?" I asked.

"I was just thinking about those creditors breathing down my neck, and why I can't do what needs to be done to get them off my back," he responded, then went silent again.

"Say more?" I asked.

He answered, "I was thinking about why my mind goes blank when creditors harass me or I start to write checks but doesn't go blank when I talk with you, even if 'my mind going blank' is the subject of what I'm talking about."

"What about the distinction?" I asked.

"Talking with you is something I want to do; so, when you ask me something, I want to answer you, but that's different from writing checks because that's something I don't want to do," he replied.

"Are you saying then, that when your mind goes blank,

it is your mind's way of refusing to do something you don't want to do, especially if someone is forcing you or breathing down your neck?" I asked.

He was silent several moments, nodded, then remained silent while he appeared to be reflecting on the question.

"Can you think out loud?" I asked.

"I was thinking about what you just said about my mind going blank as being my way of refusing to do something I don't want to do," he responded.

After waiting several moments for him to continue, I asked, "Perhaps your silence now is saying 'my mind is blank because I don't want to talk about this'?"

"I'm going to answer you because the reason we're doing this is so I can get over my problem, but I can tell you that I'm starting to feel with you right now the same way we're talking about," he said, with anxious irritation. "Your persistent questions about what I'm thinking make me feel that you, just like the damn creditors are trying to force me to do something I don't want to do, and then I start feeling like I don't want to answer you, and my mind goes blank. And that's peculiar, because I want to get over my problem, and I want to do this work with you to get over it, but I'm reacting as if I don't want to do the very thing I do want to do. It's so screwy, because if it were just that I didn't want to do this, that would be one thing, but I'm reacting this way even though it's something I really do want to do."

"You seem to be saying that it was a feeling of resistance to my questions that turned into the blank mind. If the resistance feeling could talk, can you sense what it would say?" I asked.

"It would say, 'Screw you, take your damn questions and shove 'em up your ass,'" he exclaimed, then quickly averted his eyes. "It's how I feel when you keep asking, 'Can you say more? Say more? Can you think out loud? Can you sense what the resistance would say'?" he blurted out sarcastically, then sat back in his chair, folded his arms, and glared at me.

"You said you're aware that there's a difference between those times when you want to answer my question, and can do so freely, and those times you want to refuse, and to tell me and the creditors to 'shove it.' What more can you sense about the distinction?" I asked.

"You just did it again with your damn question!" he exclaimed, throwing up his hands. He narrowed his eyes and regarded me for several seconds. "Sometimes it's subtle, but it's the difference between whether it's your idea or mine, or whether it feels like we're doing this for me or you. When it's something I want to know or am interested in, then I don't have any trouble talking, including answering your questions, but if it's your idea, or you get pushy—and sometimes it doesn't take much of a push in the way you ask—then my dander gets up and I want to tell you, or anyone else who does it, to go straight to hell."

"You're saying, then, that somehow these feelings get translated into a blank mind. Can you sense how that works?" I asked.

He shook his head, looked me in the eyes, and gave a sly smile. "There you go again with another one of your damn questions. The way it works is that I must have discovered somewhere along the way that you just can't go around telling people to go screw themselves, and still get along in the world. So I guess I learned to do it in a way that wouldn't get me into trouble.

Again he shook his head, then, with a sardonic smile, added, "I guess I figured it was better to get into trouble with myself, although I have to admit that up to now I haven't thought of being in trouble. I know, given the trouble I'm in up to my eyeballs, that that sounds ridiculous, but it has seemed all along that that's the way life is, and, that if I don't have a manager, then there's nothing I can do about it."

Having seen me look at the clock and move my legs from the ottoman to the floor, he said, "Well, I know where I'll start next time," then nodded, smiled, and left.

Two days later, he began by saying, "I want to continue with that 'something's missing' feeling I talked about last time." I nodded and extended my open hands as a gesture for him to continue. Then he added, "But I'm not sure where to begin."

I said, "Your thoughts last time suggested that the 'something's missing' feeling might be connected to your anger and blank mind."

"When I first said 'something is missing,'" he responded, "I thought I meant that I didn't have a manager to do things for me, or to tell me what to do. And now my mind is getting blank again."

"It feels like I'm breathing down your neck?" I asked.

"I know I'm feeling under pressure right now, and I know I'm reacting to you as if you were doing it to me, but actually the pressure is coming from inside me," he responded.

"How can you sense it's coming from within you?" I asked.

"I first noticed it when you asked if the 'something is missing' feeling is connected to my anger and blank mind, because it was clear to me that I wanted to know the answer, and that I was the one, not you, who was putting pressure on me. And that's really crazy because I'm treating my own pressure on me as if it were coming from you, and then I blank my mind to you as if you were the one demanding it of me," he replied.

"What occurs to you about the function, or gain, when you feel the pressure, even when it's from yourself, and then turn the 'go screw yourself' anger into a blank mind?" I asked.

He hesitated a moment, then said, "I don't know why, it's really crazy because it feels so natural, even though it makes things a lot worse. But I do know that when I thought of calling the eye doctor, I had the same kind of "buzz-off" feeling toward him that I just had toward you, even though he would've told me what to do to save my eye, just like the surgeon would have told me how to save my life." He half-smiled, shaking his head. "I had no idea I was this crazy. Whoever heard of needing a shrink to tell you to see your eye doctor for a serious eye problem, or for your surgeon to have to tell you more than once that if you don't do something about your cancer that it's likely to kill you. I don't know what would've happened if you hadn't picked up on it, because I didn't know then how my mind could play tricks on me, like it did a few minutes ago with you, so I could get back on track."

"What can you sense about the gain in what you just told me?" I asked.

He said, "I think it has to do with whatever, or whoever, is missing. I know that if my manager is there, I can go ahead and do things even if she doesn't do it for me. But even then, there's a vague feeling that something, or someone is missing." He stopped and became silent.

"Did your mind go blank just then?" I asked.

He responded, "Yes, and I still don't understand why it happens, because the only pressure I felt was coming from me, because I want to get over this thing. What I was thinking about was why I refuse to do things for myself. I think it's because, like a moment ago, I felt that you were putting pressure on me to answer your question all by myself. When you asked me what I gained by turning my 'go to hell' feeling into a blank mind, I was mad because you were asking me to answer you and there was no one to help me, and I think the gain was that by blanking my mind I didn't have to tell you to go to hell and then be afraid you would be mad at me and go away.

"I know the obvious answer to, 'whoever,' is Booba, but that doesn't feel right because Booba was always there, and that still didn't make the 'something's missing' feeling go away."

"What else occurs to you about the 'something's missing' feeling,'" I suggested.

He said, "I don't know, I started wondering about it the moment I said it, and whatever it is had to have happened very early, because the feeling has been there as long as I can remember. I guess I'll just have to piece together some things I know, or have learned, to find the answer." He leaned back in his chair, holding his hands in front of him as though he were holding pieces of his early life together. "Like I said before, I don't think Booba caused it because no one could have been better to me than she was, but even she couldn't make the feeling go away completely. It had to have come from when both my parents went away to the war when I was two and a half, and before that, too, because, and I heard this from Booba and another aunt and my grandmother, both my parents worked full time and were hardly home even before the war. That all happened before I could remember anything, but it feels right because, even when they lived at home later on, I don't remember them being around."

I said, "As you've been talking about the 'something's missing' feeling, and of your parents being away, have you sensed how your anger and blank mind fit into your feelings?"

He replied, "That's easier to answer than how I felt about them going away when I was two, because as I got older I can remember missing my mother, until she came home for good after the war."

"When you said, 'came home for good after the war,' were you making a distinction between that time and some other times they came home?" I asked.

"Yes," he responded immediately, "my father was off fighting the war, and he didn't come back until after it was over. But the shipyard where Mother worked was just two hundred miles away, and she did come home, but only about once a month, because, I learned later, she worked ten hours a day, six days a week. I didn't know at the time that I was angry, I just remember that I wouldn't do anything I didn't want to do until she came home to do it with me, and I just kept waiting for her to come so that I would feel good and she could do things with me. Booba, and my other aunt and grandmother made me feel that way because when I was upset they would say 'Everything will be all right when your mother comes home,' but once a month seemed like forever." He wiped his eyes with a tissue he took from the lamp table next to his chair.

"I never knew what war was except that there were a lot of people fighting, or why she and my father had to go away for it. But I remember I got to where I ignored her every time she left and came back, and now I realize that that was like refusing to do something I really wanted to do because even though I was sad when she would leave, I was so happy to see her when she came home.

"But I couldn't let myself feel happy, because that made it hurt too much when she'd leave again the next day. Her going away, and then coming home, and then going away again and again, was too upsetting, so I guess I just learned not to let anything make any difference to me, whether it was her coming and going, the sadness I felt when she wasn't there, or the happiness I felt when she was there. I guess that's like today when I don't let anything bother me, whether its losing my business, owing money, or facing a serious illness."

He sat back, then covered his eyes and cradled his head with his hands.

"No one, including Booba, could ever take the place of Mother to make me feel good, or make doing things seem worthwhile. This may sound like I was depressed, but I don't remember feeling depressed. It felt more, then and now, like the world could go to hell around me, and it wouldn't make any difference to me if Mother weren't there," Mr. Morris said, and became silent.

This was Mr. Morris' eloquently described version of a small child's reaction to the repeated trauma of the loss of his mother (discussed earlier in this chapter).

"When you said a minute ago, 'I wouldn't do anything I didn't want to do until she came home to do it with me,' could that have been like refusing to do what you're supposed to do unless your manager either does it for you, or together with you?" I asked.

With sad eyes, he looked at me, nodded, and said, "Yes, and that's when I started digging in my heels and refusing to do anything until my manager came back. The managers I wait for never come of course, and I think that's why I've always had that vague 'something's missing'_feeling. But even when my mother was there, I had to put her out of my mind so much that I never accepted she was home even when she was actually there. And I think that's the feeling that makes it seem like I have to have Booba and the other managers, because when they were there it felt like that whoever was missing had come back and was with me."

The step of temporarily foregoing protective mechanisms so one can uncover underlying emotions is always challenging, but it was more difficult for Mr. Morris because his underlying feeling of "something's missing" had arisen in his earliest days before words were available to identify his feelings. We all can define, describe, and remember emotions—anger's strength, love's security and pleasure, and shame's humiliation—we experience in later childhood, because by then we have enough reasoning ability and vocabulary to conceptualize and articulate our emotions, but how can one recall feelings that his mind had not yet developed the capacity to identify, describe, or explain?

Little Michael's profound losses in his infancy and early childhood prevented him from developing either a sense of secure, self-assured individuality or the abilities to recognize and verbalize his feelings of helplessness and nothingness from those early years. Even before his father went off to the war, and his mother to the war effort, when he was two and a half, his nurturance was in the hands of several unconcerned and inconstant baby sitters. With them he learned to fear the unbearable pains of loss and emotional nothingness, hurts his denial mechanism could numb but not erase, hurts that were reinforced each time his parents abandoned him. Since a measure of aloneness is inherent in independence, these hurts became reminders of the devastating pain awaiting him if he even considered acting on his own.

Michael used denial as his primary mechanism to cope with his losses: first with the devastating emptiness of losing his parents, and then from the fear of reliving that emptiness—or as he put it, "something's missing"—when even normal duties and other activities would call on him to act on his own.

His use of denial to cope with these losses increased his plight since his emotional loss would become more profound and, in doing so, deepen his steadfast refusal to budge from his demand that his caretaker return. The feeling pattern of demanding that his loved one return then became engraved in his emotions, and he used it whenever he felt that he was, or feared he would be, abandoned by Booba and her successors. As a result, he became stubborn with innocent others who, intolerant of such infantile behavior, would also leave him and reinforce his fear of feeling alone and acting independently.

Booba's indulgence and excessive protectiveness served only to harden his flawed development. When Mr. Morris's progress allowed him to look at himself more objectively, he said, "Booba's love and care in my early years saved my life, but then, when I was older, she couldn't let go, and let me, and certainly not force me, to become independent. Then I made my problem worse, because I felt so needy and desperate, I blackmailed her into always being with me, and anyone who was as soft-hearted as Booba would've had a hard time resisting me.

"I remember one time I refused to study for a test if she didn't sit in the room with me, and another time I told her I wouldn't run in a track meet unless she came. And both times I knew she had other things she wanted to do, especially her church work. In fact, I think that when I knew she had something else she needed to do, I was even more demanding than other times, because I felt so desperate about her being away from me."

When strengths fail to develop healthily, they usually create havoc, as did Mr. Morris's flawed autonomy and independence. Children normally build into their own emotions the confidence parents and caretakers give them through love and pride in seeing their children grow and develop. This internalized feeling of lovable worthiness develops into strengths of self-assurance and secure individuality that remain even when the parent or caretaker is no longer present. If these strengths fail to develop adequately, however, the growing child is unable to become confident and emotionally independent, and, consequently, must turn to others, as Mr. Morris did to Booba, Donald, and Susan, or, as many people do, to institutions, to supply their missing strengths.

As he repeatedly used his observing mind to examine his difficult-to-define sense of helpless emotional absence, he learned he could endure the fearsome emotion long enough to identify and understand the feeling—knowledge that, in turn, gave him the strength and power to overcome his helplessness when facing challenges alone.

With these discoveries, Mr. Morris soon learned that he could independently rely on strengths that earlier had been available only when he was accompanied by Booba or her stand-in. By integrating Booba's admiration and Donald's affirmation into his own emotions, he could, for example, deliver speeches and respond to media interviewers without a manager nearby. This was particularly useful in situations that, in the past, had made him feel helpless, as when he had to defend challenges to his professional opinions from colleagues or critics.

These now independent strengths also benefitted him in situations that required he face what seemed to be demands and displeasure from people and institutions who had their own agenda, advocated their own cause, or were absolutely uninterested in devoting themselves to being his manager-on-call. Now, rather than being daunted by these situations, he could enjoy others' interest in his work and interviewers' recognition of his expertise.

As Mr. Morris came to understand emotionally as well as intellectually the ideas and feelings driving his life, he found he no longer needed a Booba-type person to organize his day or manage his every action, any more than a child who has learned to walk needs physically to hold someone's "pinkie" when taking steps.

He became a better judge of people—particularly prospective office personnel and a potential spouse—and more realistic in his expectations of them. He no longer sought others based on their ability to be a Booba surrogate, nor did he misinterpret the special feeling aroused by an admirer as evidence that the person would eagerly fulfill his unrealistic wishes.

He hired a new office manager based on her reputation and demonstrated capacity as an effective administrator, rather than on a fantasy that she would be an admiring puppeteer. As she organized his office operations and his new staff, he took charge of his near bankrupt finances, quadrupled his income, arranged to pay his obligations to the federal and state revenue agencies, banks, and credit card companies, and freed himself of debt in two years.

And he met and married Erica, an intelligent, sensitive businesswoman with whom he formed a relationship based on mutual love and respect, rather than on illusions patterned after his childhood image of Booba. Both cared deeply for each other, had a healthy admiration for each other's values and work, and enjoyed thinking and planning together. She did not give him, nor did Michael now need, the hands-on management he had felt as a boy with Booba and had striven to recapture as an adult. When Mr. Morris no longer felt driven by needs for Booba, or for a "pile of junk," we terminated his self-knowledge therapy, and, a year later, when we sidled off at a corner table to converse at a social gathering, he told me that he and Erica were happy, his business was flourishing, and his medical tests had shown no recurrence of the colon cancer.

9

So Big and Long

Angela Armagh arrived ten minutes early for our appointment on a snowy day in late February. Dressed normally for a seventeen year old, she wore an expensive red blouse, holey blue jeans with a tear in the knee, galoshes covering ragged running shoes, and a beautiful purple parka, with mittens stuffed in its pockets, that she had already hung on the coat rack.

As soon as we greeted each other she asked, with an embarrassed smile, "Can I use your phone? My cell is dead."

I nodded and, after we entered the consultation room, pointed to the telephone on my desk. She glanced at a card in her wallet, dialed, and, after a long wait, said into the phone, "Is this Triple-A?" then, after a pause, "It's a black Honda Accord, and it's stuck in the snow on the D.C. side of Western Avenue at Pinehurst Circle."

Looking at me, she asked, "How long is our appointment?"

When I answered, "I've set aside an hour and forty minutes, but we can adjust that if you need to," she turned back to the phone and said, "That's fine, I'll be waiting for you."

After hanging up, she informed me, "My car slipped into a rut about a mile from here, and I couldn't get it out.

The man I just talked to at Triple-A said it would be at least two hours, so I'll have time to get back there after we finish."

Her smile sparkled as she moved to the chair, sat, and looked expectantly at me.

I began, "When you called you mentioned you wanted to talk with me about school problems. Is that a good place to start?"

Her smile vanished, and she looked away.

"Yes, that's what I want to talk with you about, but I'm not sure how to start."

"Why don't we start where you feel comfortable, and we can take it from there," I replied.

Settling herself in her chair, she said, "I've always been an 'A' student, but this semester something's wrong. I can't study like I used to, and my grades have sunk." She glanced out the window.

When several moments had passed, I asked, "What do you think happened to account for it?"

"I don't know," she responded, looking at me tentatively. "Everything else seems all right. I'm active in student government like I've always been. So really a lot of things are okay, but I'm worried about my grades because that's mostly what colleges look at, and I'm already a junior so I have to keep up my GPA [Grade Point Average]. My science and English courses are all AP [Advanced Placement], and I thought I could ace them like I always have, but now I'm getting worried."

"When did things change?" I asked.

She responded immediately, as though certain of the moment. "It happened a month ago, at the beginning of this term."

"What happened?" I asked.

"My mind just stopped working when I tried to take tests and do homework," she said, frowning.

"When your mind stops working, what happens next?" I asked.

"I sit down and look at the test, or book, and try to think about it, but I get scared."

"Talk about getting scared?" I urged.

Her eyes widened, and she gave me a fearful look before glancing away.

"Its like something very bad is going to happen that I can't stop, and then I can't think, no matter how hard I concentrate. I've always enjoyed studying with Mother before, but that doesn't help now. And it's gotten worse. At first I could at least answer questions and discuss ideas in class, but I can't even do that any more."

"Have you found anything that's helped?" I asked.

Appearing puzzled, she said, "At first I was so scared I didn't know what to do. Then I talked to Dad, and he told me to see our family doctor, but the doctor didn't have the training to help me and suggested that I see a psychiatrist. But the psychiatrist didn't help me either. She said my problem was caused by a 'biochemical imbalance' and gave me some medicine to make me feel better, but it made my mind relax so much my concentration was even worse than before."

She shook her head. "Then I talked to the school psychologist, who said I had 'Attention Deficit Disorder,' and arranged for me to take tests alone, so I wouldn't have the pressure of other students around. I guess that helps some people, but for me it only made things worse. I need to know that other people are with me, because working alone makes me more scared and more afraid something bad is going to happen."

She pursed her lips for a moment, then took a deep breath.

"I knew by then I had to find something that made more sense and could help me, because the doctors I talked to sounded like they didn't understand what was wrong with me. I was terrified that if I didn't find out soon what was making this happen, and fix it, I'd never get over it. So, on my own, I called my pediatrician, who's helped me before when I've had a problem, and when I told her what had happened, she gave me your name right away."

Angela's voice had lightened, and she sounded encouraged.

"What do you think is making it happen?" I asked.

"I think it's because Mother has such high expectations of me that I'm afraid I'll disappoint her. She's so performance minded, she constantly pressures me to do well in school." Angela spoke with a whine she had not used before. "And, uh, uh, then I get distracted and can't think," she added, twirling her hair with her fingers.

Her hesitation and changed tone of voice suggested to me she both believed and did not believe what she was saying.

"The higher in school I get, and the more difficult my courses are, the more I'm afraid of failing. Mother's always unhappy with me if I don't do well, even if she doesn't say anything. I don't get 'B's' often, but when I do I can tell she's disappointed.

"But I'm mixed up about this, because I really love to please her with my good grades. She tells everyone I'm her pride and joy, because I love to learn and do well in school, and when she says things like that, the bad feelings go away until I try to study again."

"What about Mother's pleasure in your school work?" I asked.

With a happy smile, she folded her legs underneath her and clasped her hands over her knees. "It's not just her pleasure, I also enjoy doing my school work with her. As far back as I can remember we've always sat together and talked about the new things I've learned. By kindergarten I knew the alphabet, how to put letter sounds together, the names of colors, how to read, and how to add and subtract. In elementary, junior high, and even now in high school we've done my homework together every afternoon. It's fun, and I always enjoy it, but I can't do it anymore because I get too upset and anxious, just like I do in tests."

"What else do you recall about when these feelings began?" I asked.

Her eyes wandered, and she said, "What? Oh, uh, it was during a test on the last Monday in January. I remember because we'd gone to New England over the weekend, and I hadn't studied."

"Do you ordinarily study on a trip?"

She nodded. "Usually, but this trip was different. I didn't open a book."

"Different in what way?" I asked.

Frowning, she said, "Oh, Mother and I were just looking at colleges."

After a moment, she asked, "What were we just talking about?"

"You had said, 'Mother and I were looking at colleges.' Can you sense what there might have been about the trip that made you frown, and then push out of your mind what you had said?" I asked.

She looked out the window at a male cardinal sitting on a snow covered branch, then moved around in her chair for a better view before responding. "That's such a beautiful red bird, what kind is it?"

Before I could reply, she said, "I just got that bad feeling again," then continued to watch the cardinal as it flew away.

After a moment, I gently asked, "That bad feeling?"

She shifted restlessly in her chair, then shot back, "Yes," in a hard tone.

"Can you say more about it?" I asked.

She scowled, as though she had hoped her firm, "Yes," would have forestalled any more questions. After several moments, she said, "It's like the feeling that happens during tests."

Her crossed leg moved up, down, and around in circles, while she shifted her gaze to a squirrel climbing the tree just beyond the window.

"And were you saying the bad feeling began on your college scouting trip?" I asked.

Her leg moved faster. "Yes," she said with irritation, "that's when it started, and it keeps happening every time I remember that trip."

"Say more about 'That's when'?" I encouraged her.

She looked outside for more than a minute, then continued in a subdued voice. "When I saw those college dormitories, I knew that if I went there, I'd be there without Mother."

"What did you mean, 'if'?" I asked.

Sounding annoyed, she replied, "I'm not sure I'm going. I'm afraid if I go away to school, I'll have that bad feeling all the time."

"The bad feeling again asks us to understand more about it," I said.

She cupped her hands over her face as she broke out in tears. "I just want to make this whole thing go away," she cried.

When her crying persisted, I said, "I know this is difficult, but I'm sure, as I think you, too, know, that this self-knowledge work, like many medical procedures, often requires one to endure pain temporarily in order to get relief and be cured, and we must understand this feeling so you can overcome what would keep you from being and doing what you want with your life."

By the time I had finished my comment, her tears had stopped.

"It feels like I'm all alone, and it's the end of the world," she said, in a small voice, as she stared outside with a far-off look. "I don't really need her any more, not like I did when I was little, or even a few years ago. I mean, I can feed myself and can study and take tests without her, but she's always been with me and helped me, and I always feel so good when we study together, and she praises me. I don't know what I'd do without her."

Her gaze returned to the woods outside, though she didn't seem to be looking at anything in particular.

"It seems like the closer I get to graduation, the worse I feel. Sometimes I think I'm so dependent on her that I'll have to go to one of the colleges around here so I can live at home, but I don't really want to do that because most of their physics departments don't have what I'll need for the graduate school and career I want."

We both happened to glance at the clock and see that our time was almost up.

I said, "From what you've told me today, I think we can make inroads into overcoming your problem by the time you're due to leave for college, and, though we likely can't complete the work by then, we can either continue by telephone, or I can refer you to someone near wherever you go who can help you. For now, as I mentioned on the phone, we can meet at this same time next week, and continue where we left off today."

"Good. I'll see you then," she responded.

The next session she sat and, after observing the snow covered woods, began, "I told you about Mother last time, and I've been thinking a lot about my two brothers since we talked."

"What are you thinking about them?" I asked.

She said, "I've never really gotten to know my big brother, Sidney, very well. He's eight years older than I am, and went away to college when I was in fifth grade. My little brother, Sam, is three years younger than I am. Sidney was already in school when I was born, and Mother says that she and I were alone together most of the day, and that I got so used to thinking I was her only child, and she was my personal possession, that when Sam was born I acted like he didn't exist," she said, with a self-conscious giggle.

"What about Mother being your personal possession?" I asked.

"My Aunt Rachel, she's Mother's best friend, says that Mother acted as if that were really true. Mother never told me this, but Aunt Rachel said that after Sidney started school Mother had wanted another child and when she couldn't get pregnant she gave up hope. But then I came, as Aunt Rachel put it, 'as a gift from Heaven,' and Mother told her that she felt she could 'have with me all the joy she'd had with Sidney plus the mother-daughter relationship she'd missed with a son.'" Angela blushed faintly.

"I remember that when I started school, I wanted to be a straight "A" student so Mother would be happy with me— and I was from the beginning—and to live up to the way she talked about me."

Angela covered her face with a magazine from a nearby stand to hide a giggle. "I'm embarrassed to tell you this, but people say I'm such a 'nice, sweet girl,' and, that Mother named me Angela because God had told her I would be an angel." Then, she added, "Our next door neighbor said she knew my thoughts were pure because I've never said an unkind word to anyone," with a coy, but-you-and-I-know-the-real-truth look.

"A lot of people say things like that about me, and I know they're partly true, but there are a lot of other things they don't know about me." She hesitated and twisted a lock of hair. "I didn't go to pre-school, because I was afraid of being away from Mother, and I would only go to kindergarten when she promised me she would sit right outside the door. By first grade I did a little better—I agreed to go if she went with me and sat outside until I knew I'd be all right and had the telephone number where she'd be. In second grade I still insisted that she walk with me to school, but by then I could stay without having to know where she was. And by third grade," she was sounding stronger and more confident, "I was walking with my friends to school two blocks away, although Mother told me later she'd watched me from a distance until I was inside the school building. I guess lots of parents do that.

"I wasn't so scared after that. But I still usually stayed at home, or near home, other than school, unless Mother went places with me. Even when I was thirteen, I wouldn't go to birthday parties or get-togethers with my friends if they were more than a few blocks away, because by then I would have been too embarrassed for her to go with me. And I definitely would not go on sleepovers."

Several moments passed while she scowled.

"You're hesitating to say something?" I asked.

She responded, "I got a little scared when I started to tell you about a crush I had on a boy two years ago. It didn't last long, and I wouldn't spend time with him, unless we were at my house and Mother was there. Mostly we talked on the phone."

Twirling a curled lock with her finger, she said, "This past year I've gone to movies and school activities, but I always feel like something is pulling me home. I don't spend time with friends after school the way other students do, and when I do hang out with them I leave as soon as I can, unless it would be too embarrassing. I like to go to sports events with Dad and my brothers, but to be really honest, I'd rather talk with Mother about my studies or something in the news."

Over the following weeks and months, Angela continued to approach the therapy sessions with the interest and enthusiasm she had shown from the beginning and with an increasingly mature tone.

One day, about four months into our work, she came into the office, sat up straight, and said, "I don't really need Mother any longer to take care of me, or even study, but I feel like I have to be near her all the time. Actually, it's more that I feel secure when I'm near her than it is dependency on anything she does, so I feel awfully scared just to think of going off to college without her."

She paused and hid her face in her hands.

"I feel so childish talking like this."

Dropping her hands in her lap, she half smiled. "I've read that a part of everyone wants to stay a child, and I agree with the Bible when it says we ought to 'put away childish things,' but sometimes I wish I could be like Peter Pan and stay a child forever, so I would never have to be afraid of leaving home. My friends rebel against their parents and authorities all the time, and I guess that makes going away to college easier for them, but when I start thinking about leaving home, I get too afraid, and I don't want to go anywhere."

Suddenly, she raised her eyebrows and looked outside.

"Did something startle you?" I asked.

Hiding her face in her hands for a moment, she gave a self-conscious smile, "It's the whistle of that train going by. I've never been on a train, and I don't even see one very often, because there aren't any where I live, but you have some tracks about a mile from here, and whenever I pass by them or hear the train whistle, I get that scary feeling because I see myself on it alone."

As the sound of the train became distant, her body and face relaxed.

"What I'm really worried about now are my grades and looking at colleges, because competition to get into a good school is really fierce. I want to go to a university with a good physics department, so I've got to keep my GPA high, but I get scared when I talk about these things. I don't know how I sound to you, but when I think about leaving home and going to college without Mother, I feel all empty and alone inside, like those feelings I told you about that something really bad is going to happen. I just feel like I can't do it," she said, bursting into tears.

"You've brought us back to the bad feelings. Do you remember ever having those feelings before the college scouting trip?" I asked.

She took a few minutes to wipe her eyes and compose herself.

"When I was little, I wanted to stay with Mother so much I didn't think about anything else," she said, as a tear rolled down her cheek. "But I'm seventeen now, and I get more and more embarrassed about it with my friends." She wiped away her tear. "They don't make fun of me, but when I always say, 'I can't go out because I have to stay home and study' or, 'I have to go home now,' and it's just nine o'clock, they look at me like they're wondering what's wrong with me. I really want to be more independent than that, but I'm afraid that if Mother thinks I'm trying to push her away, she'll feel hurt and pull away from me, and then I won't have her and I'll feel guilty too."

By this point in her self-knowledge work, Angela had begun to realize her problem was not whether Mother was nearby, but why she needed her mother around to feel secure.

The next session, she smiled, and with deep breath, began, "I want to talk about those 'bad feelings' today. You asked me last time what I remember about the bad feelings from when I was little. In many ways they're the same now as when I was afraid to go to kindergarten without Mother, because then I was afraid I'd be all alone, and something bad would happen if I left home without her, and now I'm afraid I'll have all those feelings if I go to college and she's not there. But it's different now, because when I was little, there was nothing bad at school, I was just afraid to leave Mother at home without me, but now I'm scared something bad will happen at college if she's not with me."

"Say more about scared?" I asked.

Her face became red, then she crossed her legs and tugged the hem of her skirt as far below her knees as it would go.

"When I think of going off to college now, I keep seeing that dormitory and . . ."

Her eyes grew wide with alarm, she looked out the window, and then asked if I would close the drapes.

I leaned over, drew the drape cords, and said, "You said 'I keep seeing that dormitory and,' and then interrupted yourself. Was there something hard to say?"

She moved her crossed leg around in circles, realized her skirt had crawled up, and again pulled the edge of the skirt down as far as she could.

"I get afraid when I see that dormitory," she said.

"When you say 'that dormitory,' you seem to have a specific dormitory in mind?" I asked.

"Yes, I mean the one I saw on that trip." Her eyes widened again, then she gasped, "I just realized it was a coed dormitory."

"What about a coed dormitory?" I asked.

Almost breathless, she said, "I can't believe this. I've known all along it was a coed dormitory."

"There's something about it being a coed dormitory that makes it harder to remember?" I asked.

She blushed again, began breathing rapidly, drummed her fingers on the arm of the chair, and briskly moved her right foot up and down. "I keep having pictures in my mind of the students having sex. I don't know why. I certainly never thought they had anything to do with my fear of going there."

She began scratching her thigh, but stopped abruptly, as if self-conscious about what she was doing.

"What about the mental pictures of students having sex?" I asked.

Glancing out the window, she said, "That's what I kept picturing when Mother and I went on the New England college tour." She quickly added, with a slight smile and red face, "But I really don't want to talk about this."

Pulling a bottle of fizzy water from her tote bag, she said, "Is it all right for me to drink this while we talk?"

I smiled and nodded, although she had taken a quick gulp before I could reply.

Covering her face with her hands again, she said, "I know what you want me to say, and I don't want to talk about it."

"Do you know why you don't want to talk about what you think I want you to say?" I asked.

With an unsuccessfully suppressed laugh of exasperation, she said, "Yes, but if I tell you that, then I'm talking about it, and those pictures are too scary."

"Scary in what way?" I asked.

She rolled her eyes and sighed in resignation to my unrelenting pursuit of understanding her scary feelings, and said, "Because they're just like the ones of my parents having sex, and . . ."

Abruptly stopping herself, she blushed, suppressed a smile, looked out the window, and again stretched her skirt over her knees.

Sensing her embarrassment, I asked, "Could your unease suggest that what you were going to say next would have been even more difficult to talk about?"

After several moments, she blurted out, "I thought about the scary pictures of Sidney and me."

"Say more about the 'scary pictures'?" I persisted.

She rolled her eyes, and said, "The ones I get in my mind, they're so real I'm afraid they'll come true. I feel safer if I'm with Mother, because then I know that nothing like that will ever actually happen," she quickly added.

"You seemed to feel even more scared about the images of you and Sidney than of your parents having sex. Can you sense how come?" I asked.

She glanced at me, looked out window with a determined expression, took a deep breath, and turned back to me. "One thing I haven't told you before is that my thoughts are not as pure as that neighbor lady I told you about said they were. The pictures of my parents are like sex scenes on TV or in movies. They upset me a little because they're sexual, but they don't scare me. It's the other ones that I can't stop from going through my mind that are scary."

"Thoughts about you and Sidney?" I asked.

Like a baseball pitcher shaking off a sign from the catcher, she shook her head to make clear she did not like my question. After several moments of staring out the window, she said, "Those are really big oak trees out there. I've never noticed them before, but I don't know why, because I've seen those squirrels jumping from one tree to another."

She was silent again for several moments, then, looking irritated, burst out, "The answer to your question is, yes. That's when I really want to be close to Mother, because those pictures make me have tingly feelings all over my body."

She turned her body sideways in her chair and pulled her skirt edge down over her now exposed lower leg.

"I never talk about this with my girl friends, but I hear them talk about getting excited over some rock singer, or movie star, or boy friend. That doesn't make much sense to me, they don't even know most of the men they talk about. I've felt close to Sidney my whole life, so when I have these feelings it seems more natural than to have them about someone I don't know."

"You said you've had these feelings for Sidney your whole life." Then, knowing that puberty brings feelings one has never experienced before, I asked, "Have they changed any over time?"

She twisted a lock of her hair around her finger.

"I've always adored him, but it's only been since I was thirteen that I've had these pictures of him and me that give me those tingly feelings. Sidney and I have never done anything like that, but I'm always afraid he might want to, and that's when I especially have to be near Mother. I wish I didn't have these thoughts because they make me scared, and I feel so guilty, but I can't stop them." She blushed, and added, "And in a way I like them, too."

"Could there be a connection between liking the pictures of you and Sidney and not being able to stop them?" I asked.

She stared at me, clearly startled.

"I don't know, um, I don't know. I hadn't even thought about liking the pictures, until you just made me say it, and I certainly never thought that liking them had anything to with why I can't stop them."

"What about liking them?" I asked.

She blushed.

"If the blush could talk, can you sense what it would say?" I asked.

She fidgeted, then said, "Well, they're exciting." After a few moments, she added, "Maybe that's why I can't stop them."

"Can you say more about exciting?" I asked.

"Well, they kind of make my body tingle." She fiddled with a ring on her finger. "That's why I don't want to think about them."

"How so?" I asked.

"I feel guilty about having these feelings for Sidney, because he's my brother," she fiddled with her ring again, "but I don't know what it would be like to have tingly feelings if they weren't about Sidney."

Angela gazed outside.

I asked, "What are you thinking?"

She looked at me in silence.

"I'm thinking about why I want to be near Mother."

When an apparent change in topic occurs, a self-knowledge therapist must consider whether the shift is an actual change to a different topic, or is an amplification of the topic at hand. If the change is to a different topic, no matter how small the change, and is functioning as a defense, the self-knowledge therapist will ordinarily interpret the defense as a protection against some disturbing element in the original topic, and then pursue the disturbing element.

But the change may also be a subconscious indication

that, while work on the first problem is still incomplete, the person has progressed with the topic as far as she can at the moment, and for now, some other issue weighs more heavily.

In view of this uncertainty, I followed up her last idea by asking, "What else are you thinking about?"

She looked at me, glanced away quickly, and, after a few moments, took a deep breath and turned back.

"It's those 'all alone' and 'end of the world' bad feelings that keep me from studying and taking tests," she said, with haunted eyes.

"What more can you sense about what brings on the bad feelings?" I asked.

Angela replied, "I know they happen when I think about going to college without Mother, but I don't know why they happen at other times, too. They always happen when I'm afraid of not being with her, but sometimes I just get afraid something very bad will happen to her for no reason at all."

"What about the fear something bad will happen to her?" I asked.

She furrowed her brow in thought.

"I remember when I was in first or second grade I heard someone, maybe Aunt Rachel, say I had a 'school phobia,' and that was why I didn't want to go to school. I didn't know what 'phobia' meant at the time, but somehow I figured out that she thought I was afraid of going to school. I knew that she was wrong even then, but I didn't know how to argue with her. 'Phobia' was such a unusual word it stuck with me, and a long time later I found out that 'school phobia' meant being afraid of school, and I thought it sounded crazy. I was never afraid of school, I liked school, I liked learning, and I liked my teachers and friends. I wasn't afraid of school, I didn't want to go to school because I was afraid of leaving home."

"Afraid of what?" I asked.

She stared at me.

"I was afraid something bad would happen to Mother."

"What do you mean?" I asked.

"I've always been afraid something bad would happen to her, but when I was little it was much worse," she said, picking nervously at the hem of her skirt.

"What kind of much worse?" I asked.

She smiled. "I'd rather talk about that pretty cardinal on the windowsill." Then resuming her serious expression she continued. "I know I was afraid for a long time, even before I started school, and I especially remember worrying," she spoke rapidly, as if she wanted to get beyond the ideas as quickly as possible, "that Mother and Sam might accidentally fall down the stairs and get killed, or a robber would break in and shoot them, or the house would catch fire and they'd burn up."

"And staying home helped you not be so afraid?" I asked.

She pursed her lips and squinched her eyes shut in a deep frown of concentration. "I had to stay home so I could be sure Sam would be all right if Mother fell down the stairs with him, and I could hit the robber with a poker, and I could put out the fire or call the fire department. If something bad happened to Mother, then I wouldn't have anybody, I'd be all alone, and it would be the end of the world."

She sank back in her chair, relaxed her tightly closed eyes, and exhaled deeply.

"Telling me about those thoughts took away some of the fear?" I asked.

"Yes," she nodded, "I thought you'd get mad at me or something bad would happen if I told you about them."

"You've had to live with those memories cooped up inside a long time," I said.

She opened her eyes wide. "I've always been afraid of thinking about them, and I've never told anyone before."

I said, "You remembered those fears of terrible things happening to Mother and Sam when you were wondering why you'd feel 'all alone' and it's the 'end of the world' at times other than thinking of going off to college without Mother. What more occurs to you about fearing that Mother and Sam would fall down the stairs or get killed by a robber or burn up in a fire?"

"I don't know, I don't think about it much, those fears just seem to come," she said. "I never think about her falling down the stairs with him anymore, that was only when I was really little, and she was still carrying him around." Her face suddenly became expressionless.

I asked, "You stopped abruptly after you commented that you weren't afraid anymore that Mother would fall down the stairs with Sam. Could that suggest that you sometimes still have other fears about scary things happening to them?"

Silence.

"If your silence could talk, can you sense what it would say?" I asked.

"I'm not thinking anything, so there's nothing to say," she responded.

Several moments of silence later, she said, in a subdued voice, "I don't have those other fears anymore either."

Her silence continued, as she furrowed her brow and pursed her lips.

"Sometimes I do have thoughts about bad things happening to Mother and Sam, but they just flash through my mind and don't upset me."

"Do any particular thoughts come to mind?" I asked.

After a brief pause, she responded, "Sam plays football at school, and when I read one day that a player had broken his spine and was paralyzed, I've worried ever since that that would happen to Sam. And almost every day when I read about car accidents, I'm afraid that will happen to Mother, too. I don't get anxious and afraid like I do when I think about going off to college, but anytime she's out driving somewhere, like to the grocery store, I worry until she gets home."

"Can you sense when these worries come on?" I asked.

"No, they just happen," she said.

"You mentioned you worried about something bad happening to Sam when he played football. What occurs to you about football?" I asked.

"I hate football, I don't know why anyone would like it, I never watch a game, and I sure wouldn't go to see one," she said.

"What about Sam's games?" I asked.

"NO!" she shouted. "I would never go to one of his games, I'd be too worried about Sam to think about the game. I don't know how Mother stands it. She loves going to his games, and then she waits for him after the game so they can drive home together. She can't wait to tell him, 'Oh Sam, you were great today, that was such a beautiful pass you caught, and when the guy on the other team intercepted, you tackled him and saved the game,'" Angela spoke in saccharine, sarcastic tones. "I hate it when she carries on like that, I wish they were both dead." Surprised with what she had just said, she quickly added, "Well, not really, but I do remember one time I got worried they would have a car accident driving home, and they would both get killed."

"What occurs to you about what you just said," I asked.

"What do you mean?" she asked.

I said, "You recalled worrying about Mother and Sam having a car accident and getting killed just after you had wished they were both dead because Mother had made such a big to-do about Sam's game."

Wide-eyed and speechless with astonishment, she clasped her hands to her face and looked at me for several moments. Finally, she said, "Maybe what you said is true, it's just hard for me to believe." She shook her head slowly. "I've always known how much I hate them when Mother fusses over Sam like he was some great prince or something, but I never realized that it might be connected to my being afraid, or, I guess, why I have to worry about protecting them."

She glanced at the clock, and I suddenly realized our time was up, so I said, "Well, it sounds like this is one of those times when the power of what we've talked about today sets the agenda for next time."

She smiled perfunctorily, nodded, and left.

The next session she began, "I've been thinking about this constantly since last time. I think I've always known it in the back of mind, but I never knew enough about it to talk or even think about it. People have told me that when I was really little I was always happy and loved to be with Mother, and that I was so confident and secure I was never afraid when she went away for hours, or even days." Angela spoke in a voice filled with sorrow while she looked at the floor.

"There's something about people telling you how happy you were that makes you sad?" I asked.

She nodded.

"Can you sense how come?" I asked.

"It's because of what they said next. They said that I changed after Sam was born, and that from then on I would never leave Mother, or let her go away from me. I don't have actual memories of when I was really little, but I know I was happy, I can just feel it."

"What occurs to you about the change?" I asked.

She brushed away a tear before it could fall.

"I don't remember when he was born, or when he came home from the hospital, but everyone in the family remembers that I kept saying," she half-smiled, "'Mother, take him back to the hospital.'"

"What do you think, 'take him back to the hospital' meant?" I asked.

She frowned.

"I know I've always loved Sam and wanted to take care of him, but I've never felt like he really belonged in our family. I've always been afraid something really bad would happen to him, and the main reason I liked to take care of him was that I knew he'd be safe with me."

"What do you sense about 'something really bad' happening to him?" I asked.

"Well, like I said a minute ago," Angela began, as her frown deepened, "I've always loved Sam. I just never felt like he really belonged with us, at least not when I was little. I always wanted him to go away, and sometimes when I took care of him, I was afraid I would hurt him."

She closed her eyes and grimaced, as if she wanted to blind herself to what she saw in her mind's eye.

"Can you say 'hurt him' how?" I asked.

"I remember once when he wouldn't stop crying . . ." she abruptly stopped talking, as her eyes remained closed.

"You stopped yourself," I prompted.

She sat in silence several moments, then opened her eyes wide, as if by an act of great will. "And I wanted to throw him him down the stairs. These are horrible things to say, but I guess I have to. I remember hearing once about someone burning up in a house fire, and I thought how I wished that would happen to Sam, so he wouldn't cry any more, and I wouldn't have to take care of him." She rubbed her eyes with the heels of her hand. "But then, when I thought those things, I felt guilty and blanked my mind so I wouldn't think them any more.

"You said that when you had the 'school phobia' you had to stay home because you were worried about Mother, too," I said.

She looked puzzled as she uncrossed and recrossed her legs, then her eyes grew big with alarm.

"What do you mean?" she said.

I replied, "When you spoke of being afraid that your wish that Sam would burn up or fall down the stairs might actually happen, I remembered what you had said earlier about being afraid something bad would happen to Mother if you went to school. So it made me wonder if you could have wished something bad would've happened to her, too, like we were talking about last time when you wished they both were dead."

"No! Absolutely not," Angela declared. "I could never have wanted anything like that to happen to Mother."

She looked outside for several moments, then turned back to me.

"Uh, uh, I do remember, though that when I hated Sam for just being there, I blamed her for bringing him home, but I never would have wanted her to fall down the stairs, or burn up, or anything like that. And even if I did, I don't remember it."

She again looked outside, while she swung her leg from side to side.

"I blamed her even more when she tried to send me off to school, so she and Sam could stay home and play together. I can't remember any more about that, but I do remember that when I was eight or nine, Mother liked to get out the family pictures, so she could show her friends how she breast-fed Sam, and I couldn't stand to look at them."

"How come?" I asked.

"I just wasn't interested, that's all, I'd seen them all before," she said.

"That you may not have been interested, or even bored, in seeing them for the thousandth time is one thing, and certainly understandable, but not being able to stand it would seem to be something else," I said.

She looked blank. "I don't understand what you're getting at."

"When you look at those pictures in your mind's eye now, how does it feel?" I asked.

She looked away from me, and said, "I can't."

"'I can't' what?" I asked.

Appearing irritated, she said, "I can't look at those pictures."

"Are you saying, 'I can't see them'?" I asked.

Her crossed leg moved up and down in agitation.

"No, I can see them," she exclaimed, in an angry, hurt voice, "but just for a second, and then I can't look any longer."

"Can you sense what happens to your feelings during that second that makes you not able to look any longer?" I asked.

She pressed her lips tightly together, then burst out, "I hated them, both of them. Sam was sucking away, looking up at her with his big eyes, and she was looking down at him with such an adoring smile that . . ." She stopped abruptly.

"That, what?" I asked.

She broke into tears, and sobbed, "I thought she felt that way only for me."

She cried for several minutes, and I did not interrupt her. When her tears had lessened enough to talk, I asked,

"Did you sense any other feeling in that moment you let yourself see the picture?"

After looking at the floor for several seconds, she said, "I couldn't've told you if you hadn't asked because I forgot it almost as soon as it happened."

"Can you say more about 'it' that just happened?" I asked.

She fidgeted in her chair and looked around the room. "I hated them, and when I saw them look at each other like they were in love with each other, I wished they were dead." Her face was ashen and expressionless. "I feel terrible saying these things, but I remember this is how I felt when I got afraid they would fall down the stairs or burn up in a house fire.

"I got all mixed up between wanting these things to happen to them and then being afraid that they really would happen, and that's why I wouldn't go to school, and why I had to stay home, to be sure they would be safe."

We both sat without speaking for a few minutes to allow her feelings to settle and for both of us to grasp the power of what she had said.

She glanced at her watch, then buttoned her sweater, put on her woolen cap, and said, "I'll see you next time."

With a slight smile, I nodded, and she left.

The next session, still subdued from the previous time, she sat silently a few moments. "I've thought a lot about what we talked about last time. I don't remember exactly when, maybe when I was twelve or thirteen, but I started hating mother all over again when she doted on Sam."

"What more do you remember about it?" I asked.

"It would happen when I was enjoying being with her, or studying together, and when she praised me I would be thinking in the back of my mind how she had betrayed me, that her 'pride' in me was all a lie, because if she had really felt that way she never would have had Sam."

She looked as if she had been punched.

"It was so upsetting I had to blank my mind, and that was when I couldn't stand to look at those pictures of her nursing Sam any more."

Twirling her hair between her fingers, she looked out the window.

"Can you think out loud?" I asked.

She shrugged her shoulders.

"When I said just then that I couldn't stand looking at those pictures of Mother and Sam anymore, I remembered that my fears would go away after I stopped thinking bad things about her and began thinking how much I loved her and wanted to be with her and enjoyed studying together with her."

Her voice softened as she spoke of being near Mother.

"You said a moment ago that your fears went away when you stopped thinking bad things about Mother and began thinking how much you loved her. Are you saying that feeling loving with your Mother protects you from the fears that came from your wishes for her and Sam to die or get killed?" I asked.

She sat pensively for a moment. "I think that's right," she said softly, then added, "but I don't just think it's right, it feels right, too.

"It was like what happened when I was in third grade and stopped being afraid of going to school. I got better partly because Mother always assured me she was safe and took me to school and sat outside and everything, and I eventually learned she would be all right, and also Sam got older, so Mother didn't need to nurse and baby him any more. But mostly I got closer to Mother because we started studying and doing homework together, so I guess I just stopped hating her and Sam so much." She twisted her hands together. "But those fears never completely went away, they've always been in the back of my mind, just like the bad feelings."

She stared at the wall, as if deep in thought, and did not speak for many, long moments.

"Can you put these thoughts into words?" I asked.

"I was thinking about those angry thoughts I had toward Mother, and then some memories that were kind of like bad thoughts started running through my mind, although it's hard to get them back."

Angela covered her eyes with her hands.

"Perhaps you don't want to see what you're remembering."

She folded her hands in her lap and swallowed hard.

"When I got mad at her, I couldn't say anything, because I was afraid she'd go away, like now when I think of going off to college."

"Say more about 'couldn't say anything'?" I asked.

She folded her hands in her lap.

"I don't sass or even disagree with my parents, especially Mother, like my friends do," she said, quietly. "One time I watched a video of *Rebel Without a Cause*, that 1950's movie with James Dean, with some friends, and I can understand why people idolize him, but he was not 'without a cause.' I knew what his cause was; he wanted to be independent, but he was afraid to leave home. But I couldn't feel like my friends did about rebelling against their parents, even thinking about it was too upsetting."

"Say more about upsetting?" I asked.

"I got scared the first time we talked about my hating Mother and Sam and wishing they were dead. Until then, as far as I knew, I wasn't ever mad at either of them, then or anytime. Mother was so loving and good to me, I had no idea where those feelings were coming from. I thought maybe you were one of those therapists who puts false memories in people's minds. The only thing Mother did really bad," she smiled as if amused with her next thought, "was that she didn't love me enough not to have had Sam."

Over a few moments, her smile faded, and she became silent and expressionless, as her crossed leg began swinging wildly.

"There's still something I haven't told you, because every time it flashes through my mind, I get afraid, and it goes away so quickly I can't keep it in mind long enough to say it. But maybe, if we talk about it together, I can remember it. I've told you how scared I am of the sexual pictures I imagine of Sidney and me, and that being with Mother helped me not be so afraid, and that when I thought about moving into that coed dorm with all those boys, I got afraid all over again. But I don't really know why the pictures make me so afraid."

"What do you see in the pictures?" I asked.

Her face flushed, and she covered her eyes with her hands.

"It's too embarrassing to talk about. Maybe I can tell you about when they started, though. When I was seven— I remember exactly when, because I'd just started second grade—I heard Sidney and his friend, Ray, one day when they were talking and laughing about something they saw in their 'fuck books'—that's what they called them."

Her face flushed as she looked slightly embarrassed.

"As soon as they left I snuck into Sidney's room and looked at the books, actually they were more like pamphlets. They were full of pictures, actually drawings, of naked men and women. I had never seen or heard about anything like it, especially the pictures of penises that were so big and long. I knew boys and men had penises, but I never imagined penises could be so enormous. I had helped diaper Sam and saw his little baby penis, and Sidney's once when I accidentally walked in on him undressed, but I certainly had never seen one as big as what I saw in that fuck book!"

As this seventeen year old, quite proper young woman spoke unhesitatingly, even when appearing deeply embarrassed and self-conscious, about "fuck" and "penises" that were "big and long," I was struck with how dramatically societal and self-knowledge therapy attitudes about sexual feelings changed in the late twentieth century. Before the sexual revolution and the women's movement, a therapist had to approach such issues with extreme caution and sensitivity. While the emotions attached to sex can still create highly-charged, self-defeating reactions, intellectual access to the topic has become much easier.

After looking at the wall a few moments, she continued. "The penises in that book looked almost as big around and long as the men's arms and legs. And when the book showed men and women's bodies close together the penises weren't in the picture, and I didn't know what to think, but it looked like the men had put their penises inside the women's bodies, but I didn't know how that could happen, because I didn't know of any place they could go in. At the time I was too shocked, and I guess confused, to think much about it."

Angela spoke with relative ease about these topics, so I sensed she had not yet talked about the most disturbing part.

I commented, "You said, 'at the time,' like you might have thought more about it later."

Her leg began circling.

"I told you earlier that I didn't know about men and women having sex until I heard my friends talk about it when I was almost thirteen," she said with a blush, "but that's not exactly right. My room was next to Sidney's and even when I was six or seven I heard him and his friends talk and brag about sex all the time. Usually his door was open, and, even when it wasn't, I could put my ear next to the wall and hear everything they said. They would talk about putting their penises in a girl's pussy, and then laugh and laugh, like they knew all about it and did it all the time."

"Was this the part you meant earlier when you said you would feel too embarrassed to talk about it?"

"No."

Silence.

Sensing both how upsetting this material was for her and that she could proceed best at her own pace, I waited for her to decide when she felt ready to continue.

She again folded her hands in her lap, "It might be easier now that I've told you about the fuck books and what Sidney and Ray used to do, but I still didn't tell you everything." She looked at the wall for a moment. "From the time I first saw Sidney's fuck books I kept wondering how would a penis come inside me, because I didn't know then I had a vagina, and I kept trying to think about the penis coming in through my pee hole, and that really scared me because those penises were so big they looked like they were almost as long as my whole body, and I thought it would rip me apart if a man tried to put his big penis inside me." As she talked, her eyes widened, and her face became white as a sheet.

She stopped abruptly, then said, "Excuse me a minute, I need to get something," raced to the waiting room and returned a few seconds later with her bottle of fizzy water, gulped some down, and said, "I just got thirsty and realized I'd left this," pointing to the bottle, "in the waiting room."

She sat silently for a moment, then asked, "Where were we?"

I responded, "You had just said, 'Those penises were so big they looked like they would rip me apart.' That must have felt awfully scary when you were a little girl."

She looked terrified.

"I had forgotten how frightening the picture of that big penis coming inside my pee hole was. One day, when Dad and I were out walking, we saw a pregnant woman with a big stomach, and he said she'd swallowed a watermelon seed, and then I thought maybe I was wrong, and the penis didn't come in through my pee hole, maybe the penis comes in through my mouth, and that wasn't so scary because I knew my mouth was big enough for a penis. But then I got scared when I thought of the baby coming out through my mouth, and then I got all mixed up, because I didn't know which would be worse."

Some color had come back to her face, and she had relaxed slightly when she talked about her relief in thinking about the penis coming into her body through her mouth.

"And then when I got to be thirteen, and my girl friends and I started talking about sex, it got really scary, because I worried all the time about wanting Sidney to do it to me with his penis that I thought was as big as those I saw in the fuck books. That was the embarrassing part to tell you about," she said with a quick smile, "and I've certainly never told anyone else."

Angela looked relieved when she finished, then she half-smiled, and, as she sometimes did after talking about particularly upsetting ideas, made a mock gesture of wiping her brow with her forefinger.

"Earlier you said 'if a man tried to put his big penis inside me,' but this time you said, 'wanting Sidney to do it to me.'"

She nodded.

"Yes, I know. That's why it's all mixed up, because I wanted him to do it to me even though it scared me. I'm afraid even to think about a big penis coming inside me, and I certainly wouldn't want Mother or Sydney to know I wanted my own brother to do it to me." She periodically drank from her bottle of water as she talked. "And then I really got scared when I started thinking about going off to that coed dorm without Mother because I was afraid I would want those boys at college to do it to me."

Angela's dread of going to college resulted from two fundamental fears: her fear of the consequences of her death wishes toward her mother, and her fear of the consequences of her sexual wishes for Sidney. While these fears were connected at a subconscious level, each was based on a separate wish, and these fears and wishes became the primary focus of her therapeutic work.

Her observation that she was "all mixed up, because I wanted him [Sidney] to do it to me even though it scared me," expressed the fundamental principle of human nature we first observed when Mr. Masters (Chapter Ten, Skier and Conflict) discovered that his phobia of riding on the ski lift arose from his wish to jump from its dangerous height: that embedded in any irrational fear or phobia is some form of a subconscious wish or desire driving one to think excessively about a matter he consciously knows is dangerous, repugnant, or undesirable. The wish, however, is usually so remote from the fear that the relationship between the two is difficult for one to connect, until uncovered through self-knowledge.

Just as Angela was terrified of her wishes for Mother and Sam to fall down the stairs, be shot by an intruder, or burn up in a house fire, she likewise feared her sexual wish for Sydney, because it was dangerous (his monstrous penis entering her small body) and forbidden (he was her brother).

Adults often do not recognize or appreciate the depth of emotions and thoughts in the minds of small children, preferring instead to think of their little cherubs as incapable of jealous, murderous rage or of curiosity about the arousal of tingly body sensations. Children's sensitivities to fidelity in relationships are at least as delicate as are adults'; disloyalty, among other crimes, is grounds for capital punishment, though a child, like the very young Angela, cannot conceive of the death sentence's long-term ramifications. Likewise, the nerve endings of a child's body, especially her genitals, are at least as sensitive as an adult's, just as her mind is aware that something very special happens between two people whose relationship includes intimate, skin to skin, pleasurable contact, and she wants to be part of it.

Angela's experience vividly captures the problem little girls face when they are exposed to the world of sex before they are developmentally ready to understand, intellectually or emotionally, all that adult sexuality involves. Because a small child's undeveloped mind can perceive only her present state, a little girl has no way of comprehending, even if great pains are taken to explain it to her, that she has a vagina, that it will develop along with the rest of her body, and that this receptive organ can dilate to accommodate any penis size, just as it can if she delivers a baby.

Without this intellectual and emotional maturity, a little girl is left to her own sexual theories derived from her uninformed imagination, and when she tries to explain to herself how a grown male's mammoth erect penis can enter her tiny body, most often through the urethra or anus, her undeveloped mind can become terrified of the mutilation and horror she envisions. Little girls often find great relief in imagining that the penis enters through the mouth since it provides a much larger opening, and Angela was eager to believe her father's explanation that a woman becomes pregnant by swallowing a watermelon seed. The mental pictures of mutilation can later cause her to avoid sex altogether, or, if she does participate with a male partner, she does it by using an emotional process that manifests as a physical reality of genital numbness, often referred to clinically as "frigidity," which deprives her of sexual, including orgasmic, pleasures.

By the time Angela was a teenager, she had consciously forgotten the events that had caused her to feel betrayed and angry—Sam's birth when she was three and a half, her knowledge of her mother and father's intimacy when she was five and her sexual curiosity, wishes, and fears that focused on Sidney, beginning when she was seven. But her subconscious mind, where the feelings had been etched, had not forgotten, and she developed mechanisms intended to keep these disturbing emotions out of her awareness.

Managing these emotions meant that at the same time Angela was desperately needing her mother in order to feel secure, she was also refusing to acknowledge her rage toward Mother by being a sweet girl and good student— the kind of emotional juggling act our complex mind pulls off regularly without our conscious awareness.

Angela's suppression of her feelings into her subconscious mind had been successful. Too successful. Because she had hidden from herself all anger toward her mother, Angela stifled everyday differences with her mother, and, by extension, with others. She could not allow herself ordinary, healthy gripes common to everyone—especially to a teenager struggling to achieve independence and her own self-identify. She could not understand why her friends were so angry with their parents, and their protests always sounded foreign and ungrateful.

Similarly, since her sexual fantasy life had been bound up in conflict over her erotic feelings for Sidney, she was prevented from experiencing sexual ideas and feelings about boy friends and rock stars she heard her girl friends talk about with great excitement.

When Angela began self-knowledge therapy at seventeen, she had needed Mother to reassure her that Mother would be safe, just as when Angela was a little girl. But at seventeen the haven of Mother's nearness served an additional purpose—protecting Angela from the fear that her sexual feelings would run amok when she went to college. Because Mother's presence as a sanctuary against Angela's fears had been well-established since Sam's birth, when Angela had wished her mother and Sam dead, Angela naturally turned to this defense when her sexual fears about Sidney, and by extension other men, entered her emotional life. As long as her mother was near, Angela could avoid her sexual fears, but when she envisioned living in a coed dormitory without Mother's protection Angela became anxious and emotionally paralyzed.

Just as Angela's easy handling of words like "fuck" and "penis" reflects a sea change in society's attitude and use of language about sexuality, so therapeutic work with teenagers about sexual fears has also changed. Yet, in spite of the sexual revolution, and social mores becoming less restrictive, a self-knowledge therapist has to tread a fine line so as not to lead the young person to misconstrue the therapist's interpretation of irrational fears as the therapist advocating or encouraging loose sexual behavior.

In a session near the end of our work, Angela smiled, and said, "I don't have those fears about sexual pictures of Sidney and me any more, and I'm not so afraid of losing Mother either. It would be terrible if she died or something happened to her, but I don't feel like I'd be all alone or it would be the end of the world like it used to. The more I've worked out these feelings, the less they bother me, and they've become so weak already sometimes it's like they never existed."

As Angela resolved her conflicts, her anxiety diminished, her ease in studying and taking exams returned along with her excellent grades, and she pursued interests and personal relationships she had avoided earlier. Her social activities were no longer confined to home, nor did she limit her dating to one boy. Increasingly free to engage in whatever interested her, she joined the chess club and entered competitions away from home several days and nights at a time.

A year and a half after we had begun our work Angela entered her first-choice university three thousand miles away. She was sad about leaving home and our work but not anxious.

Once into the academic year her scholastic work went well, and she soon found a new boyfriend. Over the first year, we spoke occasionally by telephone, usually about unexpected events related to her basic problem, but we had no regular schedule.

Even at a young age, Angela had learned to use her intellect as she enjoyed the process of learning, the discovery of new ideas, and the ability to debate concepts. Neither an ivory tower dreamer nor remote academician, she eagerly integrated knowledge of science, literature, and psychology with other fields and world events; she saw the oscillations of human emotions as they occurred in the alternating liberal and conservative trends of political history, and applied the cause-and-effect principle to psychology as well as a wide range of sciences.

Angela's good mind had also done two other things—one that almost ruined her intellectual powers, and one that saved them. It had created great anxiety from conflicts about her murderous jealousy and sexual wishes, anxiety that caused Angela to be in danger of losing her mind's great productivity and benefits, anxiety that was relieved only by Mother's presence, anxiety that became crippling when Angela feared living in a coed college dormitory without her mother. And this same good mind had been Angela's saving grace, since she could also use it to uncover and master the underlying emotions causing her fears.

Angela went on to pursue a Ph.D. in laser physics, planning to become a college professor so she could teach and exchange ideas with students. She particularly relished the prospect of occasionally working in a think tank where, freed of conflicts and anxieties, she could discuss ideas with colleagues and other academics and recapture her now unconflicted, treasured memory of those wonderful afternoons when she studied together with her mother.

10

My Only Escape

"I'm having panic attacks. I'll tell you more when I see you. How soon can we meet?"

"How about tomorrow morning?" I replied, concerned about the desperation I heard in Louis Masters' voice.

"That's great. How early?"

"Will ten work?"

"I'll be there," he stated.

Five years earlier I had seen Mr. Masters to help him resolve conflicts in his career and earlier marriage. In his work, he had struggled with whether to continue as a creative artist or to enter management, and at home he and his second wife, Anne, couldn't reconcile their frequently differing views. His first marriage had ended in divorce after only a year when he was in his early twenties. When we had worked together earlier neither his career nor marital problem had caused severe anxiety, and since he had concluded that his ill-conceived second, like his first, marriage was beyond repair, he had not felt the need to explore further his emotions that might have contributed to the problem.

When this fifty-five year old man of medium build and height arrived thirty minutes early the following day, he was dressed informally, as he usually had when we worked together before, this time in T-shirt and slacks. His customary casual demeanor, however, was completely absent; he dragged his feet, his eyes had dark circles, and when we shook hands his palms were wet with sweat.

Sinking heavily into his chair, he took a few minutes to look around the familiar room and gaze out the window to the woods beyond.

Our previous relationship made introductory formalities unnecessary; he didn't feel like speaking, and I waited silently out of respect for his preference.

When he did begin talking, he spoke rapidly, shaking his head.

"These attacks started a month ago when Donna [his current wife] and I were on a skiing trip. The first time I went up the chairlift I panicked. I had to stay on until I reached the top, and then I skied down, but I was so terrified I didn't try to go up any more that day. The next day I wanted to, and Donna expected I would, so I got in line for the chairlift, thinking the day before might have been a fluke and some magic might have happened overnight, but there was no way I could do it," he said, running his hands through his hair.

"I couldn't understand what happened. We'd skied those slopes for several years, and I'd never been afraid." He shifted in his chair, crossing and uncrossing his legs. "And to make the trip worse, Donna got upset with me for ruining our vacation, although to be fair to her, she had no idea what I was going through inside."

He briefly rested his head in his hands.

"I should've called you as soon as I got back to Washington, but the chairlift was two thousand miles away by then, and I didn't have to think about skiing, but then I started having other fears, and one got so bad yesterday afternoon I knew I had to see you."

"Other fears?" I asked.

He wrinkled his forehead and glanced nervously out the window.

"I had to take a tranquilizer to get on the plane home from the ski trip, and I've been on the verge of panic ever since. Now I'm too afraid to fly or go to any high place. I get afraid just thinking about tall buildings, not just because of their height, but—and here's something else new that scares me—I'm so anxious about being in elevators I've been skipping business meetings above the second floor.

"And another thing, whenever I have to sit for more than a minute, I start getting a closed-in feeling that makes me so restless I can't concentrate on my work. That's why I called you, I panicked yesterday when I got stalled in rush hour traffic for thirty minutes." His voice was plaintive.

"Tell me more about the 'closed-in feeling'?" I asked.

"I don't know, it started about a year ago, long before the ski trip, but it's much worse now."

He began tapping his foot on the floor.

"Do you connect it to anything about a year ago?" I asked.

"Not really, but it was around the time Donna and I started having problems." He was still for a moment, then resumed his foot tapping. "I started seeing a side of her that I didn't like, and hadn't known before."

Seeming suddenly aware of his restlessness, he planted his foot, leaned back in his chair, and said, "You know I haven't seen you since Anne and I divorced, so I probably ought to bring you up to date.

"Donna and I started having an affair several months before either of us got divorced from our spouses at the time. We both felt that what we had found in each other was—and I know it sounds corny—made in Heaven." The tension in his face eased with the hint of a smile. "Donna was soft and sensual, and gave herself totally to me. I had never known such admiration and voluptuous devotion, and she knew I adored and respected her, which she had never known with her first husband. Most of what she says about him is that he was selfish and mean.

"Then, a few months after we got married, what I'd thought was our 'perfect' relationship started to fall apart." A bitter edge had crept into his voice. "We discovered things in each other we hadn't expected, and didn't like. I wanted things to stay the way they were before we got married, and she wanted to be independent and do whatever she pleased no matter how I felt."

"Say more about independent?" I asked.

"Maybe it's more naive than independent. Men come onto her and she does nothing to let them know she's not available, even when they do things like call her at work, or send her silly emails, or try to arrange secret conversations with her. Some of them have had the stupid nerve to tell her they'd leave their wives for her," he said, his face red with anger.

"She's a beautiful woman. She has a way of dressing with understated elegance that's very appealing, and men flip their lids over her. I don't think she's ever actually done anything sexual with them, or given any real indication she takes them seriously, but the fact that she refuses to make clear she isn't available drives me crazy."

He paused and took several deep breaths.

"She's only thirty-eight, and our seventeen year age difference makes things worse. I know I'm getting older all the time, and I'm afraid that someday she'll leave me for a younger man." As he spoke, he slumped deeper and deeper into his chair and stared at the floor.

"But that's not all," he exclaimed, raising his head, "she constantly keeps me waiting, usually for trivial reasons, but sometimes for no reason at all, and I really resent it. She often works late, sometimes because she's helping someone, usually women rather than men—she's truly generous that way—but her explanations are always inadequate, especially when she won't take thirty seconds on her cell phone to let me know she'll be an hour late getting home. She always apologizes, but then she's late again the next evening without calling me, and I'm completely helpless to stop her."

His voice had gone flat, as though he were trying to push away his anger.

"And when she's really late, I worry about her safety because she takes outrageous chances. Her downtown parking lot is underground, it's unattended, and it's a block away from her office, so when she works until midnight, she has to walk alone on an isolated and unguarded Baltimore street to get to her car. What *really* ties me in knots is how I can't get through to her. She's doesn't seem to care at all that I'm worried to death something terrible might have happened to her." He seemed unaware of his clenched fists.

"She's not an idiot, she's intelligent and highly regarded as a clothing designer—we work for the same company, I'm in marketing—but sometimes she has no common sense. She says the problem isn't hers, its the men's, because, after all, she doesn't try to seduce them. She says that since women also admire her attractiveness and friendliness, she shouldn't have to worry about men just because their animal hormones get aroused. She reasons that she would have to actively show her disinterest in the men for them not to be turned on, and, since she doesn't intend to excite them in the first place, she sees nothing that should concern either her or me." He threw up hands, then slumped back into his chair.

"Of course that kind of logic might hold if that were the only problem, because technically and legally she's obviously right, men are responsible for their own behavior. But what Donna does is not just a problem for the men, it's a problem for her, for me, for our marriage, and for some of the other men's wives. Two of the wives were so upset they called Donna and me and warned us that if Donna didn't stop leading their husbands on, they—the wives—would ask her employer to intercede, and if that didn't work, they would sue her in court for alienation of their husband's affections. Even after that, Donna still didn't see a problem about her behavior with the men any more than she did about walking alone at midnight in downtown Baltimore." Again he threw up his hands in frustration.

He sat quietly a moment, then for the first time a slight smile appeared. "I remember from our earlier meetings how you think and work, and right now I'm thinking that you're thinking, 'Yes, I believe everything you're saying, and there's probably a need in this for marital counseling, and, if Donna is motivated, for her to get her own therapy.

But right now you're the one having panic episodes, and, since they're happening entirely within you, they are our main order of business.'"

I smiled. "I see your memory is as good as ever," I said as we both glanced at the clock, "so let's take advantage of it and begin there next time."

"Same time?" he asked.

"Yes," I nodded, and when we shook hands goodbye to show our pleasure on seeing each other again, his palms were dry.

The next session he walked in with a lighter step, sat comfortably, and said, "I'll just start where we left off before.

"Donna says that if I weren't so thin-skinned and would talk with her calmly, that she could hear me and might change her ways." He rolled his eyes heavenward. "Maybe that's true, but when we fight about the way she behaves with men my feelings get so strong I don't see any other way of looking at it. She isn't honest about it either, because when I try to reason with her about her flirting, she denies it, and then gets angry and digs in her heels, and we end up fighting even more."

In a gesture I remembered from our earlier work, he took a pen from his shirt pocket and twirled it between his fingers.

"What's depressing about this is that even though our marriage isn't really in jeopardy right now, I know she'll go on like this until she feels threatened enough to change." He looked out the window into the woods as tears formed in his eyes. "Our divorces caused both of us so much heartbreak we're both desperate for this one to work, and, in the end, we'll go to almost any length to make it happen.

"I think Donna will mature and eventually grow out of this, but I also know that in the meantime I have to cope with how I feel and, if I have to, change some of my own ways. My coming to see you was primarily to get relief from these panic attacks, but it also may be the only way for Donna and me to get over our impasse. We both want a happier marriage, but that means we'll have to reconcile our conflict about her behavior, and right now the initiative for that lies totally with me."

He leaned back in his chair and stared outside at the snow-covered trees as though remembering his days on the slopes.

Apparently sensing I was getting ready to ask him about his thoughts, he shook his head, so I waited. After a few more moments, he turned back to me and spoke.

"Almost from the beginning of our marriage, or at least as soon as I learned about the way she turns men on, I tried to talk with her about it, but she acted so innocent of any wrongdoing, I couldn't reach her. She thought I was unreasonable to get upset, and said that all I really wanted to do was control her. Well, unreasonable or not, I felt so helpless that, at least early on, when she wouldn't discuss the problem with me, I sometimes got rough with her." He sat up suddenly, as if startled by what he had said.

"Got rough with her?" I asked.

"A couple of years ago we took a vacation to Asia and, while we were in Tokyo, we got into a really hot argument when we were driving around," he clamped his lips together as if to brace himself for his next words, "and I stopped the car and pushed her out. I knew enough Japanese to get along, but she didn't know a word, not even how to tell a taxi driver the hotel where we were staying, which wouldn't have helped anyway because her purse was still in the car so she didn't have any money. I cooled down in a few minutes and came back and picked her up, but we were at it again as soon as she got in. A few days later, I tried to get her attention by grabbing her by the throat, as if I would choke her, and even though I knew I'd never actually hurt her, I felt desperate to get through to her, whatever it took." He shook his head as his face fell. "Jesus, I don't know why I get out of control like that.

"I've *got* to stop doing those things, physical solutions not only don't work, they backfire. After I almost throttled her, Donna threatened to leave me if I ever touched her in anger again." He had fallen into his now customary slump in the chair. "I understood why she said that, because I know it scared her, but everything else I'd done to reach her hadn't worked, and I didn't know what else to do. After that, when she said she'd leave me if I ever did it again, I was so afraid of losing her I just resigned myself to her being the way she is."

He had slumped so deeply in his chair, he was almost supine, and his face drooped with despair.

"The worst thing that's ever happened between us was the day before we left for our ski trip. I was walking by her computer while she was reading her email, and when she saw me look at the screen she quickly changed the window. When I demanded to know what the email said, she, grudgingly, allowed me to read it. One of the guys in her department had sent her a note—I guess he assumed it would be private—that said something like," Mr. Masters struggled to an upright position, "'You are the prettiest woman I've ever seen and I want you to know how much I love having coffee and talking with you, I'd leave my wife and family for you in a minute.'" He spoke with deep sarcasm.

"Say more about what made it the worst?" I asked.

"I was furious with her," he exclaimed, livid with anger. "I went out of my gourd and screamed at her, 'What kind of an idiot are you, leading some man on like that? What do you get out of it?' I know that what the guy said was adolescent and superficial, and that he isn't an actual threat to me or our marriage, but what makes me furious is that she keeps encouraging this stuff, especially since she knows how it makes me feel. But her reaction was the same as always, she just looked at me with a blank face, like I was some kind of an idiot. I know I may act crazy when I'm mad, but I'm not crazy in how I think about her leading these men on. I couldn't reach her. She acts like she has no idea about how inappropriate it is for her to go along like that with other men. When she doesn't set them straight, it leads them to think that she and I don't have a real marriage, or that I don't mean anything to her, and that she's wide open to them. If she doesn't stop it, one day one of them will feel so betrayed he'll commit some kind of violence. I felt so helpless I didn't know what to do," he sighed.

"What did you do?" I asked.

"Nothing," he said, raising his open palms in a gesture of futility. "There was nothing I could do. She was totally unmoved. I couldn't reach her, and she'd already warned me that if I ever touched her in anger again, she'd leave me. It was all I could do to keep from breaking her neck."

"What happened to the helplessness and rage?" I asked.

"I don't know, I swallowed them, I guess. I just pushed them into the back of my mind." He gave a weary shake of his head.

"You said this happened just before you left for your ski trip. Could the timing suggest that the helplessness and rage you swallowed are connected to the panic that began the next day on the chairlift?" I asked.

Still shaking his head, he said, "No, I don't think so. One has to do with feeling angry and helpless, and the other with panic, like something bad would happen to me. But I know our time's up, so I'll think more about it before next time." He rose, gave me a sad smile and walked out, head and shoulders bowed.

The following session he opened by saying, "I know what we talked about last time, but I haven't thought anymore about it."

"That's the first thought. Let's see what occurs to you next?" I asked.

"Nothing."

"And next?"

For several minutes he shifted in his chair, saying nothing.

Body language is unique for each person, and individual traits can be especially pronounced when one is anxious or troubled. Louis showed his restlessness by slumping in his seat, glancing out the window, and suppressing his yawns, actions that helped me sense when he felt tense or uneasy.

"If your restlessness could talk," I asked, "can you sense what it would say?"

"I just feel impatient," he responded. "We don't seem to be getting anywhere."

"Is 'impatient' a familiar feeling?" I asked.

"I feel this way at work sometimes when I'm working on a project and my mind goes blank and I don't know what to do," he replied, crossing his legs.

"Maybe you're feeling that way about the project we're working on now?" I asked.

He looked down and patted his waist. "My belly is getting too big, I keep telling myself I'll lose weight, but I can't seem to get started dieting. This is one of my fears, that I'll get old and fat, and Donna will lose interest in me and take up with a younger man."

"Perhaps that fear is also part of the project we're working on, and why your mind may prefer to go blank. Let's see what comes to mind about it," I suggested.

He looked at my bookshelves, and said, "I see you have a lot of history books. I enjoy reading history, too."

"Could you be saying that reading the titles about history in the outside world is less disturbing than reading the thoughts about your own history inside?" I asked.

"I don't know what to say," he exclaimed. "Or at least I don't want to talk about what I'm thinking."

"What about what you are thinking?" I asked.

His face tensed, as though he were preparing for battle.

"I get scared," he murmured, almost inaudibly.

"Scared?" I asked.

"It's not panic, it's more like I'm going to lose everything. Right now I'm thinking about several things. One is that when you asked if what happened between Donna and me just before the ski trip is connected to the panic after we got there, I didn't know how to answer, but I do remember that while we were there, I walked around in a daze the whole time. I felt like a zombie. I was numb—when I wasn't afraid—and my mind was blank."

He shifted in the chair.

"The other thing I was thinking was that this restlessness is like when I'm angry with Donna and nothing I say gets through to her, and then I feel helpless because I can't get her attention, not even by doing something physical because she threatens to leave me."

Of the two thoughts Mr. Masters spoke, I chose to follow up the second one first since his restlessness suggested the helplessness and anger were more available at the moment.

"Are you saying that's how you're feeling right now?" I asked.

"The short answer is yes." Then, he added, "But I don't want to talk about it," in a cold tone.

"What about wanting not to talk about it?" I persisted.

After hesitating several moments, he said, "If I do it'll ruin my marriage."

"Can you say more about it ruining your marriage?" I asked.

He furrowed his brow and looked at me with an intense frown, as if to say, "I'm doing this under duress, and I resent your making me do it."

He answered, "I don't want to say anything else. I'm furious with Donna. I'm so angry I'm afraid that if I talk about it, I'll explode, and I won't be able to control myself when I get home, and I'm afraid I might do something to her. I believe her when she said she'd leave me if I ever touched her in anger again."

The fear that if one talks about his anger it will become so aroused one will lose control and act out the anger physically, can present a delicate therapeutic challenge, since experiencing the feelings is necessary for self-understanding. Mr. Masters had been attempting to manage his fear of losing control by suppressing his anger, but now he faced the therapeutic necessity of experiencing his feelings long enough to understand and overcome his fear of them, while, at the same time, not losing control when angry with his wife.

Fear one will lose control of his feelings usually begins when, during the early life formation of one's emotions, one develops only partial control over acting out his feelings and, as a result, does not learn that he can feel angry without physically acting on the anger. In self knowledge therapy one can develop the ability to experience these feelings without having to fear loss of control, by, a small measure at a time, exposing those feelings to himself as he comes to feel safe enough in the therapeutic environment. Since this was the first time Mr. Masters had brought up the issue, however, he clearly indicated he did not yet feel secure enough to undertake this phase of his therapeutic work.

When I became aware that I had misjudged his readiness to work with his fear of losing control, I returned to the first of the two feelings he had expressed: being in a daze during the skiing trip.

"You said that during your ski trip, you 'walked around like a zombie,' that you were 'numb', and your 'mind was blank.' Can you say more?"

He pulled himself up in the chair and draped his hands over the chair arms. "I know I said that, but now I realize it was only partially true. When I think back to our ski trip, what I called 'numb' was all mixed with feeling helpless about Donna, and when I said 'zombie,' I really meant resignation—absolute, total resignation—to being helpless. I just gave up," he said with a shrug.

"Anger is the only way I've ever known not to feel helpless, and before Donna threatened to leave me it seemed like the angrier I got the better chance I'd have of reaching her. But when we were skiing even my rage made me feel impotent, not just because Donna threatened to leave, but because nothing I said could ever get through to her about the way she led those men to think that pursuing her was all right. Everything I tried just made her mad. I'm sure that the reason I've been afraid the rage would get out of hand is that it was the only way I felt like I had any power.

"When you asked me if there was any link between my rage at her after she got that guy's email and the panic I had on the chairlift, I said I didn't see any, but now that I've had a little time to think about it, maybe there was."

"How so?" I asked.

He leaned back and frowned. "This is all blurry, I'm

only vaguely aware of what I'm saying, but I can sense that feeling helpless was part of the panic I felt on the ski lift, and that I've felt in all the attacks I've had since. I can't recapture the panic when I'm not in it, though, and when I'm not feeling it, the episodes during the trip, and even the time I got stuck in traffic, are so remote I can't get the feelings back. All I can do is describe it intellectually."

Left to one's emotional druthers, most people will, at times, prefer to spend their hard-earned money in self-knowledge therapy avoiding their feelings by talking intellectually about them, rather than facing the emotions creating their anxiety. As a consequence, there comes a time when a person seeking self-knowledge must actively confront the actual situation that triggers the fears so he may experience the underlying emotions he has been avoiding.

Mr. Masters' comment, "I can't get the feelings back," said that he was ready to take the next step of doing exactly that. Getting the feelings back often means using sheer willpower to confront the feared feelings and so begin to demystify the exaggerated threats the panic creates.

This step is usually best accomplished if one can encounter the actual panic-causing situation, as when a person who fears flying actually takes an airplane flight so he can experience the fear, fresh and firsthand.

Confronting fears in this way often requires the self-knowledge therapist to provide gentle but firm encouragement for the patient-client to encounter the feared situation and to stick to the task of understanding and mastering the aroused feelings. Knowing how and when to encourage the process in this way, and at the same time not endanger the efforts by causing the person to feel excessively threatened and betrayed, requires considerable training, sensitivity, and experience.

Sometimes, however, when reality, or the person's overwhelming dread, prevents him from directly facing the scary situations, one must find another way of gaining access to the feelings. One often can accomplish this by imagining oneself in the threatening situation so he can recall and experience, intimately and in detail, the fears he is trying to avoid. Because this mental-emotional event happens while he is sitting safely in the therapist's office, he can experience his emotions without the paralyzing panic aroused by the actual event.

Over the months that followed Mr. Master's observation—"I can't get the feelings back. All I can do is describe it intellectually"—he confronted his feelings by picturing the situation he feared the most.

During one session, I asked, "Can you talk about how the panic feels when you see yourself on the chairlift?"

"It's been so long since I was there, but now that we're talking about it, the memory is coming back, and I'm starting to feel panicked just remembering the ride on that chairlift," he said, running his hands through his hair.

"Can you put the panic into words?" I asked.

He crossed his legs, looked out the window, uncrossed and recrossed his legs, then looked back at me.

"This sounds crazy, I know, but I have an almost uncontrollable urge to leap!" he blurted.

He breathed deeply for a few minutes while staring at me or gazing out the window.

"Talk about the urge?" I asked.

He continued to stare out the window, still breathing heavily.

"I feel so helpless just sitting there! I've got to do something," he exclaimed, then shook his head, as if to clear his mind.

"Say more about 'just sitting there'?" I asked.

His shoulders sagged, as he retreated into his slump.

"The ski lift where we were has four fifteen minute segments, and the whole time you have to just sit there, fifty feet above the ground. And one of those segments is on a mountain's edge looking straight down a half-mile precipice!" His eyes widened as he gripped the arms of the chair. "Long before these panic attacks, I was on a chairlift that had an electrical failure and left me hanging what seemed like a mile above the ground forever, although

I think it was just thirty minutes, and I've dreaded that ever happening again. And now that it's coming back, I remember that that time, too, I was terrified because I almost couldn't resist the urge to jump." He ran his hands through his hair. "But this last time, I panicked even when I wasn't stuck way up in thin air by some kind of mechanical problem," he said, with sweat rolling down his face.

"Can you put 'panicked' into words?" I asked.

He pulled out a handkerchief and wiped his brow while he took several deep breaths.

"I know all this sounds bizarre, and I even say to myself, 'You've got to be kidding,' but when I imagine myself just sitting on that chairlift, and especially getting stranded up there, all I can think about is this urge to jump off and then imagining myself falling fifty feet, or a mile, or however high I am above the ground. I can't bear just sitting there." His face had gone pale. "That's when I feel panicked, because I have to do *something* to get away from feeling helpless, and leaping from that height would be insane, but that was my only escape."

"Can you say more about 'urge'?" I asked.

He nodded, "I know I said 'urge,' but it's not an ordinary impulse, like when I want to write a letter to the editor of the *Baltimore Sun* because I disagree with some columnist, which I've never done anyway. What I'm talking about is a deep drive, like a compulsion that is absolutely imperative."

"What more can you sense about imperative?" I asked.

"I don't know, it's too crazy," he said, clasping his hands to his head. "It's like I have to take some kind of action or do something so I can feel I have some control over my life, anything so I won't feel so totally helpless. But that's when the panic hits, because I know that leaping from that high would get me killed."

As if relieved from having survived a "trial by fire," he paused and chuckled to himself, while his breathing slowly returned to normal.

"When I go for a walk I sometimes say, 'This is the only time of my day when I feel I have any control over anything I do, I can put one foot in front of the other, and no one has any say about it except me.' The rest of the day, in one way or another I have to submit or defer to, or at least consider, the needs or demands of everybody else. I go walking for just that reason, but what happened in the ski lift was a whole different ball game. That panic was the worst experience of my life." He had glanced at his watch while he was talking, then, after he finished speaking, sat quietly and stared into space.

I said, "These thoughts occurred to you as we talked about the connection between your helplessness with Donna and the panic on the chairlift. I know the clock is telling us we have to stop now, but the power of this issue has told us it will be at the top of our next agenda."

As he rose to leave, he said, "Ordinarily I'm disappointed when the session is over because I'd rather continue, but this time I'm glad it'll be next week before I have to think about this again."

When he entered the office the following session, he gave me a quick, guarded smile, and, after sitting down, began to reflect on his insight the previous week.

"What I said last time about feeling compelled to jump from that chairlift so I wouldn't feel helpless sounded really wild," he said, shaking his head. "But it made me think more about your question as to whether my panic, and now I guess, my compulsion to jump, on the chairlift may be connected to being helpless with Donna. I know I felt helpless in both and I also know that when I had the urge to leap, I didn't feel so helpless for just a split second before I felt panicked."

He became quiet as he frowned, and his jaw slowly dropped.

Then he continued, "I think I started to understand this while I was talking," he said carefully.

"How so?" I asked.

"I felt helpless on the chairlift, like I did with Donna. But with Donna, I could at least walk away, so I wasn't completely helpless, but I couldn't walk away from a chairlift fifty feet in the air, because that would have been almost certain suicide. And it was almost as bad when I was sitting in traffic, not because it would get me killed, but because there was nothing I could do."

He stared into space for several minutes before continuing.

"I feel like I've been to hell and back with this. I still have to work out all that's gone into it, especially my differences with Donna, but I don't feel as intimidated by the panic now, because I know I can live through it. Once you've been through the worst, it's easier to know you can survive anything else."

"Say more about 'anything else'?" I asked.

"It's these conflicts with Donna," he replied, then gazed at the wall a few moments. "They're so impossible. Usually when I have to make a choice, the upside and downside are clear and I can live with whatever I decide on, but with Donna both sides are down."

"What conflicts are you thinking about?" I asked.

"Well, there are two big ones. One is, when I think I am right about something, I can't let it go, and I think I'm right about the way she gives these men the come on, but there's nothing I can do to make her stop. And the other one is I don't know what to do with my rage when I'm so furious with her and can't reach her with reason and then it feels like all I can do is choke her, and then I'm so afraid of losing her I can't do anything. Up to now it's seemed like all I could do was pretend those feelings weren't there, but I can't do that forever, especially now that I realize why I get panicked."

He shook his head, "I can understand why she won't tolerate my physical abuse, but I can't make my anger not exist. I get furious when I'm just reminded of the way she behaves with other men, and then I'm paralyzed when I realize that if I don't control myself, she'll leave me. I know I've got to find some other solution for either getting so mad in the first place or for doing something with it if I can't stop myself from feeling it."

He looked outside for several minutes.

"What's going through your mind?" I asked.

"I'm thinking about the difference between how I felt about this work when we started several months ago, and how I feel now. I was so anxious then I would've done, or faced, anything necessary to get rid of the panic, and I have been doing it, but what I'm talking about now is different."

"Different in what way?" I asked.

"Well," he began, "since I know that the feelings causing my panic came out of Donna's and my relationship, I know that you'll make me talk about my marriage, but in spite of everything I've said about her, I've always felt our marriage 'was made in Heaven,' and I don't want you to tell me it wasn't."

"Do you know why I'd think it wasn't?" I asked.

"I guess because of what I've told you," he said, brushing away tears. "I've said so many bad things about Donna, you probably feel I shouldn't have married her. But that's not true, because we both love each other and want to make this marriage work."

I replied, "Are you saying that the fear of losing Donna is so great that there is no place in what you feel is a basically good and sound marriage for getting mad at your wife when her views differ, even radically at times, from yours? I understand your frustration and unhappiness about her behavior and her unwillingness to talk to you about it, but you're saying it threatens the relationship to have thoughts and feelings that don't match your picture of a marriage 'made in Heaven,' or just to talk about them with me in the safety of these four walls."

He thought for several moments. "Well, I hadn't looked at it that way, but I feel so embarrassed talking about this."

"Embarrassed? Is this a familiar feeling?" I asked.

He looked slightly taken aback, then appeared to consider the question, and an expression of recognition slowly surfaced.

"You know, even as I said it, it seemed like I'd felt that way before, and now that you ask me, I remember what it reminds me of."

"What about 'what'?" I asked.

"Well, actually, it's not a 'what,' it's a 'who.'" He

made a wry smile. "It's my mother."

"What about your mother," I persisted.

"I've told you many times about my family, but there are some things I think I left out, so bear with me if I repeat some things. As you know, I was the oldest of three—Carl, my brother, was two years younger, and Jennifer, my sister, was three years younger. My mother was strong, and I know she loved me, but she would never talk to me when I was upset and really needed to talk to her, and I always ended up feeling hurt and empty." He abruptly stopped talking and looked at the floor.

"Did something come to mind that was hard to say?" I asked.

"Yes, but this is all so foolish, and it doesn't mean anything anyway," he responded.

He briefly watched a hawk building her nest in the beech tree outside the back window.

"When I said that my mother wouldn't talk to me when I told her about things that upset me, I thought you would ask, 'Like what?' and then I would have to tell you that I complained to her because she paid more attention to Carl and Jennifer than she did to me and she made them think they were special to her when she should have treated me that way because I was the oldest and had been her child the longest." He stopped a moment, forced a half smile, and shook his head. "I feel so silly talking like this."

"Say more about feeling 'silly'?" I asked.

"Well, this sounds so childish. I've always been strong, even when I was little, and I've felt that when I complain, people will think I'm whining and want to be babied."

I replied, "You said you felt 'silly' because you were afraid I'd think you were 'whining' if you told me your mother wouldn't talk with you when you complained that she paid more attention to Carl and Jennifer than she did to you, even though you deserved it most."

Looking sad, he stared at the floor.

"I know that's what I said when I was talking about mother not paying attention to me, but Anne was the one who hurt me the most that way."

"Anne? Say more what you mean?" I asked.

"Because that's why she divorced me—she said she just got sick and tired of me whining all the time about her paying more attention to other people than she did to me, which, she said, wasn't true anyway. Actually, Kay, my first wife, complained about the same thing, too. Now you're probably thinking I was jealous, and I wondered that myself, but I never thought I was jealous, and even Anne said that it didn't came across to her that way because I never accused her of doing anything sexual, or intimate, with anyone. She said she just thought I wanted to possess her, and that I whined if I couldn't, and that she agreed I deserved her attention more than anyone since I was her husband, but that that didn't mean I owned her every second."

He shook his head, smiling sheepishly as he looked back at the floor

"I remember that 'whining' is what mother called it, too, and that was why it hurt so much when Anne and Kay and others said it. When I tried to talk with Mother, she would just say, 'You're whining like a baby,' and wouldn't pay any attention to what I was trying to tell her that upset me. God, that felt terrible, and it still does when I think of it. I felt so humiliated, and alone. It was bad enough when she paid more attention to Carl and Jennifer, but then she just dismissed me like I was just as a crybaby who didn't count at all."

He stared at me, then at the wall, then out the window.

"But this is crazy, I was twenty-two and a grown man by the time Kay and I were married, and twenty-five when Anne and I got married, and for me to still have these feelings now with Donna doesn't make sense. I know the feelings sound alike, but it's hard to believe that something I felt with my mother when I was just a kid would have anything to do with how I feel with my wife fifty years later. Donna says, though, and I remember Kay and Anne did, too, that I create this problem in my own mind, because they all have said that whatever I think about them isn't how they actually are .

"I just remembered something else. It wasn't just that Mother paid more attention to Carl and Jennifer than to me, I was upset when she spent time with anyone, including my father. I never complained to her about him, though, because I was afraid she'd tell him and then he'd get mad at me. He was a big, strong man, and he'd whip me with a belt if I ignored him or didn't do what he told me. He didn't actually whip me very often, but when he did it hurt, and I really hated him for it, but it got my attention, and then I'd do what he said.

"That's how I learned to get Carl and Jennifer to do what I wanted when I tried to reason with them and they didn't do what I said. It seemed so natural to do it with Donna, too, until she threatened me."

I said, "As you're talking about the way you ignored your father when he tried to talk with you, and how he got your attention by getting physical with you, as well as how you learned from him this method of getting through to people, what can you sense you're saying about how these memories are connected to the problem you feel with Donna?"

He stared at me while he considered my question.

"Well, my first thought is, 'I don't know what you mean'," he answered, "but I can tell you what I thought about while you were talking, and what's been in the back of my mind all along." He set his jaw. "I feel like I never really had my mother, at least not like Carl and Jennifer did, and like my father did, too."

He stared out the window, lost in thought.

"What are you thinking?" I asked.

"Well, I touched on it earlier when I said how humiliated and alone I felt when Mother dismissed me like I was a crybaby. Maybe mother loved me when I was really little, and I don't know when she changed, but I really don't have any memories of her being happy to see me."

I responded, "Perhaps you're saying that the way those whippings by your father and your getting physical with Donna are related is that when you can't get through to Donna you try to break down the wall by getting heavy-handed with her the way your father did with you. And perhaps you're also saying how, at times, you may have felt like doing it to your mother, too."

"I don't remember ever wanting to throttle my mother, but I do know that I always wanted to feel special to her, and that I've looked for that in a woman my whole life." He quickly brushed away a tear. "The only time I've found it was with Donna before we got married, and sometimes after, too. Some people have said I expect too much, but I don't know what 'too much' is. I don't think it would have been 'too much' for mother to listen to me and talk with me about what upset me even if I was wrong and whined when I said it, or 'too much' to expect Donna to talk with me about why she behaves the way she does with men. But I do know that Kay and Anne, and I guess Donna, too, feel I've expected too much."

Until Louis's helplessness and rage had become severe and created panic in his effort to cope with them, he was more than willing to endure his helpless anger so he could maintain his illusion of a perfect marriage. Before Donna laid down her ultimatum, his reflexive anger had given him a sense of strength to avoid feeling helpless. Now, faced with Donna's threat she would leave him if he touched her in anger, he could not act on the anger without losing her. As a consequence, his self-restraint only reinforced his sense of helplessness.

Louis knew that the survival of his marriage, and his internal peace, required that he find a real solution to these emotions, since the only solutions he had tried were intolerable: accept his helplessness, which he had never learned to do; persevere in reasoning with her and risk his rage becoming physical, which terrified him he would lose Donna; or continue to push the anger out of his awareness into his subconscious mind, which he had already found he could not do because it created panic and other fears.

Our rational mind is still underdeveloped and immature in childhood, and irrational feelings we experience at that age are perceived as total and permanent reality. A child suffused with wishes for mother's special love, but who feels he does not receive it, may appear to proceed with life none the worse for his hurt, but his subconscious mind does not forget its deeply felt unrequited yearnings, and seeks to recover them later, often through an idealized notion of marriage.

Louis' admiration of his father's heavy-handed tactics became an equally powerful emotional structure. The ideal of muscle power is familiar to us all: children play cops and robbers for fun; many children, and even some grown-ups, physically fight to settle differences; throngs watch professional wrestling; and almost everyone is at least curious about *Godfather, Rocky,* and *Terminator* stories and movies.

But most people who live in the adult worlds of rationality and the law find that manhandling—what the law calls "assault and battery"—does not work well when dealing with others. And it certainly did not sit well with Donna. Louis had not fully learned that while his ability to physically coerce others had seemed to serve him well as a child, it was horribly ill-suited for settling differences as an adult. Louis' childhood emotional and behavioral patterns had irreconcilably conflicted with his life partner's view of acceptable behavior.

The collision between Louis' desperate wish to reach Donna—as he had sought in vain with his mother—and hIs notion that he could fix any problem through verbal persuasion backed by physical intimidation had caused him incapacitating panic and almost wrecked his marriage.

In spite of Louis and Donna's love for and commitment to each other, their marriage had become so heavily burdened by strains between them they could not deal with normal, everyday problems. Louis knew that to avoid these strains he had to relinquish his illusions and replace them with rational attitudes and behaviors that would serve his and Donna's marriage goals.

Louis' compulsion to overcome obstacles kept him from realizing that sometimes he had to accept the helplessness and humility life brings to all of us, like it or not, painful or not. Just as he had been unable to accept as a child that his mother was unreachable, he now was power-less to reach Donna in the way he wished. Although he had already lost two wives, he had not had to accept the loss of his fantasy of true love because the other women had never meant to him what Donna did; Donna was the sole heir to his childhood fantasy that he could have in an adult relationship what he had both actually had with his mother in infancy and early childhood, and what he sought but failed to have with her in later childhood.

Mr. Masters' second step of self-knowledge debride-ment originally centered on his emotions that created panic about leaping from the chairlift, as well as his other fears, and on those feelings causing his ongoing friction with Donna. As his work progressed, he focused more sharply on the emotions that caused him to fear he would become physical with Donna, on those feelings that made him un-able to accept a normal level of helplessness, and on his unrequited feelings of reaching his mother. Mastery of these nonrational reactions, particularly his helpless panic and his use of angry assaults to solve problems with Donna, meant that he needed to understand how these reactions worked in creating his problem.

One day he opened a session, saying, "I had another tiff with Donna last night about this business of the men at her work, although this time it was minor, and it happened mostly within myself anyway. I don't get near as upset with her these days, partly because of the work here, and partly because I recognize that she gets some kind of reas-surance about herself, that she's attractive I guess, when these men pay attention to her.

"But it still bothers me too much, and I know there's more to it than what I've talked about so far. I got some insight into it last night, because while we were arguing I discovered that the more I felt I couldn't reach her, the more I longed for what I've called our 'perfect love.'" He stared at the floor.

"You seem to be saying there was something about not being able to reach her that made the fantasy of your 'perfect love' all the more compelling?" I asked.

"Yes, but I don't know where to go with it."

"The way you described the sequence," I said, "suggests that the feeling that came with not being able to reach her felt unbearable, and that you had to replace it with the 'perfect love' fantasy that not only didn't feel bad, but felt very good and reassuring. If that sounds right, can you say more about the unbearable feeling?"

He pursed his lips thought.

"I know you've already answered this," he said, "but what feeling do you mean?"

"I was referring to the one that came when you couldn't reach Donna," I said.

He replied, "I think I know why I was confused about what you said, because even now when I try to focus on the feeling, it keeps going away, and won't stay long enough for me to talk about it."

I said, "Perhaps there is an edge, or even a tiny sliver of the feeling that you could describe?"

He chuckled. "When you said 'a tiny sliver of the feeling,' I imagined a mouse running into a hole and my grabbing it by the tail."

"Did you see or feel the tail long enough to describe what you saw or felt?" I asked.

He hesitated for several moments.

"Do you remember once very early when I said something about feeling empty when I couldn't reach Mother? That's the feeling I'm talking about. It's just so empty and devastating, and seems like it will last forever. I'd do anything, and I mean anything, not to feel that way. And I can see now that when I think about Donna's and my perfect love, even when she disabuses me of it, it feels so much better than when I feel so empty."

"What more—" I began to ask, but he interrupted me.

"I know you started to say something," he said, "but I want to go ahead with what I thought of next so I can talk about it while it's fresh. This is where my problem with my father came in, because when I felt so empty, I'd try to get close to him—and I know this sounds crazy—but it

seemed like the only way I knew how to do it was by ignoring him, the way mother did me, and then he would
whip me for it."

"Say more about feeling close with him when you ignored him and he whipped you?" I asked.

"It wasn't ignoring him that made me feel close, it
was when he whipped me," he answered. "I ignored him
just to get him to whip me. I knew he would get mad if I
ignored him, and his beatings weren't too bad anyway."
He chuckled, looking smug. "But I felt really close to him
when he whipped me because I knew it meant he cared for
me, and then I didn't feel so empty. That all stopped when
I got to be a teenager, I guess because I started doing things
outside home. But the truth is his whippings really hurt
my feelings, and I'd feel empty and rejected by him the
way I felt with my mother. It seemed like I couldn't win
with anybody."

"You felt empty and helpless every place you turned,"
I said, to underscore that I had heard the depth of his pain.

He thought for several moments while looking out the
window, then grinned slightly.

"Yes, except for one place," he said, looking as if he
had been found out, "and I guess in the end it's what brought
me here."

"One place?" I asked.

Still half-smiling, he said, "It seemed perfectly natural to me to twist Carl and Jennifer's arms and bang their
heads together if they didn't do what I told them to, because that's what Dad did to me. It even made me feel
strong and close to them, I guess because they couldn't
whip me like Dad did."

"In anticipation of what you just said, you had commented just before, that 'I guess in the end it's what brought
me here.' Can you say more?" I asked.

Looking sheepish, he shook his head. "That's how I
got into trouble with Donna. When I tried to use brute
force to make her say or do what I wanted, she wouldn't
take it like Carl and Jennifer did. I never really hurt Donna
anymore than I did Carl and Jennifer or than my father

actually hurt me, so, and I know this sounds peculiar, at first I was kind of surprised when Donna objected to my getting physical. But those are the same feelings that got me into trouble with myself even after I stopped being physical with Donna, since they were responsible for my panic on the chairlift and in traffic."

Several sessions later Mr. Masters referred to his empty feelings when he couldn't reach his mother and Donna and to his heavy-handed anger in managing the empty feelings.

"Once I got to know the feelings I'd thought were impossible to live with, they didn't trouble me like they used to. Not having been able to reach Mother doesn't seem so important any more either, so feeling helpless isn't so unbearable, and I'm not as worried about losing control physically because I don't feel so angry."

Louis' third debridement step came as easily for him as it does for most people. Once he had accepted the loss of his infantile fantasy of "true love" and learned he could endure feeling helpless, he no longer feared that his anger would become physical or excessive, and, as a result, was then able to use his healthy, well-tempered aggression to solve the marriage differences.

The idea that any kind of action, especially a suicidal one, is preferable to feeling totally helpless, can sound so preposterous that it is a particularly clear illustration of why people who think with reason and logic often have difficulty treating seriously many of the notions put forth by people who study the subconscious mind. It also helps explain why the human mind prefers magical and easy-to-digest conventional explanations to any problem, and why many people turn to treatments, like drugs and exciting psychological fads, that provide uncomplicated answers.

The self-knowledge therapeutic work that relieved Mr. Masters' panic was also a vivid example of why treatments directed toward an isolated behavior would, for most individuals, be incomplete and inadequate. People who are either unconcerned about, or are willing to live with, the far-reaching limitations and harm created by their basic conflicts may be satisfied with relieving a single symptom. Treatments whose primary aims are to provide symptom relief as quickly as possible are currently popular with insurance providers, managed care companies, and employers. But the singular relief of Louis' fear of heights, whether by drugs or other treatments with narrowly defined or short-term goals, would not even have addressed, much less resolved, his fear's cause and its extensive effects.

Louis' two underlying conflicts, the first, between his excessive demand for Donna's "pure love" and his helplessness when she behaved contrary to his demand, and second, between his heavy-handed reaction to his frustration—with her strong-minded independence—and his fear of losing her, not only spoiled his vacation, it almost ruined his treasured marriage.

As he uncovered the causes of his fears, though, instead of exploding and threatening Donna with violence, he found he could use his mature capacities to think and act appropriately, and because these abilities were already well-formed, they needed only to be strengthened and exercised. His reasoned discussions with Donna were, for the first time, effective, and his attitudes, although firm and persistent, were toned down. She, in response, was less resentful and more cooperative, and the good faith attitudes he and she showed in making changes gave them greater compatibility. Since now Louis could tolerate helpless feelings and was not crippled with impotent anger, he could, without anxiety, ride the chairlift and sit in stalled traffic, as well as participate freely and effectively in conversations with Donna and engage in other activities that had been crippled by his panic.

11

At-One

Linda Lewis, a trim, attractive, well-dressed woman who appeared to be in her mid-thirties, arrived promptly for her first appointment and, after customary pleasantries, began at once, with no cue from me.

"Paula Whitaker is a friend of mine, and she recommended I see you. She said you may not remember her because you and she met only a few times, but she said you were very helpful with a business problem she had similar to mine." She twisted a lock of hair. "I've never done this before, so where should I start?"

"Just start wherever you feel comfortable, and we'll take it from there," I responded.

Her face went blank for a few moments, then she said, "I'm not sure how to do this. Where do most people begin?"

After silently noting that she seemed not to remember having just asked and received an answer to the same question, I said, "You mentioned you had a business problem and that it was similar to Ms. Whitaker's, perhaps you could start there," I answered.

She nodded. "I'm, uh, having problems in both my business and personal life, but maybe it'll be easier to understand them if I give you some background about myself first. After high school, I got a B.A. in business from

321

the university where I met Bob, my husband. We got married after we graduated, then I joined an investment banking firm for five years before I went back and got my MBA. Then I organized my own company—I was thirty at the time—that serves business clients by offering developmental, financial, and legal consultation. I had every reason to expect my business would succeed, because I'd done well in school, my education was top-notch, and I had gained considerable experience and contacts at the investment banking house." She frowned and shook her head. "But it hasn't turned out the way I'd expected."

"How so?" I asked.

"I'm running into problems, and I don't know why. My business looked so promising in the beginning, and still does," she stared into space for several moments, "until I meet with clients. It's not that they don't need my services, they always say how much they do. But then something happens that makes it not turn out right."

"Something happens?" I asked.

She curled her hair between her fingers.

"Maybe it's something I'm doing wrong." She seemed bewildered.

After several seconds, I asked, "What's your hunch?"

"I'm not sure." She tilted her head in thought. "But most of my clients are big shots, and I don't like them."

"And you think they may sense it?" I asked.

With a wary look she stared at me, then answered, "I don't want to admit it but they must. My friends have told me forever that I have problems with certain men, and it shows. Not that everything I do with men is bad. My husband and I love each other, and we get along okay, except for normal ups and downs, and I've always had men friends, but I've never liked or gotten along with arrogant, self-important types."

I said, "When I asked you if you thought the 'big shots' sense that you don't like them, you said your friends have told you you have problems with men, and that it shows. Shows how?"

Her face went blank, and she became silent. "What do

you mean? How does what show?" she asked with an edge of irritation.

Curious that for the second time she did not remember what she and I had just talked about, and that this time she sounded annoyed, I answered, "The feeling about the 'arrogant, self-important types'."

She looked at me for a full minute.

"What are you thinking?" I asked,

With a piercing glare, she snapped, "I'm wondering if you're a Freudian, and if I came to the right place."

I responded, "I'll be glad to answer that in a minute, but I was wondering if it struck you, as it did me, that the question arose while we were talking about how much you dislike arrogant big shots, and if the feeling might show."

After another long pause, she said, "Well, I don't think you've seen it yet, but sometimes I have a sharp tongue and people get offended, and other times my mind goes blank and people think I might be dumb. I'm not aware of these things when they happen. It takes me a few minutes to realize what I've done, but other people must recognize it, and I've lost a lot of friends that way, especially from my sharp tongue. Some people just leave, although most stay around and tell me later, but I often go away from conversations wondering what I did wrong."

She resumed twirling her hair.

"Do you think these behaviors could be invading your work with clients?" I asked.

She looked at me, as though considering her answer.

"I guess that's the main reason I'm here. I told myself I came because of my husband, but that's nonsense. Maybe some of this does come into our marriage, but basically Bob's and my relationship is good, and we usually work things out. But with my clients," her eyes narrowed, "I get only one shot at making a good impression, and, if something goes wrong, then that's it, there's no tomorrow. And things go wrong too often."

"Tell me, actually tell both of us, what happens when you meet with these guys?"

I had chosen the term "guys," intentionally, reasoning, in this early stage of our work, that by diminishing their importance I could, in a subtle way, lessen their threat and make it easier for her to talk about her feelings toward them.

She responded immediately.

"Well first, I'm not talking about regular 'guys,'" she answered somewhat sarcastically. "I get along well with guys, especially nice guys. My clients are not nice guys, they're the top brass who plan policy and make decisions, and they wouldn't be where they are if they were just 'guys.'" She glared at me as if I were one of the offenders. "They're important, they know they're important, they act important, and they treat me like I'm some stupid little girl. They probably think they're just being proper, but in one form or another they're condescending, humiliating, and abusive."

"Where do you come in?" I asked.

She continued to glare at me. "If my presentation is first on the agenda, and he hasn't already seemed like a know-it-all, things may start out well, but, more often than not, I don't even get that far because things go wrong before I say a word. The last one I talked to was the CEO [Chief Executive Officer] of a textile plant in North Carolina. Before I could begin, he said, 'Well, how do you think you can help me?' His words alone, 'How do you think you can help me?' with the emphasis on 'think,' pissed me off, like I was some idiotic child who 'thinks' but doesn't really know what the hell she's doing." She was squeezing her hands around an imaginary neck, as if to throttle the man she was describing. "And his snotty tone was even worse. But whoever begins, it's always the same." Her hands dropped into her lap. "Most big shots I see are like that CEO I just mentioned, but, even when they're not, I feel the same way."

As an implied question, I observed, "You said *he* even before you spoke specifically about the head of the textile plant."

She shook her head. "Talking about that would take

longer than we have right now, so maybe we can begin with it next time." As she pulled her car keys out of her purse, she looked up, and said, "When do we meet next?"

"Would Thursday at three work out for you?" I replied.

"That'll be fine. One more thing," she said with a smile, "you never answered my question about whether you were one of those Freudians?"

I responded, "Anyone," then smiled and gestured with my open hands to her, "and now that includes you, who wants to understand how her mind works, has a bit of Freud in her soul. Freud began the science of understanding how the mind works, but since then, many other great thinkers, like Karen Horney, have added their knowledge, just as Einstein advanced Galileo's theories of physics, so that by now self-understanding has progressed far beyond Freud's, and has improved by light-years our ability to help people."

Before closing the door, she said, with a hint of a smile, "That's an eloquent answer, but I'm not sure it's the one I was looking for. I'll see you Thursday at three."

She began the next session by saying, "After our last meeting I figured you would wonder what kind of answer I was looking for when I asked, 'Are you a Freudian?' so I've been thinking about it. I don't know how I would have reacted if you had said, 'No,' but I do know I was a little disappointed you didn't say, 'Yes.'" She peered at me with her lips pursed. "Not because I wanted you to be a Freudian—God knows how women feel about that 'penis envy' crap—but, it feels like I was disappointed because I was braced for a fight with you."

"Was it similar to bracing yourself for a fight with that CEO you spoke of?" I asked.

She bit her upper lip and slowly nodded. "Like just before we stopped last time, when you noticed I'd been talking about a man, even before I'd said anything specific about him."

"Maybe you don't know it, Doctor," she said, throwing up her hands, "but there are very few *shes* in these situations. The 'shes' are all at home, barefoot and pregnant. And that's where these men think I ought to be. Most of my clients are men, and they're all Neanderthals in the way they look at women."

"What are you telling us about how you cope with these feelings when you talk with clients?" I asked.

She gaped at me nonplussed, then with a stiff grimace, said, "I don't come right out and say, 'You stupid son-of-a-bitch, how dare you treat me like I'm some imbecile who can't do what you great men do,' but it must come through anyway. I really want to cut these arrogant bastards down to size." She spoke with great heat. "And I guess they pick it up."

"How did you do it with the textile plant CEO?" I asked.

She grimaced again. "I ruined my chance with him right off, and I knew then that I had to do something about it."

"Can you tell me what happened?" I asked.

She twirled her hair with her finger. "When he said, 'Well, how do you think you can help me,' I didn't say anything for a minute, but then I blurted out, 'It's not a matter of how *I* think I can help you, it's how *you* think I can help you. You know better than I do that your profits have been down for three years, that you are running a poor third to your competitors on foreign exports, and that there's a lot of talk in the industry about dissension in your upper ranks that filters all the way down the chain.' And I know I was furious when I said it, and I'm still angry. It just came out before I could help myself, and I knew immediately that I had lost him." She heaved a big sigh. "He was polite and told me to go ahead with my presentation, but within fifteen or twenty minutes, he thanked me and said he would think about what I said and would call if he needed me. But I knew he would never call, and he hasn't." She had stopped twirling her hair.

"What galls me most about all this is that in this man's world men can behave the way I feel, and they do it all the time, and it's all right, even expected. Why in the hell is it all right for them and not for me? Why should I have to be

careful about the way I handle myself and they don't?"
Her tone was bitter. "That's why they're Neanderthals. They
do whatever they damn well please, but I have to be sure I
don't step on their fucking toes. I hate having to accept
that their stupid, might-makes-right mentality is my reality, and that if I want to succeed in a man's world, and not
look like a ball-crunching feminist crusader in the process,
I have to kowtow to them and tailor every damn thing I do
to suit them."

She fumed silently.

"You mentioned earlier that a blank mind is sometimes
part of these angry feelings," I said.

She glanced up quickly, frowned, then responded, "The
only way I can keep from blowing my top is to make everything in my mind disappear. I intend to push out the
feelings, but the problem is that whatever I'm thinking goes
with them, and at those times I probably look like a child
and an idiot."

Her brow was furrowed, as she rested her jaw on her
fist.

"It happened momentarily with that CEO, and with
you, too, during the first session, when I blanked my mind
a minute or so just before I said, 'I'm wondering if you are
a Freudian, and if I came to the right place?' But it isn't
black and white, other things come into it, too. With you, I
didn't really feel angry in the first place—I knew I wasn't
going to lose control and scream at you—and even if I
had, it probably would have been all right. But with that
son-of-a-bitch in North Carolina, I was so furious with his
smart-ass attitude, I didn't really care at that moment, and
it all came out."

I asked, "Are you saying that your mind going blank
depends, in part, on whether or not you feel in conflict
about the anger?"

Ms. Lewis paused, then, recognizing our time was almost over, said, "I don't know, I've never thought about it
that way, but I'll consider it."

As she readied herself to leave, she looked at me and
said with a smile, "I know we haven't solved all this yet,

but I feel better getting it out in the open. It's been a burden living with it pent up inside, and I feel stronger just knowing what I'm dealing with."

She fidgeted with her car keys. "But I have another problem, too, something I haven't mentioned, because I've been so involved with my business and clients. I want a family, too, and I don't know what to do about it." Holding back tears, she said, "Tuesday?" confirming our next appointment.

I nodded yes, and she left.

The next session, when I met her in the waiting area, her eyes were dark and sunken, and again she was holding back tears. I could barely hear her mumbled, "Hello."

In the consultation room, she sat and looked ill at ease.

"Last time I said I needed to talk today about having a family," she said, slowly and somberly. "I'm thirty-five, I've been married almost ten years, and . . ."

She clasped her hand to her mouth, shutting her eyes tight, then began to sob. After several more moments, I said, "If the tears could talk, can you sense what they would say?"

She shook her head for me to wait until her crying had calmed.

"I think I've been on a one-track course ever since I was five. That's when Papa took me to the docks where he worked and showed me the big boats that had come from far away and brought all those cars and television sets. I was in awe! I said, 'Papa, when I grow up, I want to own a big business just like you.' He didn't actually own the business, he operated a gigantic crane that unloaded cargo, but he enjoyed his work so much I assumed he owned it all, and I wanted to be part of the excitement, not just stand by and watch while those men had all the fun."

Her face crumpled, as though she were going to cry again.

"But Papa said, and I'll never forget how hurt I felt, 'You don't want to do that, Sweetie, that's men's work. When a little girl grows up, she wants to be a good wife and mother, just like your Mama.'" Stifling more tears, she continued, "I loved Papa more than anything, but what he said hurt me so much I never told him about my wish again. He was wrong, though, not just about me, but about Mama, too, because she resented his small-minded attitudes." She paused and smiled sadly. "Mama was devoted to Papa and us children, but she always regretted not pursuing other interests she had, so she was on my side.

"Mama and I talked all the time about my wanting to be married and have children like her," she said in a tender voice, "but we also talked about my wanting to own a shipping company like Papa, and we agreed that since he couldn't understand us, we wouldn't tell him about my dreams, or Mama's, or our special conversations." Tears formed as she slumped in her chair. "But when he put me down as just a little girl who shouldn't be thinking about doing big things, I think I decided then and there I wanted to become a big, successful businesswoman, and I've never thought seriously about being anything else since." Bursting into profuse sobbing, she cried, "But now I want to have children." Then for several minutes she released a flood of tears whose intensity showed they had been building for a long time.

When her crying lessened, I asked, "Say more about wanting children?"

"In spite of everything I've said," her voice was subdued, "my family was very close when I grew up, and now I want to have my own. Up to now, I've mostly wanted to establish a career and be free to travel, but my biological clock is running out, and it's time for my husband and me to have children."

After waiting for her to continue, I said, "You spoke of wanting a family like the one you grew up in. Can you say more?"

She twirled a lock of hair, as she thought. "I'm the second of four children. I have a four-years older brother, Ralph, a sister, Sue, who's three years younger, and Eddie, he's ten years younger. It was a love-hate thing with Ralph, we had terrible screaming and physical fights. I loved Eddie later on, but he didn't exist in my early years. I've always felt closest to Sue. I've loved her ever since she was born, and we've been close all our lives." She smiled and her voice was warm. "I'm not only her older sister, but, everyone said, and I know they were right, I was her 'little Mama,' too. I always loved being with her and Mama and Papa. Papa died when I was eighteen, and by then Ralph and I were off in college, but we'd already had so many good family times together, and that's what I want for my husband and myself now—to have my own children and family, like we had when I was growing up."

"Are you saying that your wishes for a family are now in conflict with your business goals?"

She smiled again.

"No, not any more, it isn't a conflict between those two that I'm worried about. I could arrange time to do both, or if I couldn't, I could interrupt my career long enough to begin my family. The problem isn't that, it's something else."

She looked out the window.

"What about something else?" I asked.

Turning back, she said, "I think I can work out these feelings about big-shot clients, and that I have the abilities to succeed in business, but for a long time now my work may have become an excuse—what you would probably call a defense—for something that scares me."

"Something that scares you?" I asked.

She removed her glasses and began swinging them back and forth by the ear piece.

"Whenever I start thinking about having a baby I get scared."

"Scared of what?" I asked.

She whirled her glasses in circles. "Being a prisoner at home."

"What about being a prisoner at home?" I asked.

She shifted around in her seat, then leaned forward, and pressed her hands on the chair arms, as if she were on starting blocks ready to take off.

"This is really hard, because it's the first time I've ever actually talked about it."

"Could you talk about what makes it hard?" I asked. With a sigh and deep breath, she leaned back and continued.

"I've always been active—going places, doing things —like when I played ball and fought with Ralph and the boys. People used to call me a 'tomboy,' although I haven't heard a girl called a tomboy in a long time. But if I have a baby I can't do those things so easily. I don't just enjoy being active, I'm restless and scared to have to stay inside at home. I've always hated it that boys could go out and do things girls weren't supposed to. I'm sure that was the main reason I got an MBA and created my own business where I could take charge of my life and travel anytime I wanted to."

Though she seemed a little less anxious, she rotated her outstretched foot, as she continued her thoughts.

"But now that's the problem. If I have a baby, I can't be the kind of mother I want to be, like I was with Sue, and run a company and fly all over the world at the same time. So I guess there really is a conflict." She had stopped moving her foot in circles.

"You've talked about being a mother to Sue and playing ball with Ralph and the boys. How did you work out the conflict then?" I asked.

"I don't know," she responded, knitting her brow. "I don't remember being anxious then, I don't think there was a conflict."

"What do you sense about there having been no conflict?"

"It must have been because being Sue's little Mama was something I enjoyed but didn't have to do, at least not as much as I actually did. I always knew in the back of my mind that taking care of Sue was Mama's job, and I could go outside and play with Ralph and his buddies any time I wanted to. But," she smiled, "now it's all up to me. I could hire a caretaker, but that isn't the way I want to be a mother, and that's where my conflict really is."

She seemed more at ease than when she began talking about her fear of being a prisoner at home.

"I didn't have this prisoner feeling when I was little—
I always assumed I would have an active, independent life.
I didn't know exactly what I wanted to be when I grew up,
but I knew it would be exciting, like Papa had with his
shipping company that operated big cranes, and have a
natural home life, like Mama. When Papa said, 'You don't
want to do that, Sweetie, that's men's work, you want to
be a good wife and mother, like your Mama,' I was hurt,
not because I would be like Mama, but because he was
saying that since I'm a girl I couldn't do what he did. When
I was little, I never thought about being a prisoner at home,
or anywhere, because I believed I could choose to do in
life whatever I wanted, and that my life would be good
whatever I did. Feeling afraid of staying at home to be a
mother for my own children has happened only since I've
been grown, and it's come as a big surprise."

"You said a 'natural' home life, like your mother," I
said.

"Yes, both sides of what I want to do feel natural, but
it's hard to find a way of having both. My generation lied
to me when it told me I could have it all, and all at the
same time. I said natural a minute ago because between
the two careers—owning a business or being a mother at
home—being a mother at home feels more natural, because it's like Mama was, and I feel more like her.

"Maybe Papa was right, but not for the stupid, self-
serving reasons men believe. A man thinks a woman's place
is in the home so she can take care of him, when, in fact,
being home taking care of a baby is a woman's place, because, after carrying, and delivering, and nursing a baby,
taking care of the baby comes naturally."

Over the next several weeks, Ms. Lewis continued to
sharpen her goals and identify the emotions preventing her
from achieving these goals: conflict with big shot men that
impaired her business career, and a fear of being prisoner
at home that kept her from fulfilling her wish to have children.

She began one session by saying, "I know that many
women have a baby and then get someone to take care of

it so they can get back to work as soon as possible, but for a woman to work while she has a small baby at home is not natural, at least it wouldn't be for me. Trying to do both while the baby is little may work for some women, but I couldn't stand being away knowing I had a baby at home. I couldn't keep my mind on my work, and I wouldn't want to anyway. Papa would have made all this easier if he hadn't put me down when I said I wanted to do what he did."

"How so?" I asked.

Shaking her head, she adjusted herself in her chair and frowned.

"Papa really loved me, but his attitudes about women came from his days in the cave, or at least his Italian background. He expected girls to be pretty, loving, and submissive, and he was so pleased when I smiled and was a good girl and made my mind go blank. And that was the problem, because I hated acting like I had no brains and wanted only to play with dolls. I was always afraid he wouldn't love me if I did what I really wanted to do, which was to play sports with Ralph and the other boys."

She smiled as she gripped and swung a make-believe baseball bat, and, with a wider smile, said, "I loved to play ball, and I could hit and field better than a lot of the boys."

"Papa behaved as if only boys had brains, so girls should blank their minds?" I asked

"Yes, and that's crazy. Papa and most other men don't understand that when it comes to thinking, their penis is just excess baggage. You don't think with your penis, you think with your brain. When I got older and learned about women's struggle for equality, the story of the women's movement really helped me get rid of Papa's way of thinking."

She made a fist and delivered a knockout punch on an imaginary sexist male, providing sound effects by clicking her tongue against her palate.

"I've always had a good brain, and I was a good student, including at graduate school, but I could never enjoy it, because Papa brainwashed me into thinking only a boy should have a good mind. I especially hated his attitude, since I made better grades without even trying than Ralph and most boys did studying hard. I genuinely enjoyed learning and knowing things, and the idea that I should give that up just to please Papa is a crime against women and humanity. Yet, as much as I enjoy the business world, I've never really been sure why I've wanted to do the same thing Papa did. Did I really want to be a businesswoman to be like him because his work seemed so exciting or important? Or did I just want to do something he thought girls shouldn't do?"

She looked at me as if she expected an answer, but then continued before I could speak.

"I knew something was wrong with Papa's ideas, because if God had intended boys to have better brains than girls, He, or She, wouldn't have given me such a good one. All through school, I almost never spoke up in class, because I was self-conscious about showing off my mind at school like I sometimes did at home. I have a sense of victory when I remember those times, because Papa never quite knew what to say when I got good grades, and he was speechless when I knew things he and Ralph didn't." She smiled, then added, "But Ralph made it worse," and her smile faded.

"Ralph made it worse?" I asked.

"I guess I haven't talked about Ralph." She had a pained look. "Since Ralph was a boy, and four years older, Papa took him hunting and fishing, and even let him work on the dock, not just stand around and watch like I had to. I never wanted to hunt and fish, because it's so cruel to animals, but it did hurt me when Papa would take Ralph and leave me out. And then Ralph learned from Papa to treat me the same way. He'd put me down and push me away when I wanted to do things with him, just like Papa did. I was smarter than Ralph, but I could never enjoy it because he would find some tiny fact, like a baseball or football statistic, and then taunt me with what he knew that I didn't. It wasn't that he knew the sports fact and I didn't, I didn't mind that, because I didn't care about sports trivia, and I knew I didn't know everything anyway, what hurt was his being mean to me." The corners of her eyes and mouth drooped.

"Even when I played with him and his friends, I mostly just tagged along, because they didn't really take me seriously. I understood, even then, that they were a lot older than I was and probably didn't want me tagging along, but that didn't mean it was all right for Ralph to hurt me like he did.

"Now that I'm an adult, I think he was just insecure and had to act like Papa, but I hated him for it then, and I still haven't forgiven him, even though his life is a wreck." Tears filled her eyes. "He drinks so much he's probably an alcoholic, and he's so irresponsible he can't keep a job. When Papa and Ralph humiliated me and made me feel that being a little girl was bad, I talked to Mama about it, and I know she talked with them, but she couldn't make them understand or stop treating me that way."

"You mentioned your conversations with Mama earlier also. What did you and Mama talk about?" I asked.

She looked outside, then softly smiled and responded, "I was disappointed when Mama couldn't make Papa and Ralph stop treating me the way they did, but I always knew she understood me and how much they hurt me, and, anyway, what she and I did together more than made up for what I couldn't do with Papa and Ralph."

She leaned back in her chair and smiled.

"Mama read me fairy tales when I was very little, and Aesop's Fables when I was older. I can still repeat by heart most of the stories, and when I do I have the same wonderful feeling I did when she read them to me. She washed my hair and taught me how to comb it and make it look pretty. Some mothers are rough when they scrub their children's hair, but Mama wasn't, Mama was tender and soft."

She smiled gently for several moments, looking out the window at the wooded, hilly area behind my house.

"We had a hill behind our house, and we'd 'climb the mountain' and sit together on our special rock. We'd bring a picnic lunch and look out on the whole world and talk about girl things, like how she had wanted to be a social worker, but couldn't, because she grew up in Rio de Janeiro where her parents were poor Brazilians, and about my wanting to own a big boat company," expressing the latter wish in a deep voice to mock macho male talk. "I never did things like that with Papa, or Ralph—Mama was the one I've always been closest to.

"I've read enough lay literature about psychoanalysis to know about Freud's question, 'What do women want?' I know what women want," she said with a cat-that-swallowed-the-canary smile. "Women want their mamas, or really, they want to feel close with someone the way they did with their mamas, and I think most women, deep inside, feel the same way.

"There's a lot of talk today about gays and lesbians. I feel like I'm a lesbian at heart. I have no desire to have sex with women, but I feel closest to women, and I think in their hearts most women feel the same way." She smiled again, tilted her head, and pillowed her head on her folded hands. "If you read about what women want in sex, it's really what they had with their mamas anyway. I'm sure you know this, but eighty percent of women want to feel close with their sexual partner much more than they want an orgasm.

"Men get this all mixed up, because they think that women want men." She sat up and raised her eyebrows, opening her eyes wide, as if she expected me to be offended. "Men can have their 'mama feeling' their whole lives—they go from their real mamas, to girlfriends, and wives, and mistresses, and never have to give up their mama feeling—and since you men feel that way with a woman, you think she feels the same way with you. We don't want men, men are interlopers, and I resent the conventions that force men on us. Women can't have a 'mama feeling' with most men because a man is a man, not a woman, and most men, certainly Papa and Ralph, could never be as tender and loving as a woman. I've missed my close feeling with Mama ever since I was a little girl." Her face relaxed.

"I have many other feelings, too, and, overall, my marriage is not as bad as I might make it sound. Bob and I love each other, and I enjoy several men's friendships, but no man, even Bob, is as tender and soft as Mama. Nothing in my whole life has ever felt as good as when Mama and I climbed the mountain and looked out on the whole world together and dreamed our dreams."

As a child, Linda had consciously learned mechanisms to cope with her helpless anger at Papa and Ralph when they belittled her. Her sarcasm, sometimes with humor, had given her the strength and confidence to bring down tormentors, and her blank mind, often seen as cute, had protected her from feeling scorned.

But by the time she became an adult, these behaviors had become so ingrained and reflexive they defeated her when she used them while marketing her business services to corporate executives. When the dominating executives behaved like Papa and Ralph, Ms. Lewis had even greater difficulty controlling her behavior since they evoked her painful memories and unresolved conflicts about Papa and Ralph.

Her major obstacle to overcoming her problem was her wish to look outside herself for the cause of her anger. Since the executives' behavior provided what seemed to her to be the obvious explanation for her rage, she had allowed herself to disown personal responsibility for her feelings and actions and their function as a defense against the pain of hurt and humiliation.

But she could not control others' emotions and actions, so her rationale of attributing responsibility to her outside world meant she could not solve her problems as long as she held others, like the business executives, accountable for her feelings, even if their behaviors were egregious. No matter how much any of us attempts to change our external environment, as Ms. Lewis did when she turned against the "big shot" men, we are stuck with the reactive patterns built into our childhood emotions, and the problems those patterns cause cannot be solved unless we, our-

selves, accept responsibility for, and make the efforts necessary to change, those behavior patterns.

In the early stages of our work together, it was evident
to both Ms. Lewis and me that her first therapeutic goal
would involve overcoming her rage, the self-defeating forms
it took, and the flawed emotional structures underlying it.
She readily achieved her first debridement step— identification of the rage—because of its glaring evidence from
almost the beginning. She saw how her attempts to cope
with her rage by expressing it with a sharp tongue and blank
mind defeated her goals, and how, when she did manage to
control herself, she lived in fear of blurting out the intense
anger she harbored. Her rage was not a global reaction, it
was a specific response to the hurt and humiliation she felt
at the hands of arrogant, abusive, "big shot" men.

Her second debridement step—elimination of the
faulty structures by understanding their underlying
causes—required that she experience her "unbearable"
feelings within the therapeutic work. Unlike instances when
a person exploring such emotions must call on the memory
of an experience, as illustrated by Mr. Masters (Chapter
Ten, "Only One Escape") imagining himself helpless on
the chairlift, Ms. Lewis was able to experience firsthand,
directly with me and about me, the abuse, hurt, and rage
she felt.

Opportunities occurred frequently, particularly when
she interpreted my comments or questions as presumptuous and condescending. She recalled her feelings from the
first session when she had blanked her mind and looked at
me menacingly after I had asked her about her feelings
toward "big shots."

"That first day," she said, "all I said to you was, 'I'm
wondering if you are a Freudian, and if I came to the right
place.' But that isn't all I felt. I felt and thought then, and
for a long time afterward, 'You're just like all the rest of
these big shot bastards, you think you're so fucking smart.'"
She spoke with burning hostility. "'I've heard about smart-
ass shrinks like you, the only thing real about the *New
Yorker* magazine is the way they make fun of you and your

August vacations on Cape Cod. You're hanging on by your fingernails to a dying profession, and you don't have enough sense to know it or self-respect to accept it. I don't know what the hell I'm doing here, anyway.'"

"You're saying that a smart-ass big shot bastard does something to you that feels intolerable. Can you talk about the feeling more fully?" I asked.

"It's easy for you to ask that, Doctor, sitting up on your lofty perch, but you wouldn't need to ask if you knew even half of what it's like to be told you're not good enough, and never will be, to do something men and boys take for granted every day. The answer to your question is that there's no way to describe the hurt and humiliation I feel every time you or anyone, especially a man, acts as if he knows something I don't, or can do something I can't." Her voice shook with anger. "And there's no word vile enough to describe it. Try 'despicable,' 'pitiful,' 'worthless,' 'shit,' and helpless to do anything about it, and always will be, and yes, damn it, these feelings have been there ever since Papa and Ralph put me down every time they opened their fucking mouths."

Aware that anything I might say would weaken the impact of what she had told us, I only nodded my head to her in silence.

She waited several moments as her feelings settled, then, glancing at the clock, added, "I'm sorry these feelings came up so late in the hour, and that we don't have time to talk more about them, but I'm sure glad to get them out because they come from so deep in my gut."

She began the next session by saying, "I felt better about these 'Papa and Ralph' feelings after last time than I can remember. It was the first time, ever, that I haven't felt helpless about the way men treat me. Just getting those feelings out on the table so I can give them a name lets me feel, finally, that I can get my mind around them, and not like I'm climbing Mount Everest."

I responded, "It seemed then like their putdowns were some kind of total, permanent, cosmic truth about you, rather than what you know today, that Papa and Ralph's attitudes came from their culturally limited values, or their own demons and defective mechanisms they've been content to live with rather than grow beyond."

She nodded in agreement.

For the rest of that session and several that followed, we worked through these feelings, until one morning she came in and said, "Somehow the hurt of being 'put down' doesn't bother me as much. I don't even notice a lot of things that used to set me off, or, if I do hear them, I don't react to them."

She looked through me for several moments. "But this thing with Papa and Ralph did something else to me that, in some ways, is more of a problem than my reaction to them for putting me down."

"How so?" I asked.

"I'm afraid to really feel close to anyone," she responded, then looked out the window.

"Afraid of what?" I asked.

"I want to feel close with Bob, but I have to fight against it because I know that if I give into it, something bad will happen."

"Say more about 'something bad will happen'?" I asked.

"It's like I won't exist," she said.

"'I won't exist' how?" I asked.

She looked out the window a full minute.

"Well, how would you like it if somebody treated you like Papa and Ralph treated me, that I wasn't important like they were or didn't count like boys do?"

"I'm sure I wouldn't like it either," I responded, "but you said this feeling is like you don't exist, and since you hadn't mentioned it when you've talked about the Papa and Ralph feelings before, I was wondering if anything else occurs to you about the 'don't exist' feeling'?"

"When I don't exist," she murmured, "it feels like I become part of the person I'm close to rather than being a person myself." Her eyes drifted.

"Say more," I asked.

"I know I said earlier that this was something Papa

and Ralph did to me, but I was thinking just then that that wasn't really true. The feeling I got with Papa and Ralph is sharp, and it cuts, but this isn't like that." She sounded puzzled and tentative.

"Your tone seems to be saying that you sense there's something else about this you hadn't thought of before?" I asked.

Several moments passed.

"Just for a moment, I was thinking about sitting on the rock with Mama when we climbed the mountain together."

"What were you thinking about sitting on the rock with Mama?" I asked.

Her brow puckered as though she were in pain.

"I told you how we ate lunch and talked together about our dreams. Sometimes I'd put my head in her lap, and feel close to her and her warmth, and daydream about how good it felt, and that we would come up on our mountain together forever, and that life would always be like that. I guess it's like how someone on drugs feels, because I know that when I read the Odyssey, I wished I could have been one of those lotus-eaters who dreamed her life away. When I was with Mama I just wanted to get lost in that dreamy state all the time. When we were together like that, I felt like we were at-one with each other, and I still long for those days, and that's what I'm afraid of now."

"Say more about the fear?" I asked.

Her face filled with nostalgic bliss, then tears filled her eyes.

"I'm afraid I'd want to spend my whole life doing nothing but just being together with another woman, and be totally unconcerned I wasn't getting anything done. I think if it were only the serenity, I would love it. But it's not. What frightens me is that I'd want to be at-one with Mama, or now another woman, emotionally and spiritually, even physically, like our spirits would be at-one with each other, I would be at-one with her and she would be at-one with me, we would be joined like Siamese twins."

After we both paused for several moments—she from immersion in, and I out of respect for, her deep longing for the feelings she first had with Mama—I asked, "Say more about feeling frightened when you think of becoming at-one with each other?"

She responded without hesitation, "I knew you'd ask me that and I felt scared the moment you started talking, because the very thing we're talking about just happened. I felt like you and I were one together because it was as if you'd read my mind and knew how scared I was. It's very hard to describe, it's not like being scared of a monster or a bogeyman when I was little, or of being afraid of snakes or high places. Talking about those fears would be easier because they're about real things outside myself—if you can call a bogeyman real—some one or some thing that you can see or imagine, that you can point to and define.

"But this fear of being at-one with Mama, or someone like her, is different because it's a fear of a feeling inside myself. When I fear becoming at-one with another woman, I'm afraid I'll become nothing, like I have no form, or body, or mind. How can you describe a fear of something like that and make sense to anyone, unless they feel it themselves, and I've never heard anyone say they do?"

She frowned and shook her head.

"What's really crazy about this is being afraid of the very feeling I want so much. There's nothing like the serenity of being at-one with someone like Mama." She looked out the window for several moments. "But it's really scary, because then I get lost in her and I become nobody, like I don't exist as a separate, or real, person, or I don't have any boundaries to my mind and body."

Suddenly, she sat up straight and gripped the arms of her chair tightly.

"Could you have felt it just then, just before you gripped the chair?" I asked.

She nodded. "Yes, for just a moment before I squeezed the arm of my chair."

Her hands loosened their grip, and she sat back.

"Can you sense what prompted the feeling?" I asked.

After a moment's thought, she said, "It happened while I was talking about the serenity of feeling at-one with someone like Mama, and then I felt it with you because I knew you understood me, but that made me feel like I didn't have any boundaries, so I had to grab the chair so I'd feel real and solid.

"I know I could never be hypnotized because I get scared when I even think about turning my mind over to someone else. I've been lucky that I've never needed surgery, because I'd be terrified of having anaesthesia and putting myself in the hands of doctors. I used to have trouble going to sleep at night because I felt like I was giving myself over to the sandman. I've had only one drink of alcohol my whole life, when I was twenty, but it blurred my mind so much I've never had a drink since. I've read about 'self-identity,' and this is like I don't have any identity, I don't know who I am, or even if I exist. The feeling is so scary I don't let it stay more than a second. What's scariest is that the feeling seems like it will stay forever, and that I'll never be able to get myself back."

She had folded her arms across her chest and was clutching herself firmly, when suddenly she grabbed the arms of the chair again.

"Did you just have the 'no boundary' feeling again?" I asked.

"No," she responded, "I didn't get that far because I could sense I might, so I was holding on to myself, and then I grabbed the chair to keep it from coming on," she said, showing her relief with a hint of a smile.

"You had this feeling with Mama when you were a little girl. Whom do you have it with now, other than when you're here?" I asked.

"I could have it with anyone if I felt really close to them. I talked about this earlier as if it happened only with women, and I do have women friends that I haven't let myself get too close to because of this feeling, but I can have it with a man, too, like with you, if he's tender and soft like Mama. And when Bob is tender, I really have to be on guard against this feeling with him."

Her face had lost expression, and she spoke in a monotone, as if to subtly create distance from me.

"Say more about being on guard with Bob," I said.

"Well, most of all, it interferes with us being close."

"In what way?" I asked.

"Bob says that when he wants to be loving with me I become remote and irritable for no reason he knows of."

"Are you saying that when Bob wants to be loving and tender, your wish to be close and at-one with him comes out just the opposite, as distant and irritable?" I asked.

"Well, yes, I hadn't thought of it like that, but the answer has to be, 'yes.'"

"Why 'has to be'?"

She took a deep breath. "Because that's when it always happens, when I feel loving with him and when we want to make love. It interferes with our whole relationship, because if I can't feel close with him or tell him I love him with feeling, then he feels I don't love him, or, if we're making love, that he isn't pleasing me. It causes a chill between us that doesn't go away easily." Tears rolled down her cheeks.

I said, "You're saying the problem of creating distance with your husband comes from the fear of being close and then having the urge to merge and be at-one with him, like you used to feel with Mama, and that the feeling of being at-one with him then is in conflict with your normal need to feel your own boundaries and self-identity. How far back do you remember this happening in your feelings with Mama?" I asked.

Her eyes had begun to dry. "As far as I can recall, there was never a time I didn't want to feel really close with her. I know it didn't bother me while we sat and talked on our special rock, and we did that 'til I was seven or eight."

"Do you recall what made you stop?" I asked.

"In the past, I think I would have said something like, 'Well mother was too busy' or 'I had too much school work,' but since we've done all this work I don't really think that's what happened. I think that I stopped wanting to go because at some level, and in a way that I wasn't aware of, more like an intuition, I knew that dreaming with Mama on the mountain and wanting to be at-one with her was making me want to stay a child forever. I know it was about that time that I starting thinking how silly *Peter Pan* was for not wanting to grow up, but I guess I never got those wishes to be at-one with Mama out of my soul."

"What more occurs to you about what made the wish to be close to Mama become a strong urge to be at-one with her?" I asked.

"I can't say for sure because it usually happens so gradually, but I know that sometimes just before I start to have my 'at-one' feeling, I feel, for just a fleeting second, that if we are so close we will be one, then I know I won't ever lose her."

She thought a moment, pursing her lips. "Mama never told me, probably because she thought I might hear it as criticism, but my aunt and grandmother said I demanded that Mama hold me and carry me until I was almost four." She smiled with the warmth that always accompanied her memories of close times with Mama. "Mama and I have talked about my wanting her to read to me for hours, and that after Sue was born I insisted even more about being with Mama every moment.

"Something else happened earlier that I don't remember, but Mama told me about it," she said, as her smile began to wane. "Mama was born and grew up in Brazil, and she and Papa met and married and had Ralph while Papa was on his first job there as a heavy equipment operator for an American construction company. They went back to Brazil for Papa's job four years later, and that's when I was born. Actually in the jungle," she smiled, "because Mama was on Papa's work site at the time, and they had to call in the company doctor to deliver me. When I was two, Papa's company brought him back to the United States, but Mama couldn't come with the rest of us because something was wrong with her passport." She paused a moment and shook her head. "I never knew why there was a problem. Papa was an American citizen, and he and Mama were married, so she should have been able to come with us, but those government things were so confusing that Mama and Papa never understood them either.

"Anyway, Papa, Ralph and I moved while Mama worked out her immigration problem, and that took nearly four months. As soon as we got here, Papa's company sent him to Montana on another job and left Ralph and me in Louisiana with some people that Papa's company had hired, Ralph with one family and me with an older couple named Deloitte. Papa was so mad about them sending him away from us that he quit the construction company as soon as he got back from that Montana job, and that's when he started working on the docks."

Again she shook her head. "It all sounds strange, and I was too young to remember any of it, but Mama and my aunt told me that when Mama finally came, I wouldn't let her out of my sight for a moment, and I guess that's when she started having to carry me and read to me, and that when Sue was born I got even worse. I'm sure it was because I was afraid I'd lose Mama again, since that's how it's always felt when I've been afraid I couldn't be at-one with her," she said, frowning.

"When I got older I was always confused when I heard the story about my having stayed with the Deloittes, because you might think they were bad to me from what I've said about being so afraid of losing Mama after she came back. But I don't believe they were bad to me because we lived near them later on, and they were always so nice to me that I know they wouldn't have mistreated me when I was a baby. It must have been that I was so little, and away from Mama and Papa, that being with anyone I didn't know would have been strange and scary."

"I notice our time is up today," I responded, "but I want to be sure we both have heard what you just said, so it will be at the top of our agenda next time. You're saying that your loss of Mama for four months, when you were two, may have set in motion the fear of losing her, and that you then needed to cling to her and be at-one with her so you could be sure you'd never lose her again?"

"Yes," she replied. "We both heard the same thing, and I know it's right because I heard myself saying it even before you'd said anything. I know we have to stop now, but I'll remember where we are because I know where it leads and what I want to work on next—my 'at-one' feeling and the problems it causes—so unless something monumental comes up in the meantime, that's where I'll start next time." She smiled and left.

The next session, she entered the office looking harried.

"I'm sorry I'm so late, I got stuck behind a traffic accident, and I know we only have a short time, but I really wanted to continue with what we were talking about last time."

She took off her coat, sat, and composed herself. "All I've thought about since last time has been that when I was little, feeling close and at-one with Mama weren't problems because all I knew was it felt good and secure to be with her, but when I got older I realized that being at-one with her, or anyone, made me feel like my mind and body had no boundaries and I wasn't a person all by myself."

I responded, "You seem to be lumping together your natural wish to be 'close,' which you enjoy, with the 'at-one' feeling" that makes you feel you have no boundaries and then undermines the close relationship you want to have. But, if I hear you right, you're saying that it isn't closeness per se that's the problem, it's the at-one feeling, the merger, that makes you feel you've lost your boundaries and don't exist all by yourself."

She stared into space and smoothed a lock of hair.

Turning back to look at me, she replied, "Until you said what you just did, they both seemed the same." She paused, and thought again. "That's why this is such a problem, I want so much to feel close with Bob and some of my friends because I love how good it feels when I'm close. I even want to feel kind of close with some of my clients, not real close because they don't mean that much to me, and it's inappropriate in business besides, but certainly close enough to feel comfortable with just being friendly. Actually, I feel more real and solid when I'm close with someone, than any other time."

"Just before leaving last time, you said you knew this was headed to the 'at-one' feeling and the troubles it causes. What more have you thought about it?" I asked.

"I've noticed I've been a little less afraid of losing my boundaries over the last several days, but I think that's more due to us talking about my fear of losing Mama than because I've made any real progress on the 'at-one' feeling. So I still don't know what to do about the 'losing my boundaries' feeling."

"You showed us how you could prevent feeling the loss of your boundaries by gripping the chair so you could feel solid. Can you sense a mental or emotional equivalent of the chair that has helped you feel solid in overcoming the 'loss of boundaries' feeling?" I asked.

Shaking her head, she answered, "No, nothing like that seems possible, because thoughts are not solid like wood. Chair arms are physically tangible, you can actually feel them with your hands. How can you feel a thought?" She raised her hands and shrugged her shoulders.

I responded, "I was struck a little earlier when you said that you feel more real and solid when you are close with someone than at any other time. On the face of it, that's sounds paradoxical, because it is closeness that often leads to feeling 'no boundaries,' but surely the paradox is trying to tell us something, for if closeness has a part that's solid, maybe it can help in overcoming the 'no boundaries' feeling. It sounds like feeling close has two sides, one that is solid, and another that leads to feeling 'at-one' and no boundaries."

She covered her eyes while she concentrated, then, dropping her hands, said, "Do you remember the other day when I said that just before I start to have my 'at-one' feeling, I feel, for just a fleeting second, that if Mama and I are so close we will be one, then I know I won't ever lose her? Well, I think that's what makes the difference. If I'm feeling close with Bob, and something bad has happened between us, or if one of us has been cross, I get afraid that maybe I'll lose him and then I just automatically have that 'at-one' feeling. The crazy thing is that although I do it so

I won't lose him, the result is I do lose him, at least for a while, because he feels hurt and rejected and then pulls away."

She glanced at the clock, looked annoyed, and said, "Well, I guess our time's up. I've got an awful lot to think about. See you next time."

I nodded, and she left.

She looked thoughtful and wore a soft smile as she entered the room the next time.

"As I told you on Friday," she began, "I left here with a lot to think about. One thing that was especially meaningful, and helpful, was the distinction you made between feeling 'close' and solid and feeling 'at-one' and no boundaries. I won't call it miraculous, because I've still got a long way to go, but I noticed over the weekend, that when Bob and I were intimate, if I kept my mind on the realness of our closeness, and that I wasn't going to lose him, then I felt solid and didn't have the 'no boundaries' feeling." She frowned in concentration. "Actually that doesn't put it in the right order. I should have said, that when we are intimate, and I start to fear that some argument we've had will turn into his getting mad and going away, if I remember the solidity of our close relationship and what we have together, rather than trying to be at-one with him so I won't lose him, then I feel solid and don't have the 'no-boundaries' feeling."

She stretched her arms out to her sides, then brought her hands behind her to cup her head.

"I can already tell that things are starting to change, even though I know it may take a while, but most of all, I'm beginning to believe I can get over this fear of losing Bob. It's amazing to me that I probably knew this all along, but I didn't know I knew it," she said smiling.

Over the next several months, she not only gained deep insight into herself, but was able to integrate her insight into an intimate relationship with her husband and less conflicted interactions with her clients.

In a session shortly before completing her therapeutic work, she said, "I feel much more solid with Bob, and I really don't worry any more that if he goes away I'd feel like I did when I was two and lost Mama for four months, or that the only way I could keep him, or anyone, with me would be to feel at-one with him." She smiled with pleasure.

"Something else I've been thinking about is that my fear of losing Mama and my need to be at-one with her was also a big part of my problem with Papa."

"In what way?" I asked.

"It wasn't exactly like with Mama" she responded, "but I know now that the hurt and humiliation I felt when Papa put me down was so colored by my fear of losing him when he rejected me, that I was desperate to please him, even to the point of blanking my mind, so he wouldn't go away."

"You're saying that at two, not only was Mama everything in your life, but that the desperation you felt when you lost her became the basis of your reaction to the possibility of losing anyone, no matter who it was?" I asked.

"Yes, and I know the reason it hurt so much with Papa and Ralph was that their rejections kept me from feeling 'at-one' with them, and that's why the hurt with them was so raw. Neither had the slightest bit of tenderness, at least nothing like Mama's, that would have softened the blow and let me feel close with them. My fear of losing Mama got so mixed up with Papa and Ralph's rejections, I cannot tell to this day how much of the hurt I felt with Papa and Ralph was due to their rejections, and how much of it was from the fear of losing Mama."

In one session shortly before ending her self-knowledge therapy, she reflected on what had been her most troubling symptoms. "It's hard to believe how I used to waste my time getting into wars with male sexists, or stayed out of the wars by being a good little girl who had no brain so Papa wouldn't be unhappy with me.

"And it's also hard to remember why I was so afraid of being close with Mama, or Bob. I'm not afraid of feeling close any more, so when Bob and I make love I can sink into it and, for the first time ever, enjoy it without having to worry that I'll lose my boundaries and won't come out of it." She looked directly at me and gestured freely as she spoke. "This has made a night and day difference in Bob's and my relationship, he feels good about me and that makes me feel good about him. And of course it is so much easier to enjoy good, close friends without having to guard myself against getting too close.

"These days I can use my mind anytime I need it, and I can feel close with someone if my heart says it's right."

When Ms. Lewis came to know that she could pursue her career goals and close relationships, especially with Bob, without the crippling effects of deep-seated conflicts, she recognized that her first goal was to have a family. In her sixth month of pregnancy, she began allowing her business to wind down, and, shortly before her first baby was due, ended her self-knowledge therapy.

Five years later, Ms. Lewis called to tell me how well her life was going. Her, by then, two daughters had entered pre-school, and she had resumed her career, this time as a partner in an export-import firm. Now free of her thin-skin, reactive rage, and 'no-boundaries' feeling that had impaired her performances and relationships earlier, she blended healthy assertiveness with her genuine business skills to deal effectively and easily with arrogant "big shots," while her sense of solid boundaries allowed her to relate easily with her husband and others with whom she wished to be close. Aware of her family's importance to her, she arranged to confine her work to clients that did not require her being absent from home.

As we concluded our conversation, she told me, "There's also been a big bonus in this. When I finally understood my wish and fear of merging with Mama, it made me realize I had turned my wish to be with my children every moment into a fear of being their constant prisoner, and that's why I was afraid of being trapped at home with them. I don't have those fears anymore," she said with ease, "and now I can't get enough of just being home with my girls."